IMAGES
of America

RACINE
DRUM AND BUGLE CORPS CAPITAL OF THE WORLD

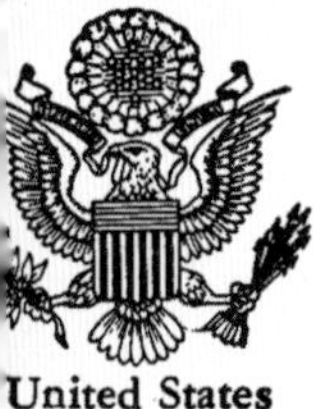

United States of America

Congressional Record

PROCEEDINGS AND DEBATES OF THE 90th CONGRESS, FIRST SESSION

ol. 113 WASHINGTON, MONDAY, JUNE 12, 1967 No. 91

DRUM CORPS CAPITAL OF THE WORLD

(Mr. SCHADEBERG asked and was given permission to address the House for 1 minute and to revise and extend his remarks.)

Mr. SCHADEBERG. Mr. Speaker, on Thursday, June 15, 1967, the eyes of America's vast drum corps enthusiasts will be on Racine, Wis., a city within my First District. On this date, the community of 90,000 citizens will celebrate its fourth annual Drum Corps Day and is being hailed as the "Drum Corps Capital of the World."

Most of us happily reflect a sense of pride when someone, something, or a community in their district produces an event or an act which is outstanding. This is true here where more than 600 young people from seven different units will exhibit their talents in a parade and exhibition.

Further, it has been pointed out that the event is being held by these various musical units in order that they might say "thank you" to the Racine community for its tremendous support over the years for drum corps activity.

Also, since there is more drum corps participation per 1,000 population in Racine, Wis., than in any other community in our land, it can rightfully claim the title of "The Drum Corps Capital of the World." Again, it is with a deep sense of pride and admiration that I call the attention of my colleagues to this accomplishment by a city within my own home district and compliment it accordingly.

A page of the *Congressional Record* from Washington, Monday, June 12, 1967, in which Congressman Henry C. Schadeberg reads into the record that Racine is the "Drum Corps Capital of the World" appears here. (Courtesy of the Racine Kilties Alumni Association.)

On the cover: The Racine Boy Scout Junior Drum and Bugle Corps is seen in Racine's 1959 Fourth of July parade. John Batikis, director of the Racine Junior Scouts, is to the left of the first row of drums. (Courtesy of the Racine Heritage Museum.)

IMAGES
of America

RACINE
DRUM AND BUGLE CORPS CAPITAL OF THE WORLD

George D. Fennell

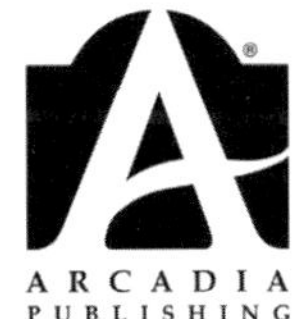

ISBN 978-0-7385-6133-2

Published by Arcadia Publishing
Charleston SC, Chicago IL, Portsmouth NH, San Francisco CA

Printed in the United States of America

Library of Congress Catalog Card Number: 2008934417

For all general information contact Arcadia Publishing at:
Telephone 843-853-2070
Fax 843-853-0044
E-mail sales@arcadiapublishing.com
For customer service and orders:
Toll-Free 1-888-313-2665

Visit us on the Internet at www.arcadiapublishing.com

This book is dedicated to my late mother, Elfriede Fennell, and to my late father, Donald Ralph Fennell, who were wonderful, supportive parents and lifelong "drum corps nuts." I also dedicate this book to my wife and best friend, Liz, whose support, understanding, and encouragement made it possible.

Contents

Acknowledgments 6

Introduction 7

1. Boys of 76 9

2. Racine Scouts 45

3. Racine Junior Scouts 67

4. Racine Kilties 73

5. Kiltie Kadets 101

6. Ambassa"Dears" and New Day 113

7. Other Racine Units 119

ACKNOWLEDGMENTS

Drum and bugle corps are, for the most part, photographed while doing what drum and bugle corps normally do: march in parades, play standstill concerts, and perform their drills on football fields. They are also photographed in a group pose. The challenge, therefore, was not in finding enough photographs to make this book possible but in finding enough interesting photographs. All images, unless otherwise noted, are from my own personal collection.

Without a doubt this book would have been a lot less interesting and a lot more work for me without the help of Dick Ammann, archivist, at the Racine Heritage Museum (RHM). I cannot thank him enough for all his expertise, time, and effort that he so generously gave to this project. His interest, enthusiasm, and dedication rivaled mine. A large number of the images appearing in this book came from the archives of the RHM.

Another major source of images for this book was the archives of the Racine Kilties Alumni Association (RKAA). Since being organized in 2003, dozens of Kilties alumni and others have generously donated photographs and other memorabilia to the association with the single purpose that they be shared and enjoyed by everyone. Many of these photographs appear in this book courtesy of the RKAA, and I cannot thank all of you enough.

I also would like to thank Jeff Ruetsche, acquisitions editor for Illinois and Wisconsin at Arcadia Publishing, for his confidence in me and his expert guidance.

INTRODUCTION

In 1964, Racine proclaimed itself "Drum and Bugle Corps Capital of the World" and set aside a day each summer to celebrate it. Called Drum Corps Day, it featured a parade through downtown Racine followed by a free drum corps show at Pershing Park where the parade ended. All of Racine's drum and bugle corps participated in this annual event as their way of thanking the community for its support. Drum Corps Day was celebrated through 1977.

But is Racine really the drum and bugle corps capital of the world? Two visiting VIPs at Drum Corps Day in 1966 were interviewed by Norman T. Monson, a *Racine Journal-Times* newspaper staff writer, regarding this question and both emphatically agreed that it is.

In the article "Noisy Boys Earn Title of Drum Corps Capital," written by Monson, which appeared in the Tuesday, June 28, 1966, edition of the *Racine Journal-Times*, Lawrence Grabowski from Glenview, Illinois, editor of the national publication *Drum Corps Digest*, told him, "There's no doubt about it. The best drum corps are in the Midwest and Racine is the hot bed of drum corps. Most cities are lucky to have one or two good corps, but Racine has got a whole bunch of them."

Edward J. Rooney, Hyde Park, Massachusetts, a highly regarded drum corps columnist, theatrical producer-director in Boston, and manager of his own drum corps, in this same article described Racine to Monson as the "Vatican" of the drum corps movement. "We in the East look to Racine as a 'headquarters' of drum corps," Rooney said when speaking at the 1966 Drum Corps Day observance.

In 1967, Ken Pias, founder and general director of Drum Corps Day, decided that as a promotional tool Racine needed to be officially recognized as the drum and bugle corps capital of the world. So that winter Pias wrote a letter to United States congressman Henry C. Schadeberg from Racine asking his help.

Congressman Schadeberg responded in a letter to Pias dated March 28, 1967,

> Relative to your desire to promote Racine as the drum corps capital of the world, I do not believe there is an official agency you go through. What I would suggest is that you contact the Mayor asking him to proclaim Racine as the drum corps capital of the world, further suggesting that the Mayor send me his proclamation which I will insert into the congressional record (which calls our intention to the attention of the Congress) along with other appropriate remarks. I'll be glad to do what I can.

Thanks to Pias's continuing efforts, that is exactly what happened. The proclamation citing Racine as the drum and bugle corps capital of the world was read into the *Congressional Record* by Congressman Schadeberg on Monday, June 12, 1967.

Racine abounds in drum and bugle corps history. In fact, Racine's drum and bugle corps history parallels that of the rest of the United States.

The civilian drum and bugle corps activity here in the United States began as a result of the bugle's introduction and utilization by the U.S. military during the War of 1812. During the war, U.S. Army rifle regiments were permitted to use bugles for the first time instead of fifes. Also during the war, the U.S. Marine Corps Band and the U.S. Army Band at West Point Military Academy incorporated the bugle into their music ensembles.

As a result of the bugle's use during the war, the instrument gained favor and became more and more popular. After the war, many civilian drum and fife corps and brass bands integrated bugles into their ensembles.

Racine's first such organization was the American Bugle Band. Organized in 1858 by one of Racine's most accomplished musicians, John P. Jones, it remained active for many years. *Bugle* was included in its name because of the then noteworthy fact that the instrument played by one of the members was a solid silver bugle that cost $100. By the end of 1858, another such organization, Leavitt's Bugle Band, was advertised in the *Racine Advocate* of December 8, 1858.

Since then, many, many other drum and bugle corps were organized in Racine. Unfortunately most of them were short-lived and now forgotten. It would be impossible for me to chronicle the history of all of Racine's drum and bugle corps in a book such as this. Therefore, the main focus of this book is on the six drum and bugle corps of the 1960s that earned Racine its title of "Drum and Bugle Corps Capital of the World." A historical survey of these six Racine drum and bugle corps—the Boys of 76, Racine Scouts, Racine Junior Scouts, Kilties, Kiltie Kadets, and Ambassa"Dears"/New Day—is presented here in scrapbook style. Amazingly three of these six drum and bugle corps are still in existence today: the Kilties, Racine Scouts, and Racine Junior Scouts. Please continue supporting these treasures of Racine.

One

Boys of 76

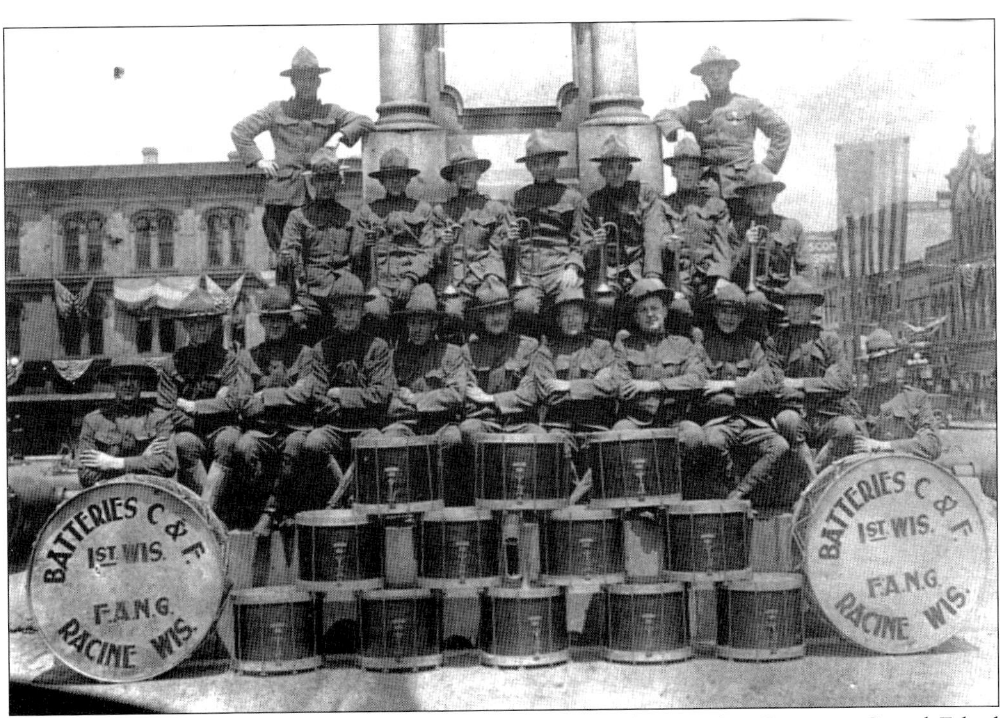

On May 28, 1917, it was announced in the *Racine Journal-News* that Batteries C and F had organized a drum and bugle corps. This photograph of the Batteries C and F Drum and Bugle Corps was taken on Monument Square in downtown Racine on Memorial Day, May 30, 1917. (Courtesy of RHM.)

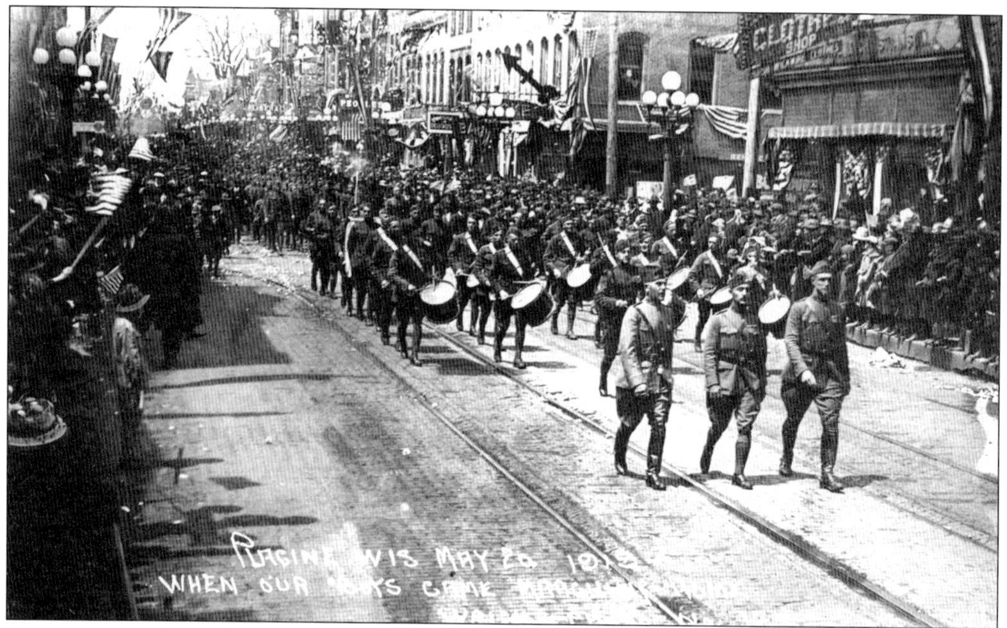

The Racine Batteries C and F Drum and Bugle Corps is marching in Racine's homecoming parade upon its arrival back from France on Tuesday, May 20, 1919.

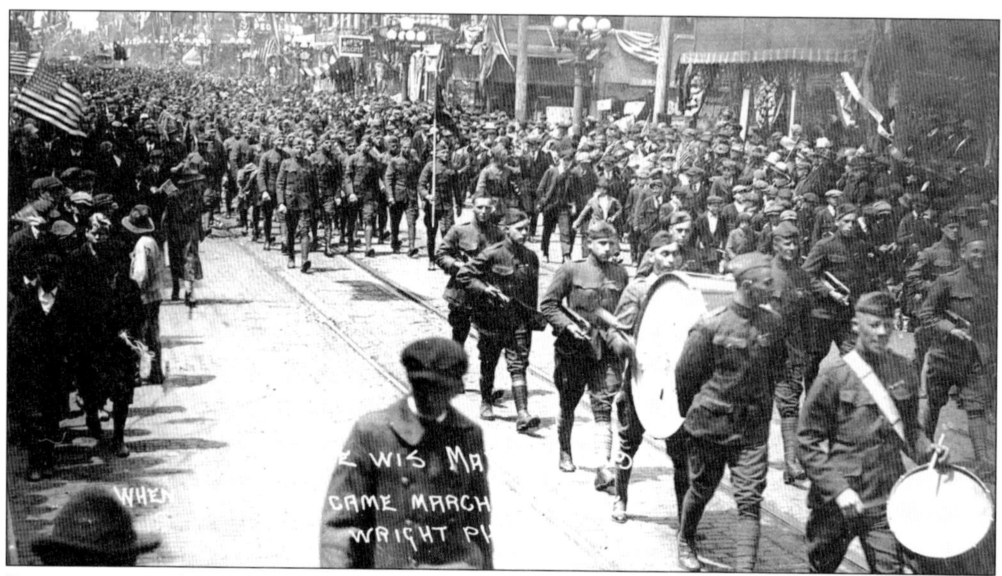

Racine was very happy that its boys were finally home. It was the most enthusiastic celebration ever seen in Racine. The marching soldiers were showered with confetti and ribbons. Guns were shot off and tin pans were banged away on. It was all a wild scene of confusion. Here Racine's Batteries C and F Drum and Bugle Corps is seen leading the homecoming parade east on Sixth Street on Tuesday, May 20, 1919. (Courtesy of RHM.)

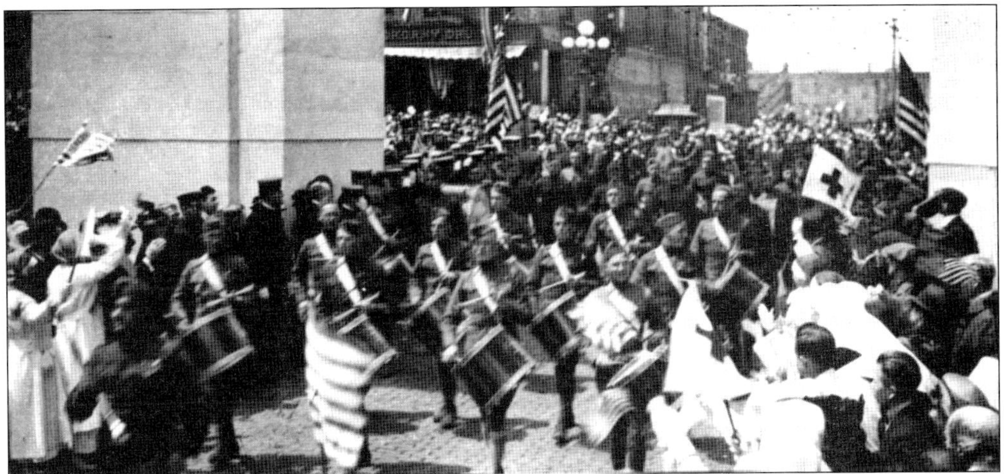

After detraining at Racine's Junction, Batteries C and F marched to the Lakeside Auditorium on Third Street in downtown Racine where they secured their packs and broke for their homes. They are seen here marching under the triumphal arch erected on Third Street just east of Main Street in downtown Racine just for the homecoming parade on Tuesday, May 20, 1919. (Courtesy of RKAA.)

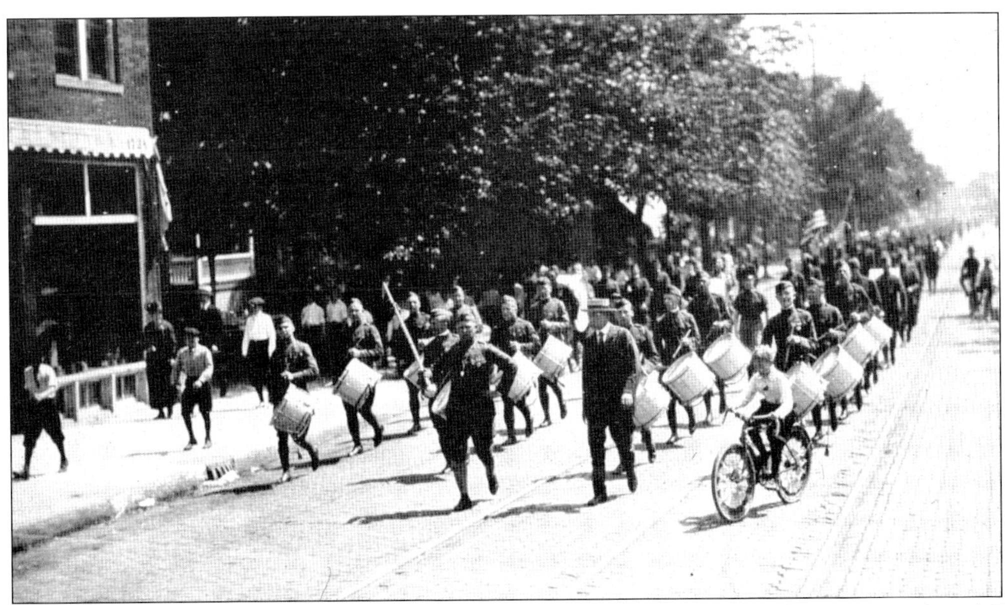

Immediately upon its return to Racine from France after World War I, the Batteries C and F Drum and Bugle Corps was reorganized as the 32nd Division Veterans Association of Racine Drum and Bugle Corps. This photograph of the drum corps wearing olive drabs for uniforms was taken sometime between May 1919 and August 1922. (Courtesy of RHM.)

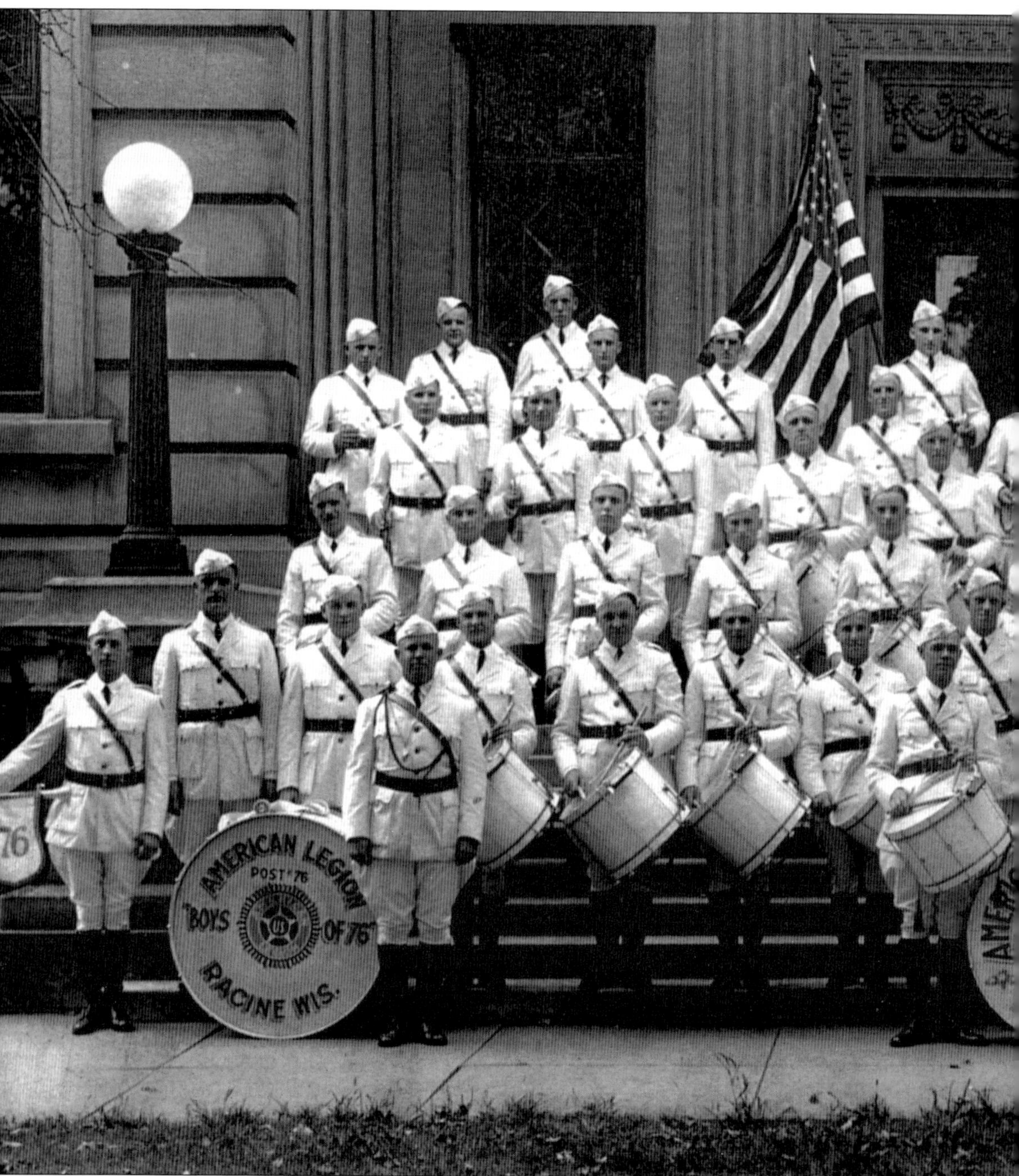

The Boys of 76 Drum and Bugle Corps began when Racine's Battery C of the 121st Field Artillery, Wisconsin National Guard, was training at Camp Douglas, August 16–30, 1916. Late one afternoon, Capt. George Rickeman, commander of Racine's Battery C, received word that it was their turn to put on guard mount that same day. Battery C had never put on guard mount before. Captain Rickeman did not panic. He had Sgt. George Wallace, first sergeant of Battery C, immediately begin training and drilling the men in how to perform a guard mount. In an effort to try to put on an impressive guard mount, Captain Rickeman also sent out Pvt. Fred Maxted,

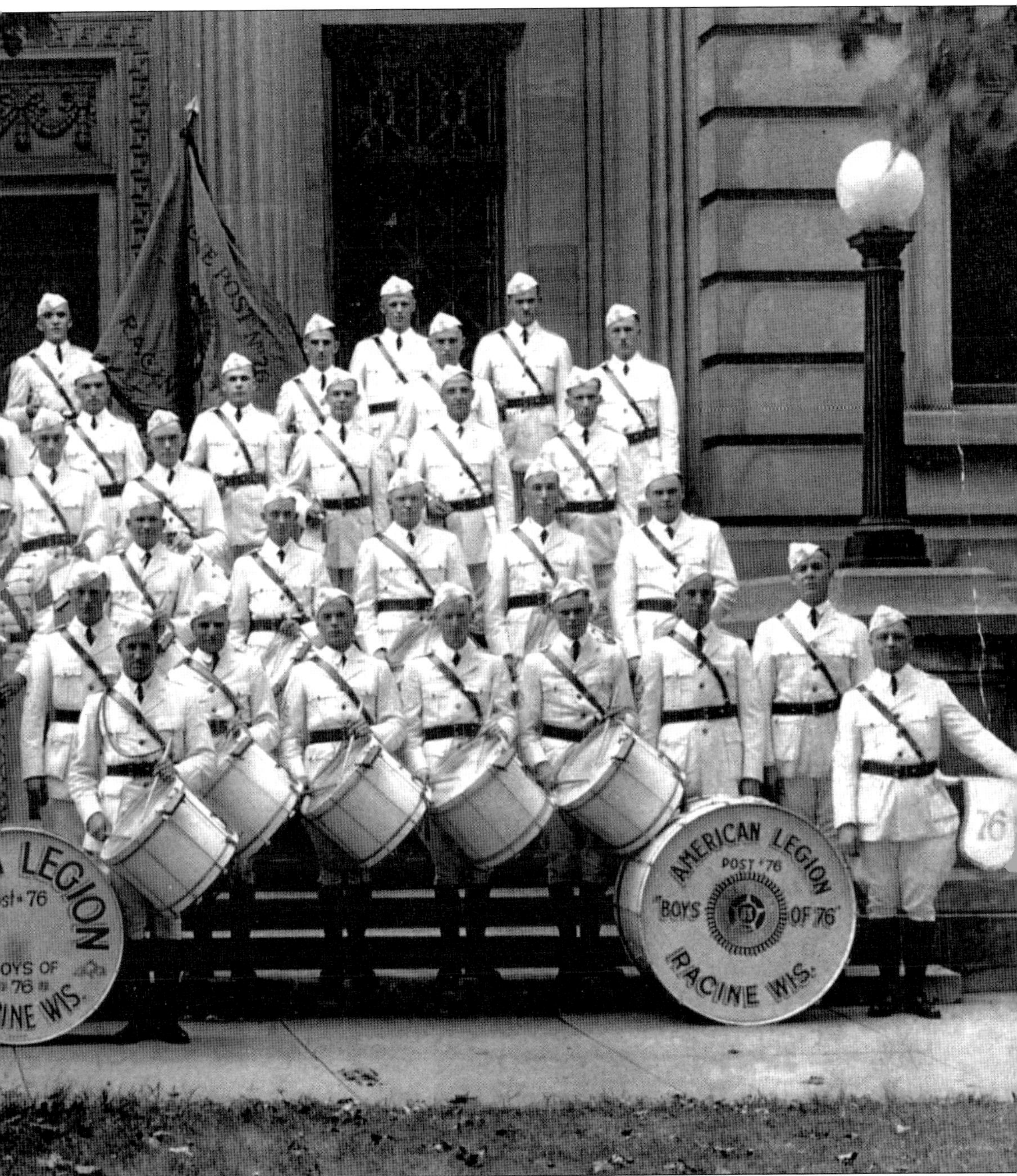

a drummer, to beg, buy, borrow, or steal some drums. He found four in the entire camp plus one bass drum. After only a brief practice that afternoon, Battery C put on an excellent guard mount. Battery C's little drum corps was such a hit that every night thereafter for the duration of this training camp it provided a cadence for each of the other batteries as they took their turns. Posing in front of Memorial Hall in Racine in the fall of 1922 is the Boys of 76 Drum and Bugle Corps in brand-new uniforms. (Courtesy of RHM.)

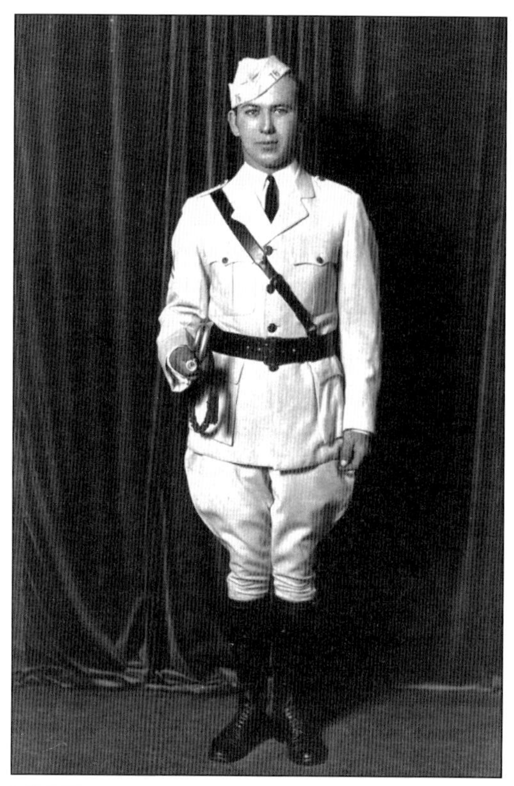

This great photograph taken in 1922 or 1923 of an unidentified member of the Boys of 76 gives a closer look of the new uniforms. The new uniforms consisted of white serge suits, white caps, black Sam Brown belts, black puttees, and black shoes. The caps are overseas style, and each bears the number 76. The trimmings on the uniforms of the drummers and buglers are blue while the trimmings on the drum major uniforms are gold. They donned these new uniforms for the first time on Monday night, August 21, 1922, when they paraded through the business district of Racine to show them off.

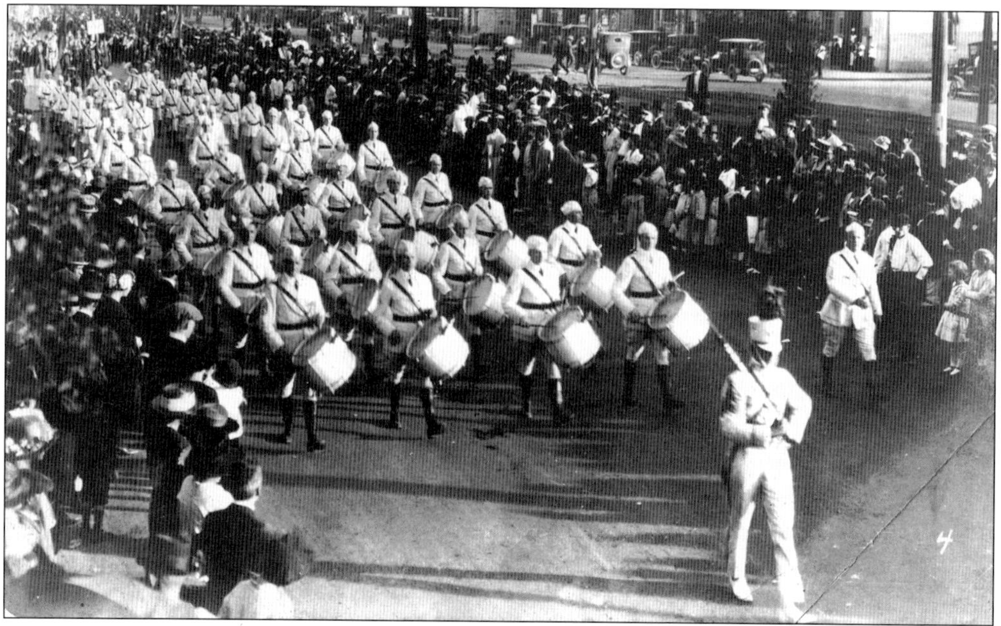

The Boys of 76 are on parade at the 1922 American Legion national convention in New Orleans, Louisiana. The Boys of 76 took first place. There was no field contest, only a judged parade. First prize was $250. Leading the Boys of 76 is drum major George Johnson, described as a "jaunty-stepping peacock." In New Orleans in 1922, he was voted best drum major and received a handsome gold-plated baton.

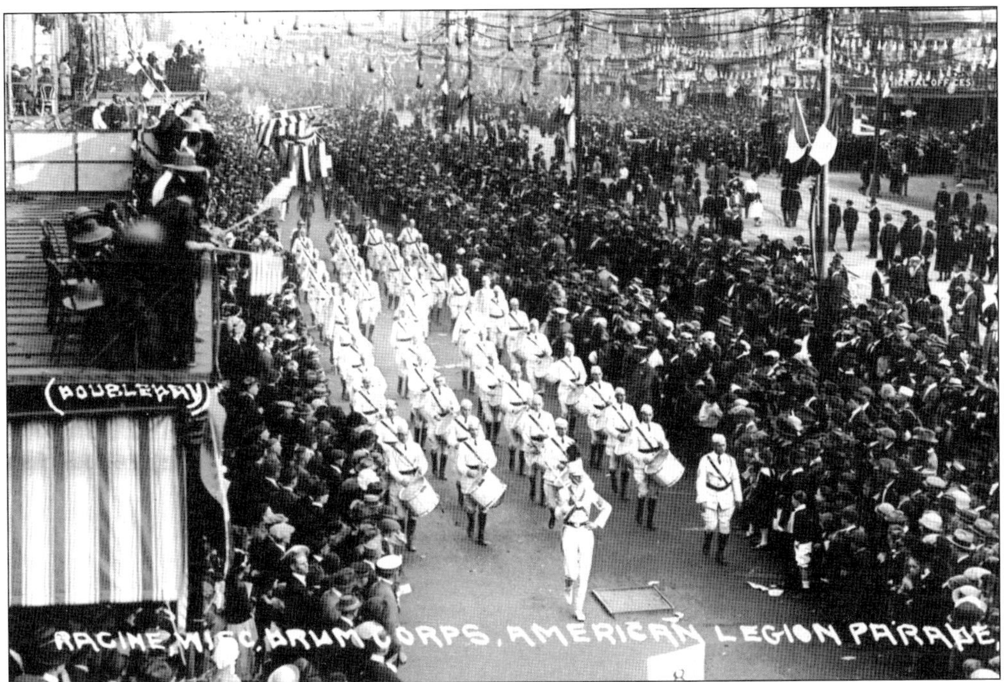

This is another view of the Boys of 76 showing their championship form in the big parade at the 1922 American Legion national convention in New Orleans. What is amazing is the huge crowd that lines the parade route.

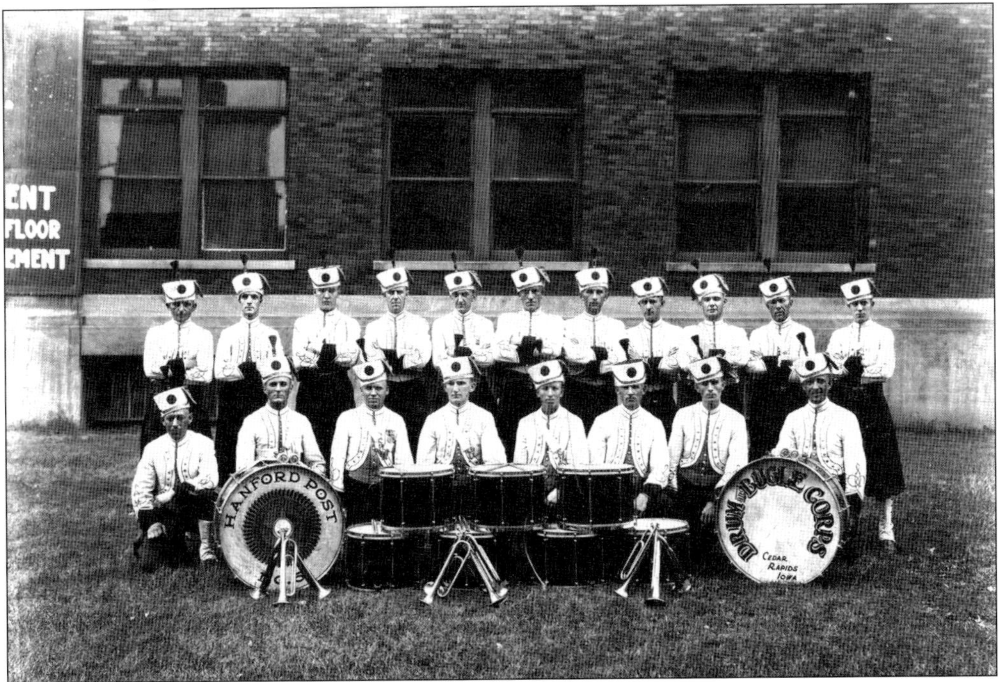

This rare photograph is of the Hanford Post No. 5 American Legion Drum and Bugle Corps from Cedar Rapids, Iowa. It was taken in 1922. This group also went to the 1922 American Legion national convention in New Orleans where it finished in second place.

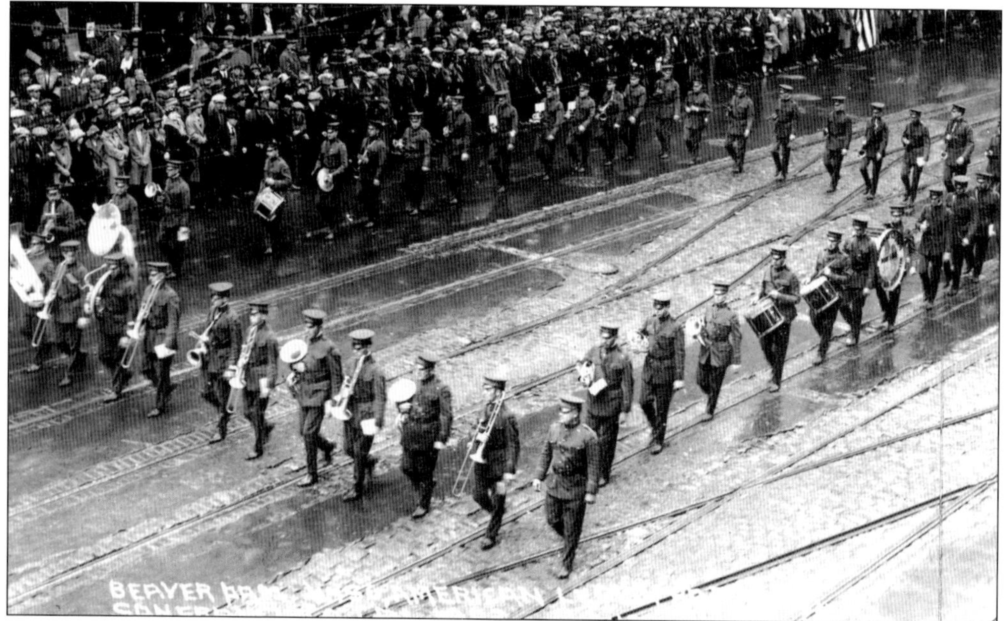

The Beaver Dam American Legion Band is seen here on parade at the 1923 American Legion national convention in San Francisco, California. The train that carried the Wisconsin delegation to this convention had three musical units on it; the Beaver Dam and Waukesha American Legion Bands and the Racine Boys of 76 Drum and Bugle Corps. For the second year in a row, the Boys of 76 took first place at the American Legion national convention.

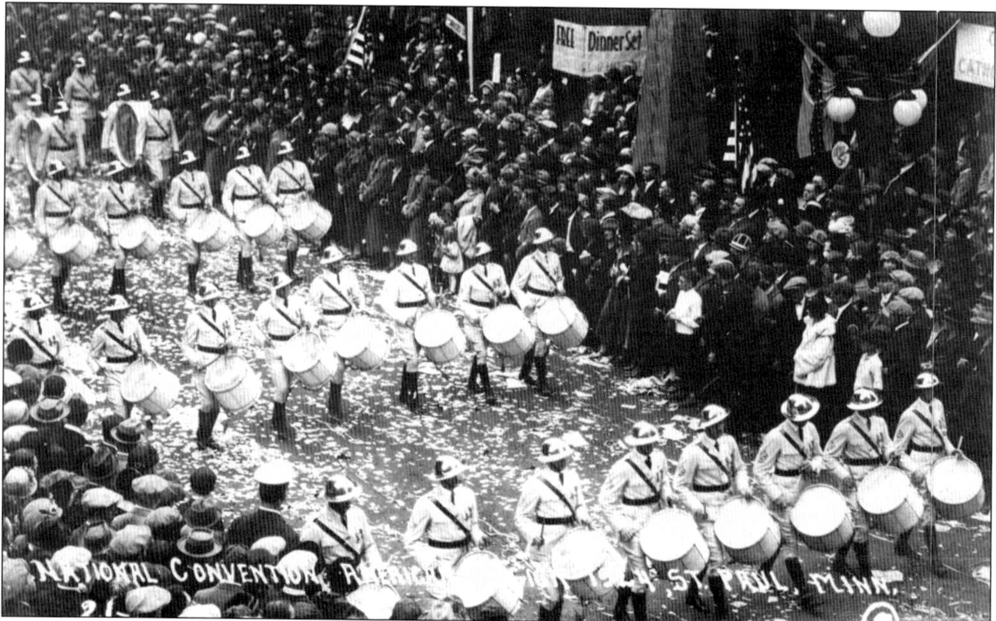

The Boys of 76 are seen here wearing their famous nickel-plated steel helmets for the first time at an American Legion national convention parade in St. Paul, Minnesota, on Tuesday afternoon, September 16, 1924. They were the original "chrome domes." The group, accompanied by two huge floats, was the highlight of the parade. The Boys of 76 won first place for the third consecutive year.

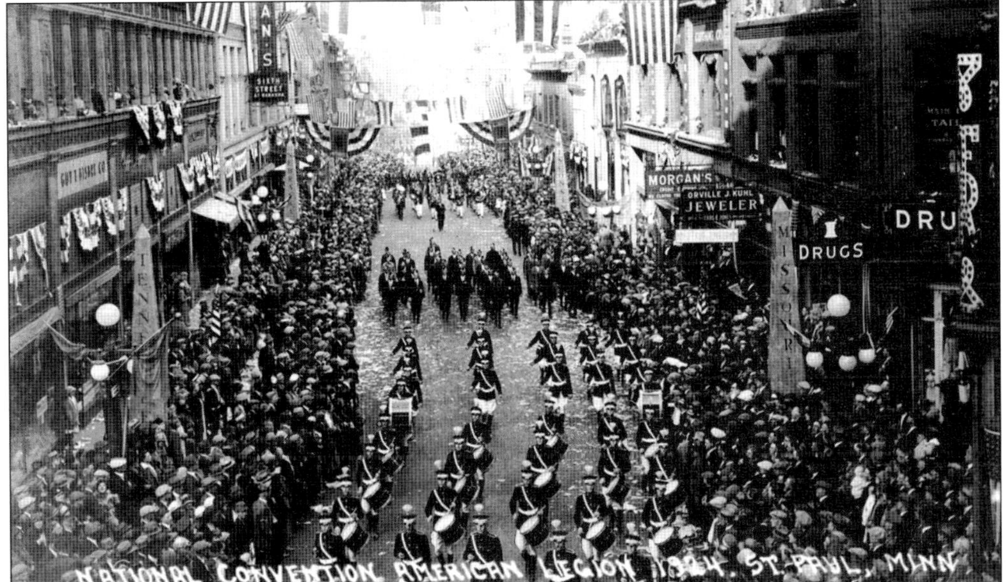

The Major A. M. Trier Post No. 75 Drum and Bugle Corps from Fond du Lac is pictured above marching in the American Legion national convention parade in St. Paul in 1924. Five drum and bugle corps were selected from the parade to compete for the championship in a finals contest at the Minnesota State Fairgrounds. Both the Boys of 76 and Fond du Lac made the five-corps finals. Fond du Lac, only six months old, made a fine showing and took third place at finals.

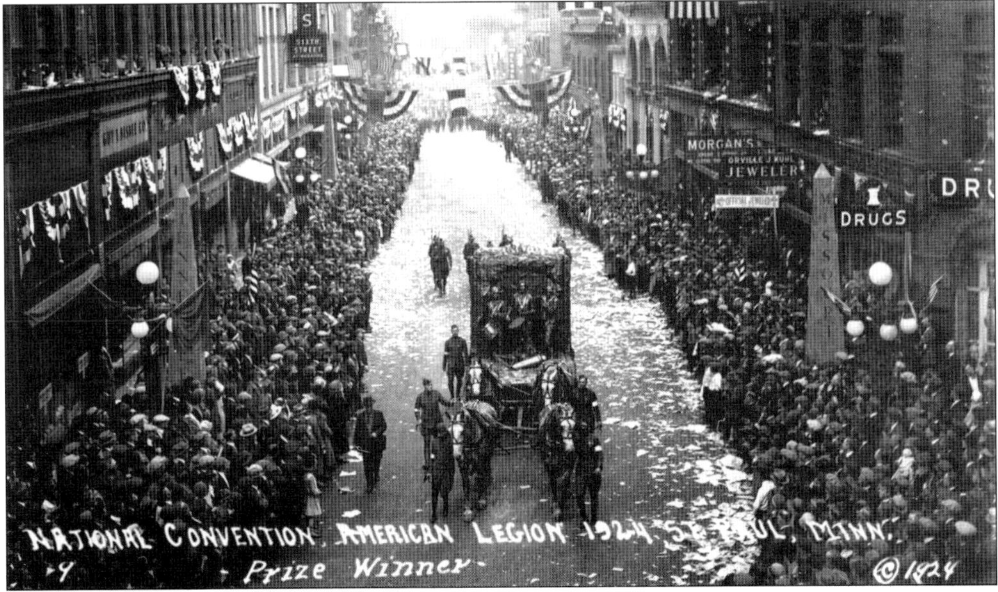

The Racine American Legion Post 76's Spirit of '76 float may be one of the oldest, most photographed, most publicized, and most paraded floats in the world. It had its debut in August 1922 at Beloit in the Wisconsin Department of American Legion's annual state convention parade, where it was awarded the first prize. It is now under the care of Racine's American Legion Post 310. The photograph on this postcard shows the float on parade in St. Paul, Minnesota, in the national convention parade of the American Legion in 1924.

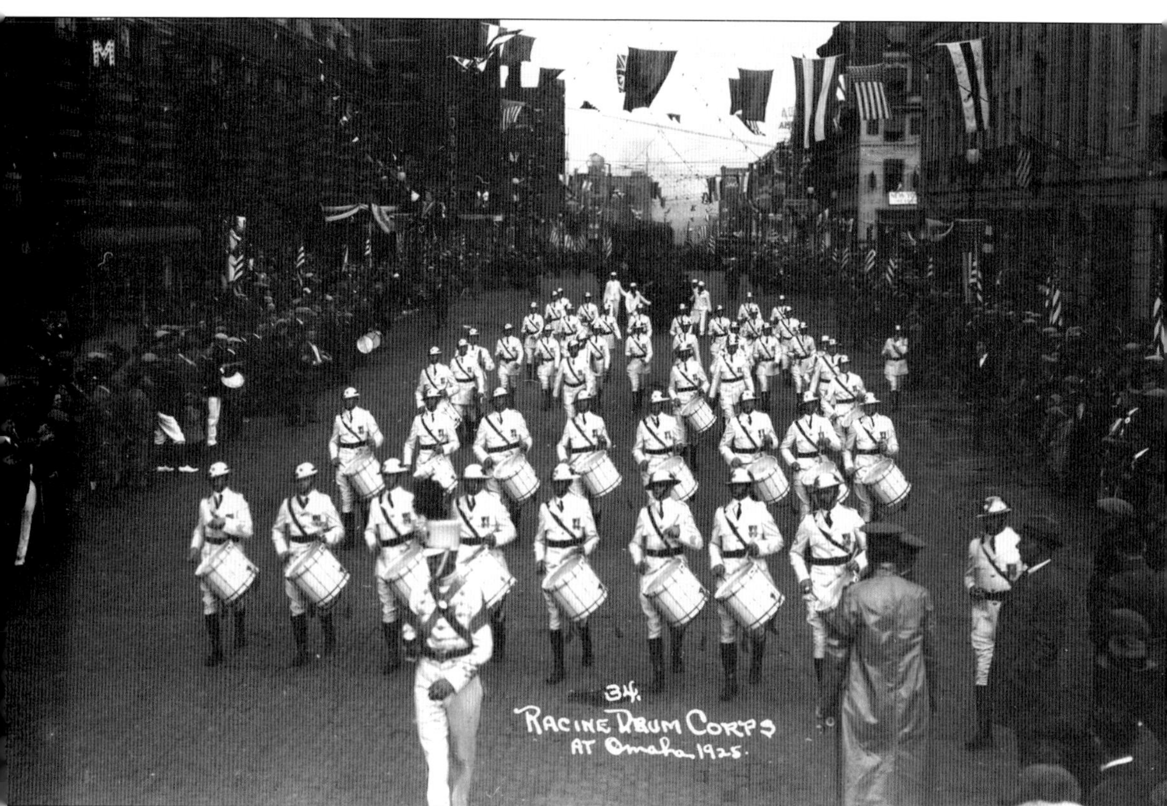

The Boys of 76 are marching in the American Legion national convention parade in Omaha, Nebraska, Tuesday, October 6, 1925. The Racine Boys of 76 won the American Legion Drum and Bugle Corps National Championship for the fourth consecutive time in Omaha in 1925. (Courtesy of RHM.)

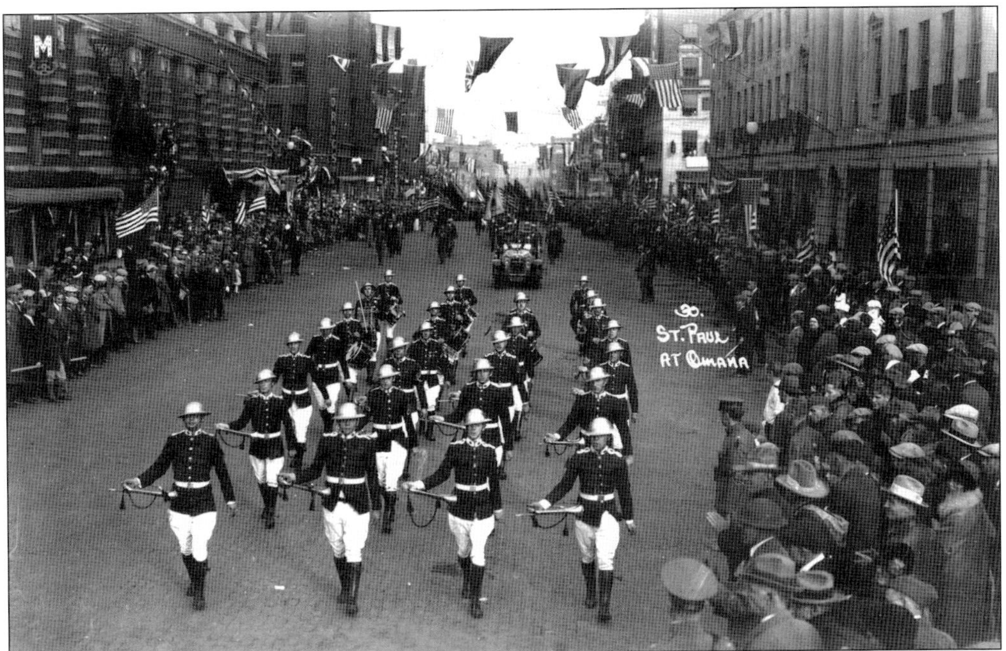

The American Legion Post No. 8 Drum and Bugle Corps from St. Paul, Minnesota, is seen in the American Legion's national convention parade in Omaha, Nebraska, in 1925. The group finished in second place at finals at the 1925 American Legion Drum and Bugle Corps National Championship in Omaha. (Courtesy of RHM.)

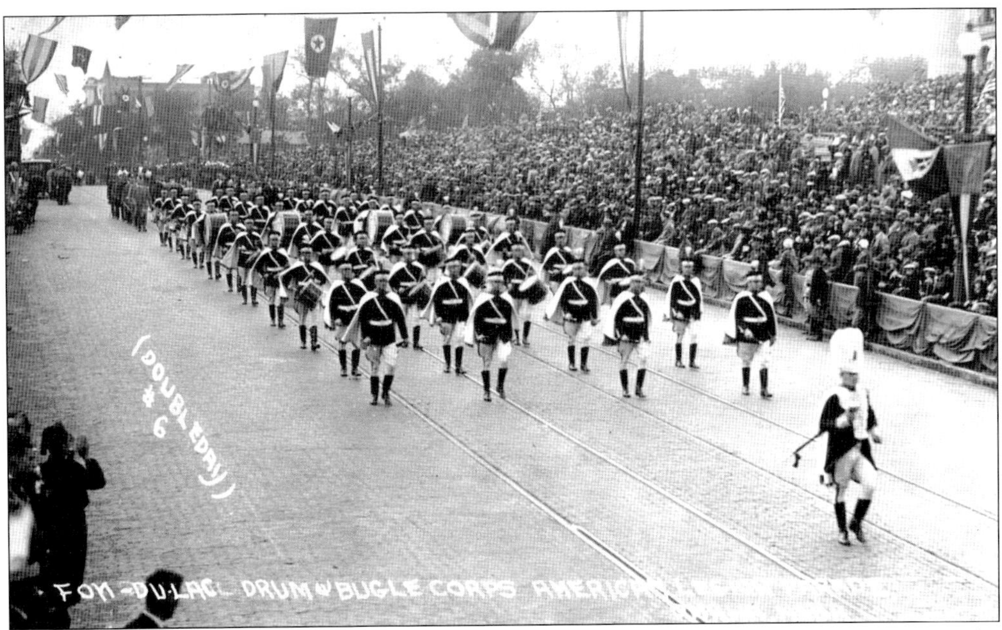

Now wearing capes, as seen here in the American Legion national convention parade in Omaha in 1925, the Major A. M. Trier Post No. 75 Drum and Bugle Corps from Fond du Lac was selected for the second straight year as one of the top five corps in the parade to compete in the finals contest. Fond du Lac came in fourth place in both the parade and at finals.

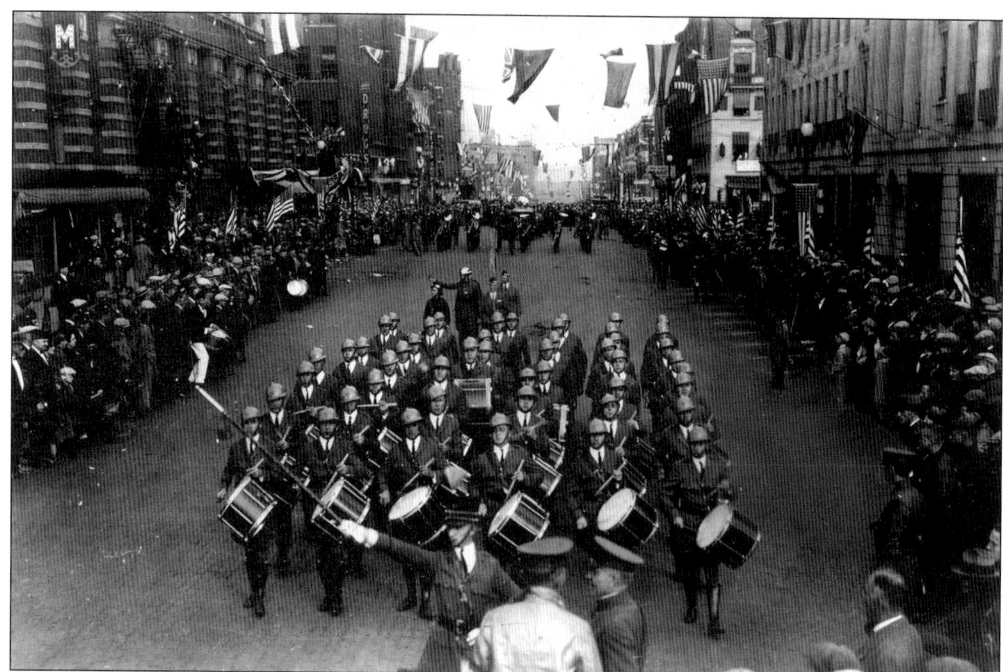

The Myron C. West Post 48 American Legion Drum and Bugle Corps, Beloit, is on parade at the American Legion national convention in Omaha, Nebraska, in 1925. The Beloit drum and bugle corps finished in sixth place, just missing making the five-corps finals.

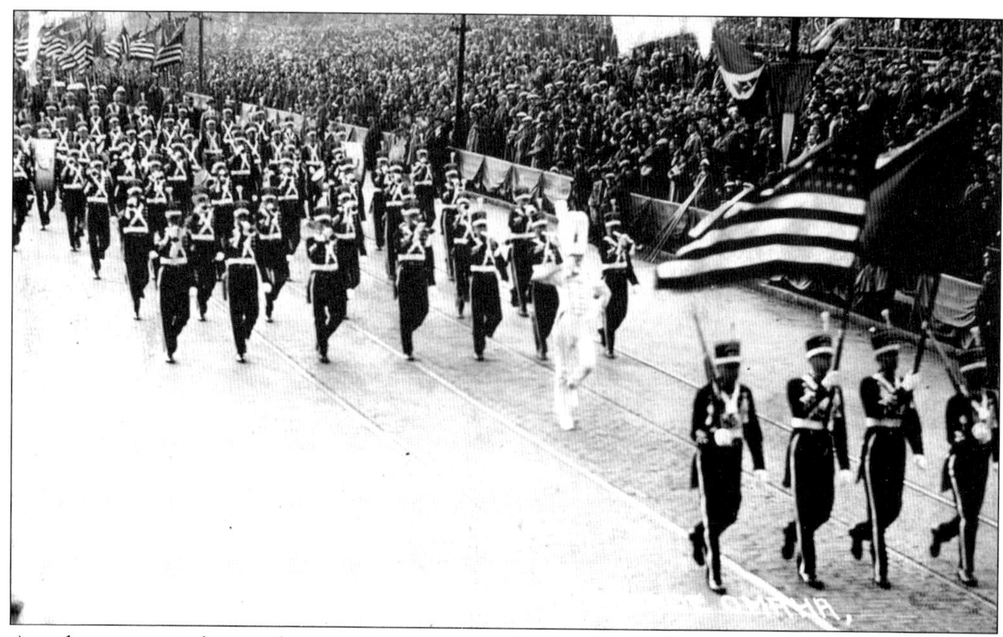

Another perennial powerhouse, the American Legion Post 85 Drum and Bugle Corps from Kankakee, Illinois, is marching proudly in the American Legion's national convention parade in Omaha in 1925. It came in third place at finals after receiving the top score in the parade. Kankakee made the top five for four consecutive years, 1924 through 1927.

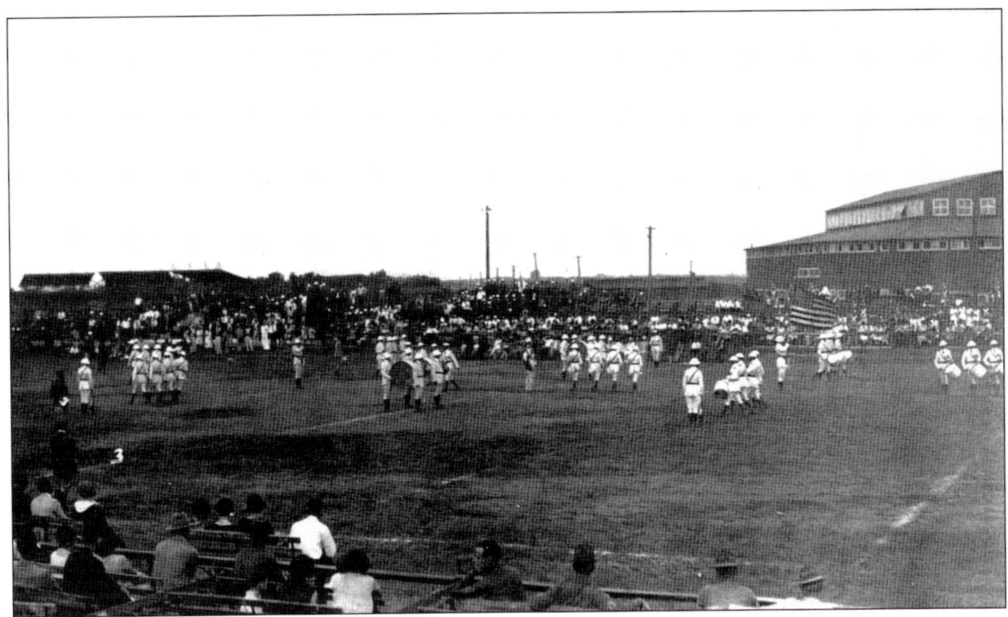

This is an extremely rare photograph of an American Legion drum and bugle corps in action on the field of competition during the 1920s. In this case, the Boys of 76 Drum and Bugle Corps is pictured performing in competition at the American Legion Drum and Bugle Corps National Championship in Omaha in 1925. (Courtesy of RHM.)

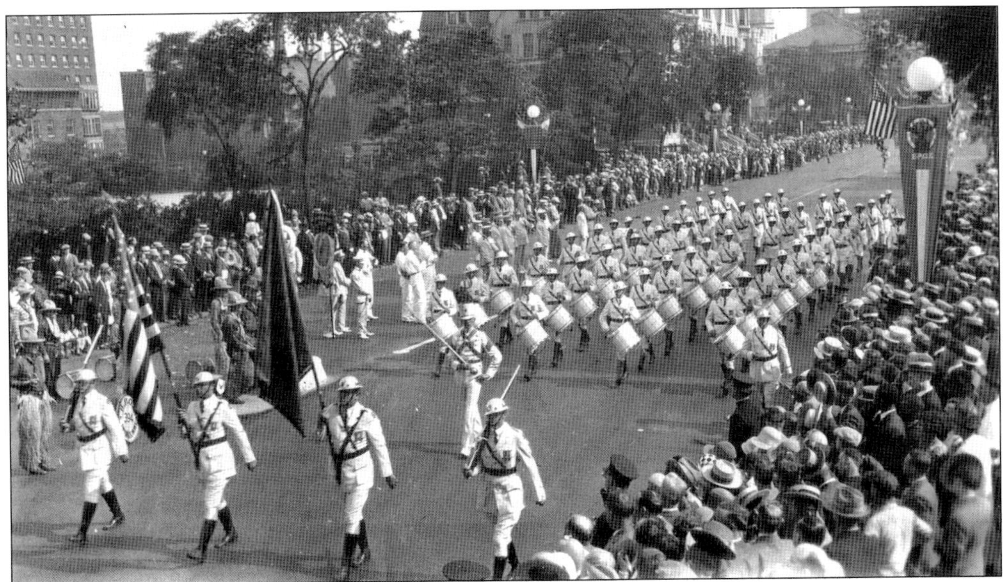

In addition to participating in most state and national American Legion convention parades during the 1920s, the Boys of 76 also marched in many state and national Elks and 32nd Division Veterans Association convention parades. Here is the Racine Boys of 76 Drum and Bugle Corps on parade in an annual Elks convention parade, most likely the national Elks convention parade in Chicago in August 1926. (Courtesy of RHM.)

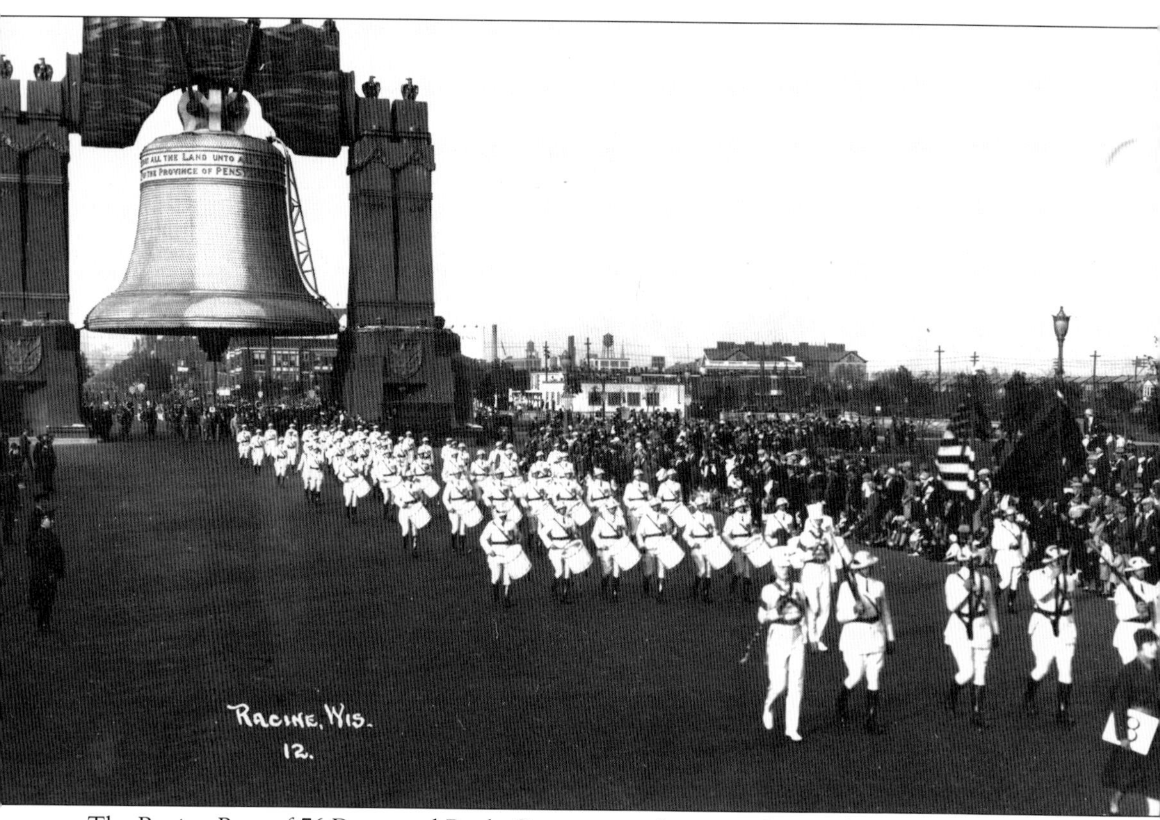

The Racine Boys of 76 Drum and Bugle Corps is seen here parading under a huge Liberty Bell during the annual American Legion national convention parade in Philadelphia, Pennsylvania, in 1926. The corps came in third place, thus ending its string of four consecutive American Legion national championships. (Courtesy of RHM.)

In 1927, the American Legion's national convention was held in Paris, France. This was the only time that the American Legion held its national convention outside the United States. Six American Legion post drum and bugle corps from the United States made the trip to compete for the American Legion national title. The Boys of 76 came in fifth place. Here an unknown member of the Boys of 76 is modeling pajamas. (Courtesy of RHM.)

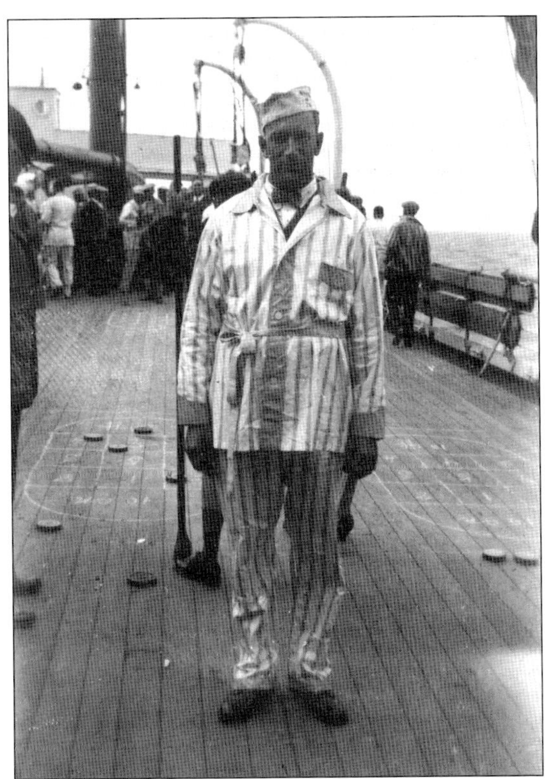

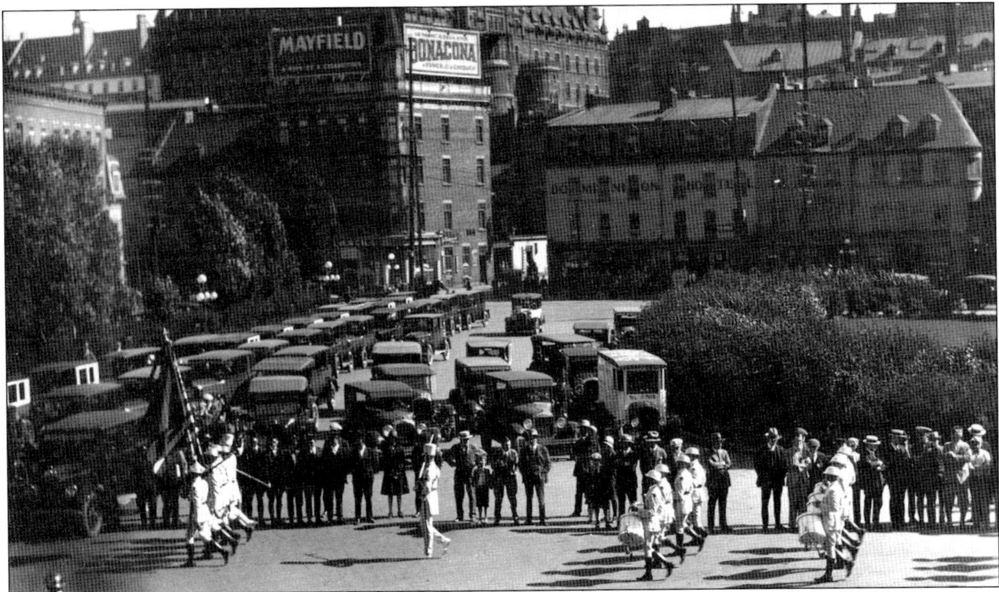

The trip to Paris actually began with the Boys of 76 Drum and Bugle Corps, numbering 52 men, leaving Racine via train on Tuesday, September 6, 1927, for Quebec, Canada. The men arrived on September 8 and were assigned staterooms aboard the SS *Mont Royal*, the passenger liner that would take them to Antwerp, Belgium. At noon, the drum corps assembled and marched to the Palais Station, where it put on an exhibition drill. The principal streets in Quebec were then paraded by the drum corps as seen in this photograph. (Courtesy of RHM.)

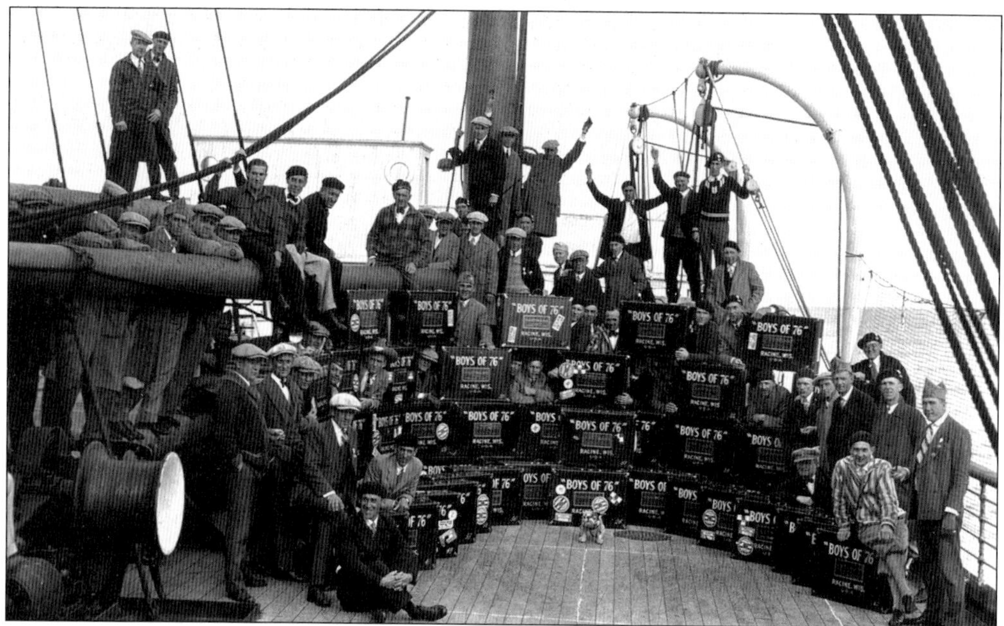

Friday morning, September 9, the SS *Mont Royal* pulled anchor and left Quebec, headed up the Gulf of St. Lawrence, and sailed to Antwerp, Belgium. Some members of the Boys of 76 are seen here having a little fun on board the SS *Mont Royal* during this voyage. Members are posing with their stacked luggage for this photograph. The luggage was made and donated by Hartmann Luggage of Racine. (Courtesy of RHM.)

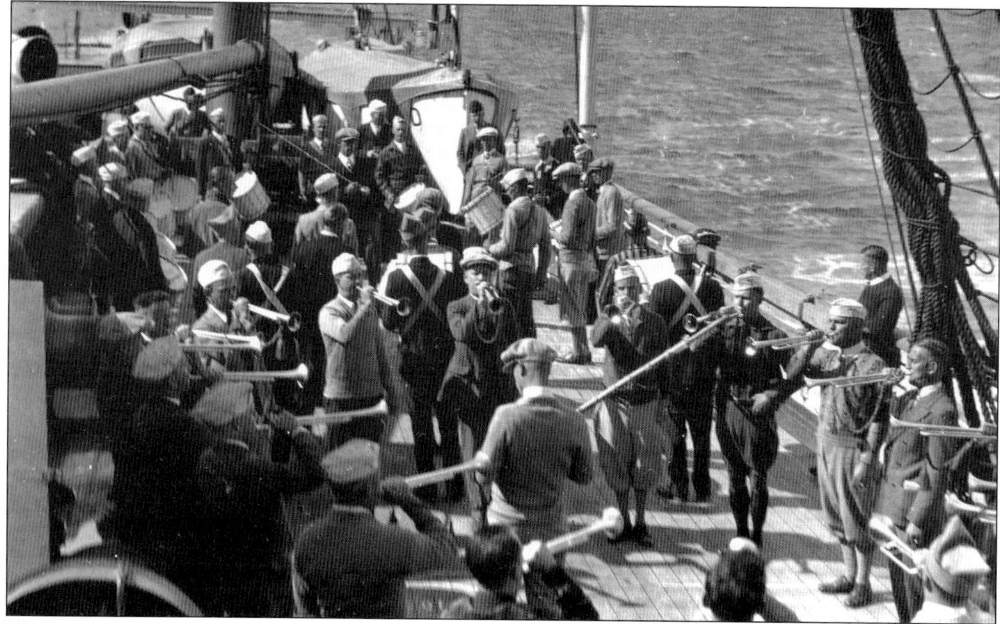

The members of the Boys of 76 practice their drums and bugles on the deck of the SS *Mont Royal* during their voyage from Quebec to Antwerp in September 1927. Early in the morning on Saturday, September 17, the SS *Mont Royal* steamed into the harbor in Antwerp. The drum corps almost immediately boarded a train and, with a stop in Brussels, Belgium, arrived in Paris that evening. The drum corps did perform in both Antwerp and Brussels. (Courtesy of RHM.)

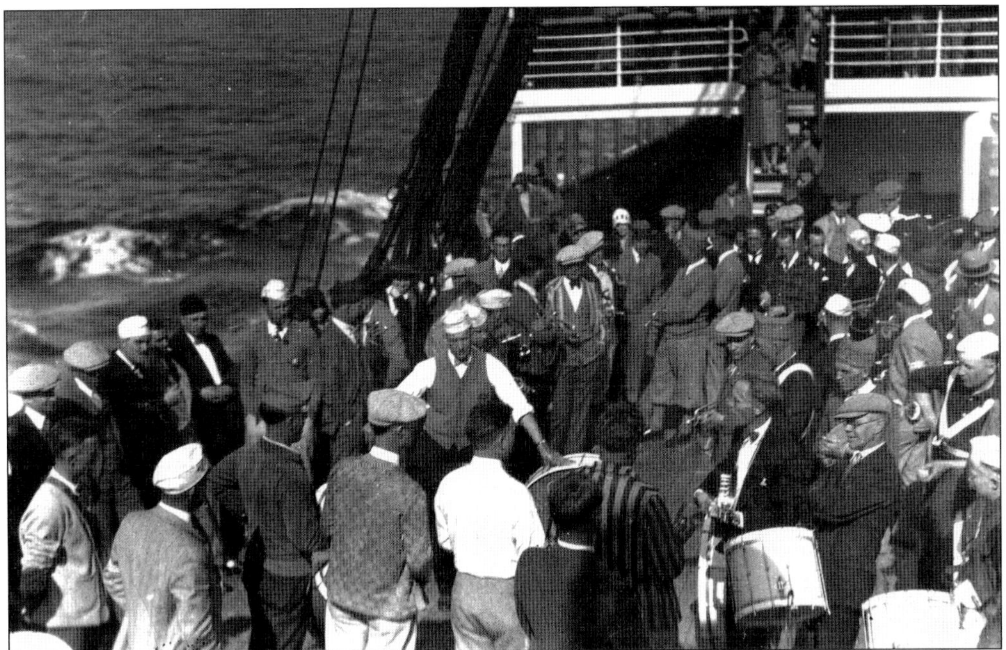

The SS *Mont Royal* was stated to be one of the largest ocean-going steamers. En route, practice drills were held on deck. The SS *Mont Royal* was also quite an elaborate ship for its time. The SS *Mont Royal* featured a promenade deck, a palm garden furnished in wicker furniture and palms, a complete gymnasium, a beauty parlor, a barbershop, and a beautiful dining room. (Courtesy of RHM.)

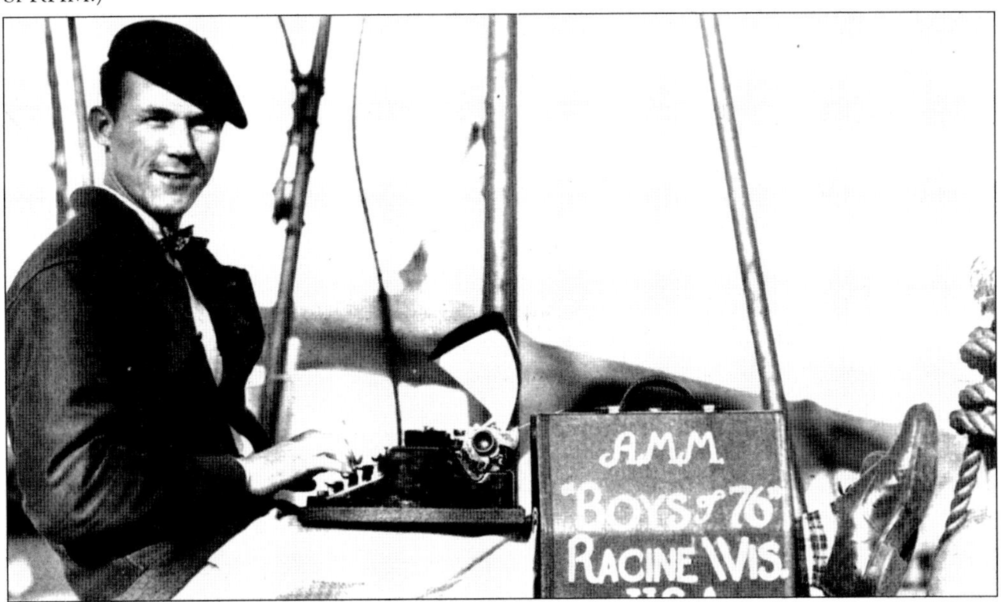

Arnold M. Malmquist, a member of the Boys of 76, is seen here typing away on the deck of the SS *Mont Royal*. He acted as a special correspondent for the *Racine Journal-News*, sending the newspaper numerous cablegrams describing the drum corps' trip to Paris in 1927. These were printed on the front page of the newspaper, keeping Racine informed about the trip's progress on almost a daily basis. (Courtesy of RHM.)

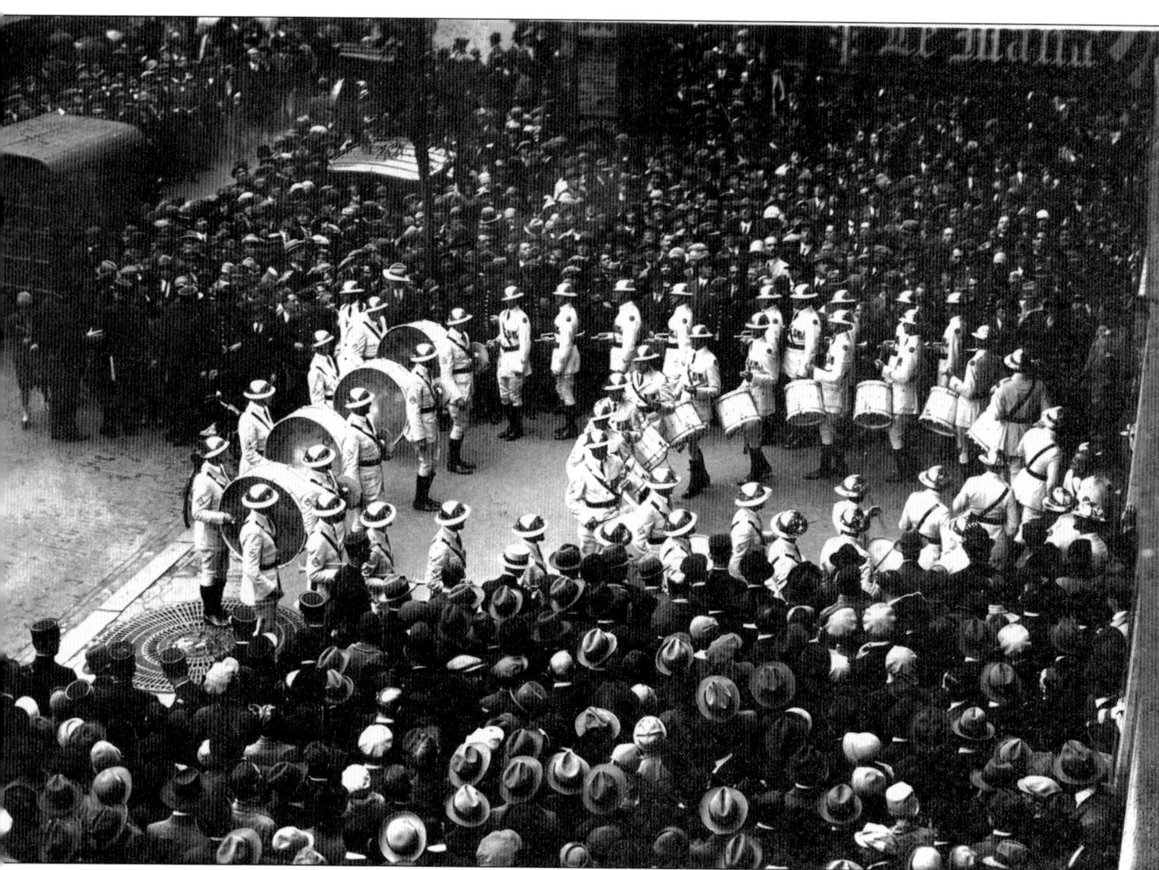

Barnstorming, marching about downtown and stopping at various locations such as in front of a hotel or on a street corner to play a song or two, was a favorite pastime for American Legion bands and drum corps while visiting cities. Here the Boys of 76 are seen barnstorming in 1927 somewhere in Paris. (Courtesy of RHM.)

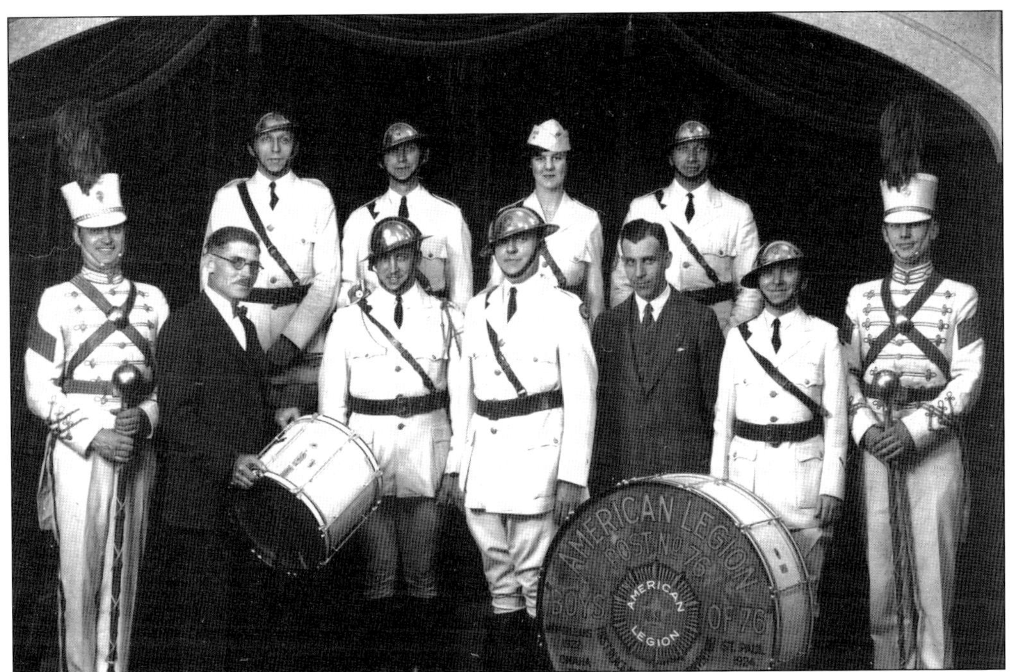

At the Capital Theater in Racine, Matthew Andis, holding the drum, is seen symbolically presenting the Boys of 76 with a gift of drum equipment on Monday night, September 17, 1928. His gift actually included 25 beautiful Avalon pearl drums with inlaid hoops and four large bass drums of the same style. The drums were the finest made at the time by the Ludwig Drum Company of Chicago. William Ludwig, the manufacturer, is wearing a suit and standing directly behind the bass drum. (Courtesy of RHM.)

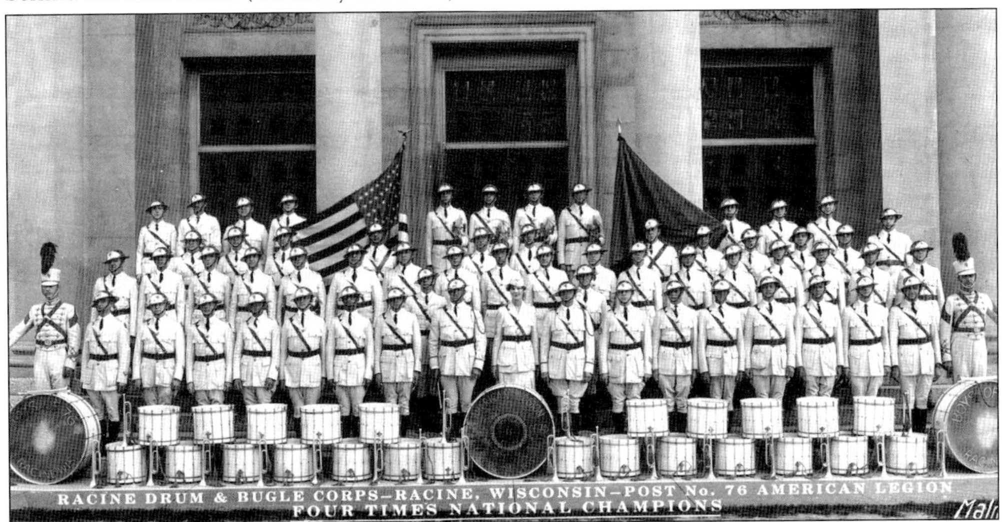

This photograph of the Racine Boys of 76 Drum and Bugle Corps was taken in front of Racine's Memorial Hall in 1928 before the group left for the American Legion national convention in San Antonio, Texas. In preliminary competition for the American Legion Drum and Bugle Corps National Championship in San Antonio, the Boys of 76 placed in the top 15 to earn a spot in the finals competition. In the finals contest at Foch Field in Fort Sam Houston for the American Legion national championship, the Boys of 76 finished in 10th place. (Courtesy of RHM.)

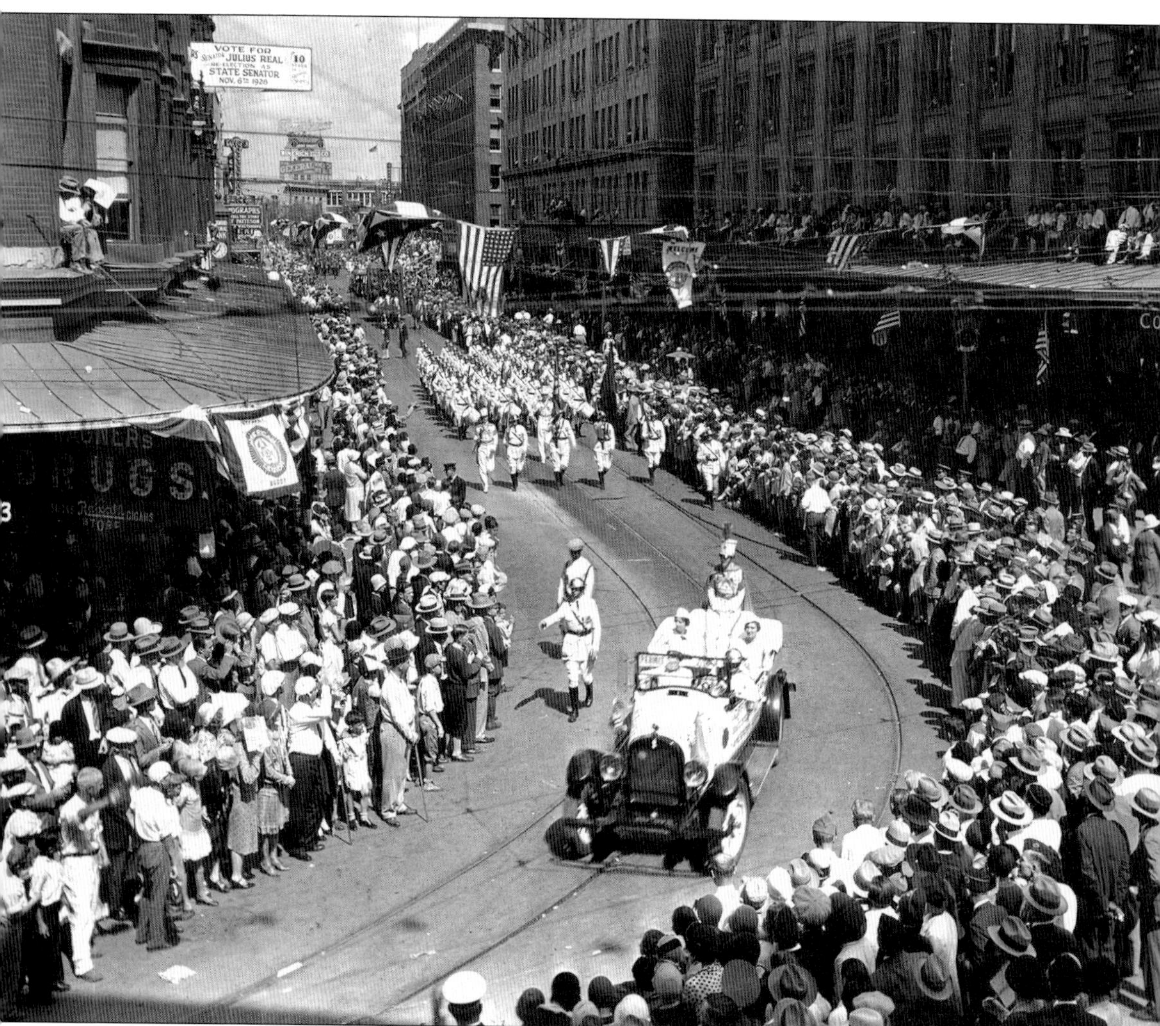

The official car of the Racine American Legion Post 76, a 1924 J. I. Case White Streak automobile, leads the way for the Boys of 76 Drum and Bugle Corps in the annual American Legion national convention parade in San Antonio, Texas, in 1928. In July 1924, the motorcar division of the J. I. Case Company presented Racine American Legion Post 76 with an automobile, which was intended for use on official business and on all future official trips of Racine Post 76. The car was enameled white with purple trimmings and carried the American Legion insignia in gold. The car was manufactured and assembled entirely in Racine. (Courtesy of RHM.)

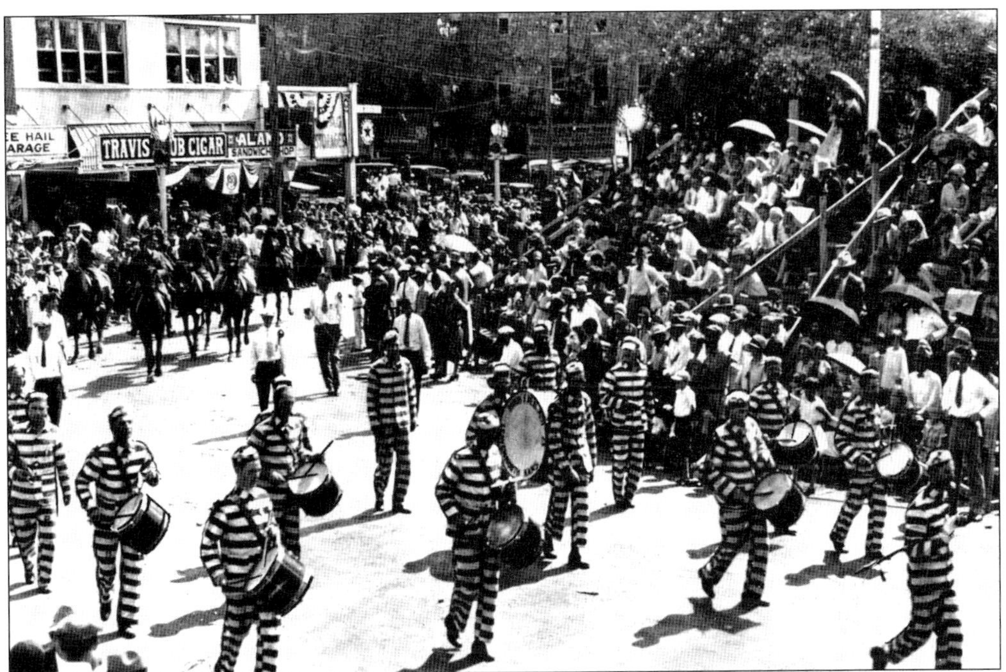

Many American Legion post drum and bugle corps wore very colorful and distinctive uniforms. Seen here, wearing prison-stripe uniforms, is the Byron H. Mehl Post 23 of Leavenworth, Kansas, during the big parade of the 10th annual American Legion national convention on Tuesday, October 9, 1928, in San Antonio.

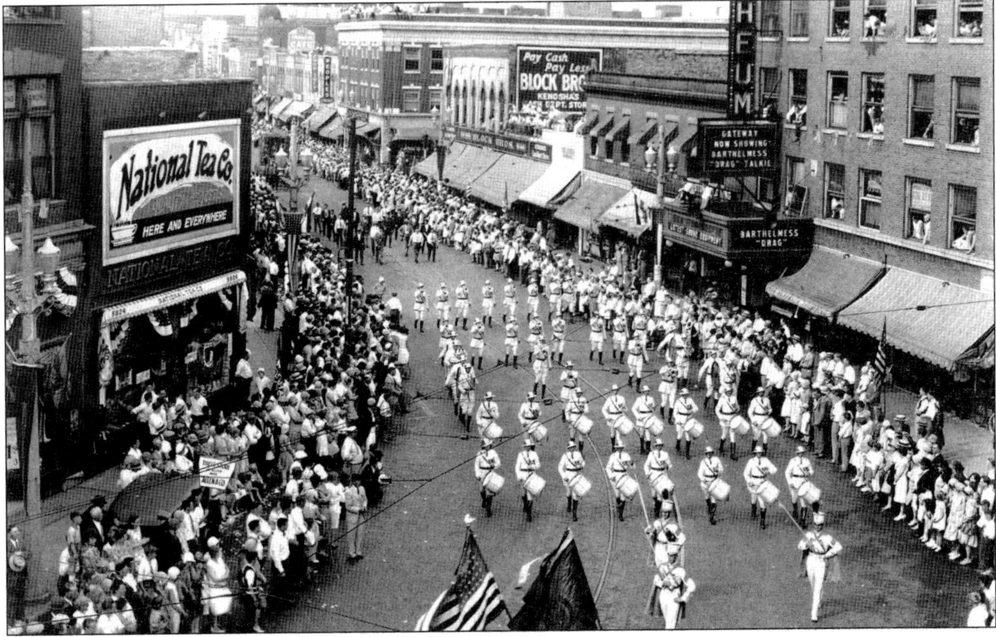

The Boys of 76 on parade are seen in Kenosha in the annual Wisconsin American Legion state convention parade held at 1:30 p.m. on Tuesday, August 13, 1929. Eight drum corps competed on Tuesday night at Simmons Ball Park in Kenosha for the 1929 Wisconsin American Legion Drum and Bugle Corps State Championship. The Boys of 76 won convincingly. (Courtesy of RHM.)

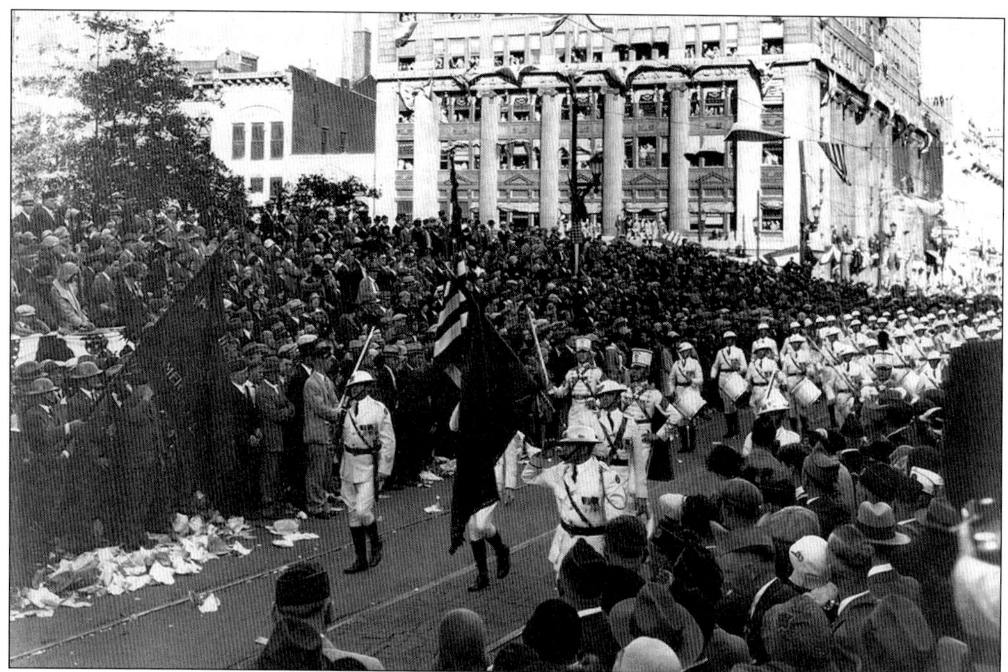

The American Legion national convention parade was the main attraction on Tuesday, October 1, 1929, in Louisville, Kentucky. Marching in the big parade are the Boys of 76. More than 30,000 legionnaires took part in the parade, which also included around 100 floats and about 129 bands and drum corps. (Courtesy of RHM.)

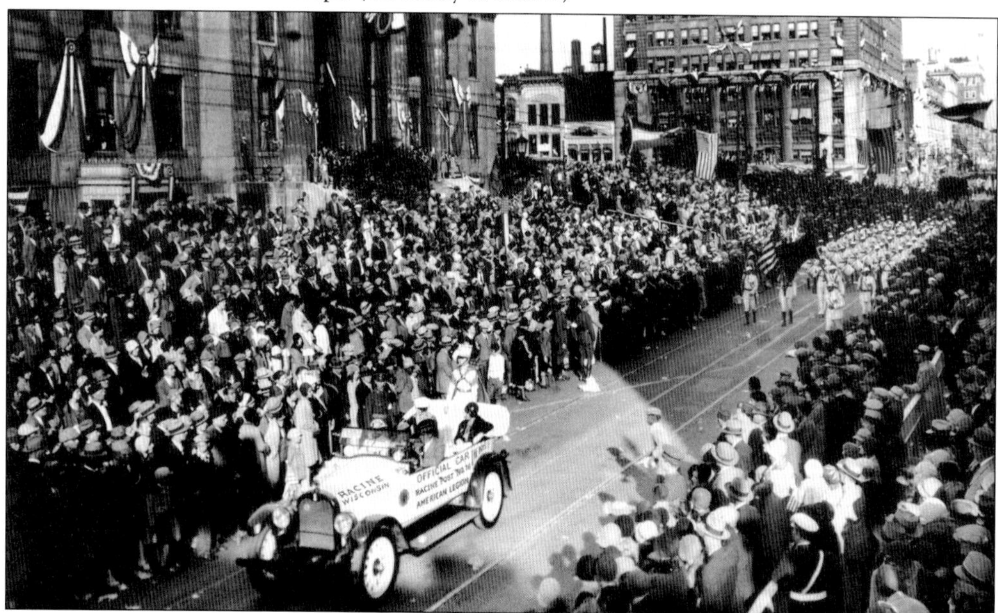

Clearing the way for the Boys of 76 Drum and Bugle Corps in the annual American Legion convention parade in Louisville in 1929 is the J. I. Case White Streak automobile belonging to the Racine American Legion Post 76. In its quest for the 1929 American Legion Drum and Bugle Corps National Championship, the group finished in 15th place in preliminary competition. Unfortunately only 10 drum and bugle corps made the finals. (Courtesy of RHM.)

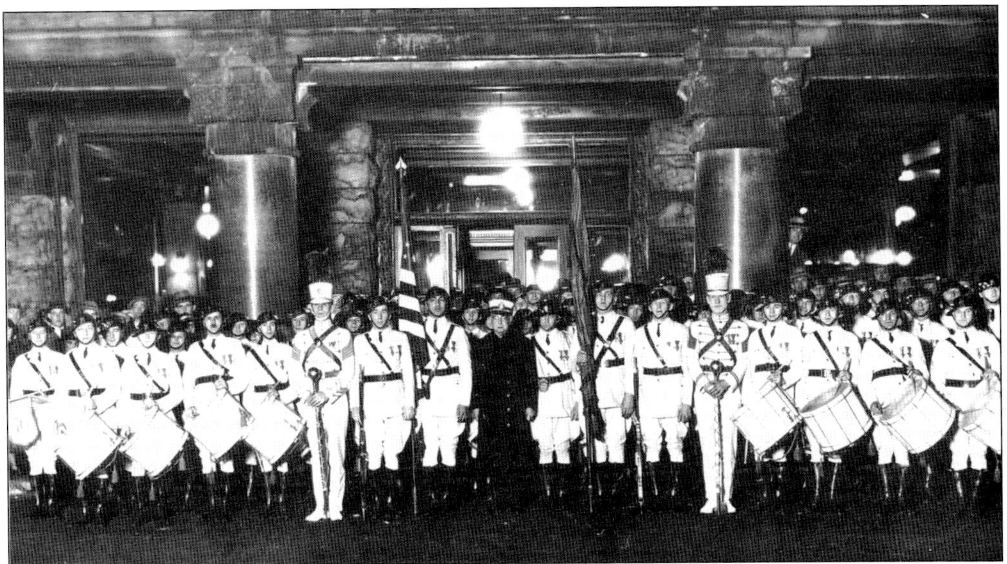

The Boys of 76 Drum and Bugle Corps is seen at the entrance of the Hotel Pfister in Milwaukee with the famous bandmaster John Philip Sousa in the center. Sometime during the 1920s, the Boys of 76 traveled by train to Milwaukee where the group escorted Sousa from the Hotel Pfister to the Milwaukee Auditorium prior to his Sunday night concert there. After the parade, but before his concert, Sousa directed the Boys of 76 Drum and Bugle Corps in the playing of one of his marches outside the Milwaukee Auditorium. (Courtesy of RHM.)

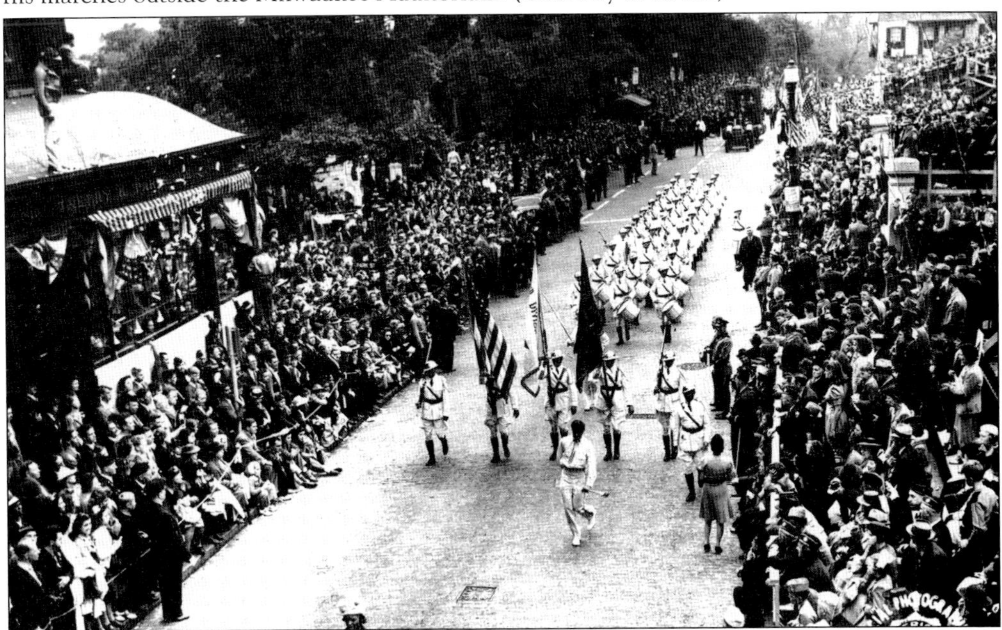

The Boys of 76 Drum and Bugle Corps is heading the Wisconsin delegation in the American Legion's annual national convention parade staged in Boston, Massachusetts, on Tuesday afternoon, October 7, 1930. The Boys of 76 placed seventh at the preliminaries, which earned the group a spot in the finals contest of the American Legion Drum and Bugle Corps National Championship. At finals, the Boys of 76 put on a splendid performance and took second place, just missing winning the national championship by 0.18 of a point. (Courtesy of RHM.)

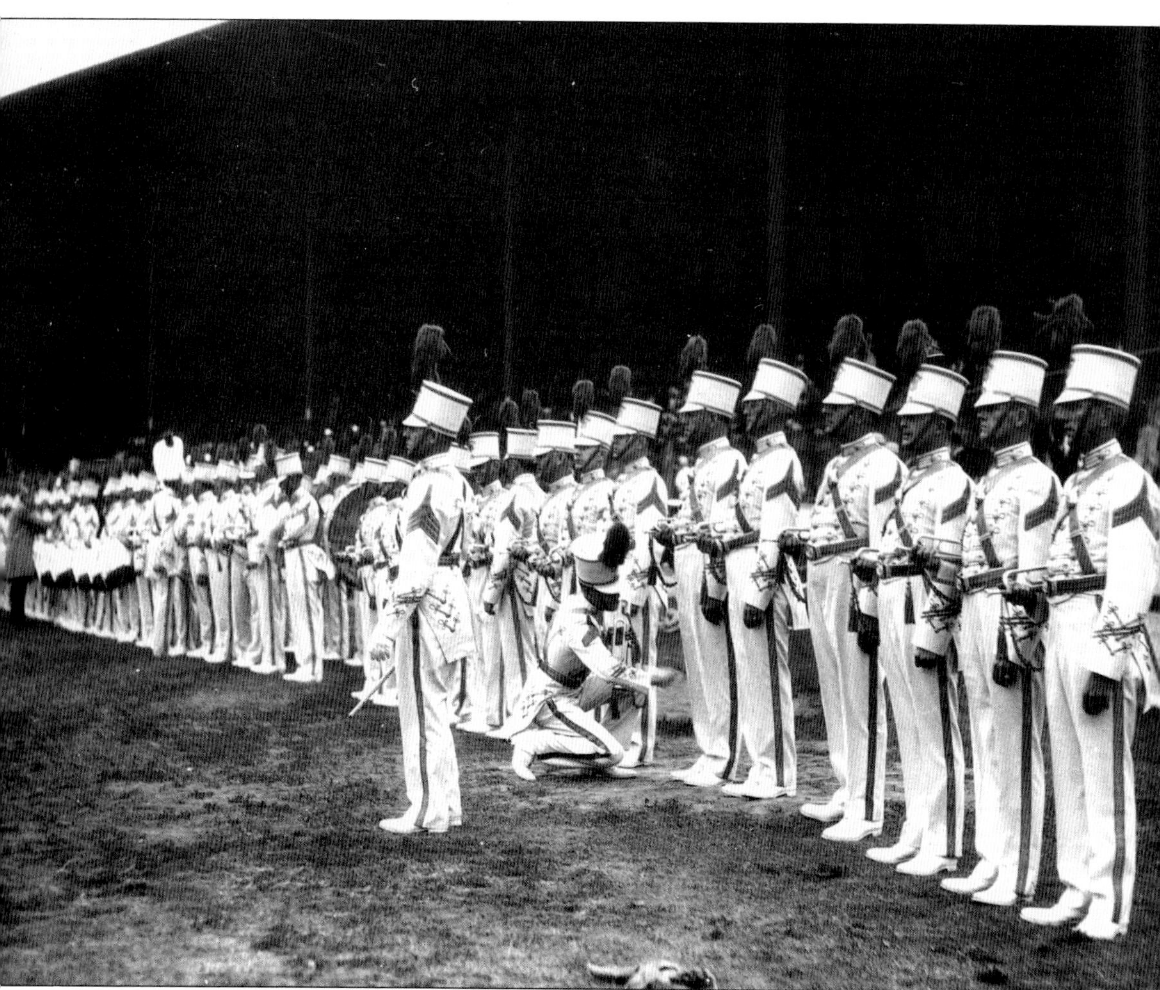

Members of the Boys of 76, resplendent in cream-colored West Point–style uniforms, appear to be getting ready for inspection at a state or national American Legion competition during the 1930s. Inspection of uniforms, equipment, and personal appearance was a part of all state and national American Legion contests. These West Point–style uniforms, first worn by the corps in 1930, were replaced in October 1939 with new uniforms. These new uniforms were duplicates of the original 1920s-style uniforms, which had been worn by the corps when it won its four national championships in 1922, 1923, 1924, and 1925, with the exception that gold shoulder cords and white and gold American Legion insignia were added. (Courtesy of RHM.)

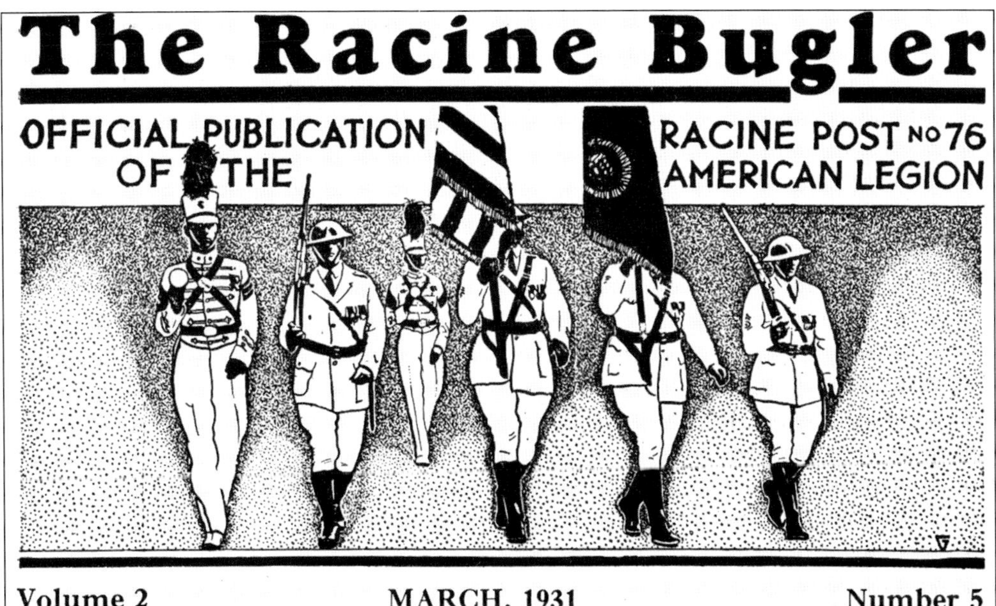

The Racine Bugler

OFFICIAL PUBLICATION OF THE RACINE POST No 76 AMERICAN LEGION

Volume 2 MARCH, 1931 Number 5

A drawing of the Boys of 76's color guard is the masthead for the *Racine Bugler*, the official publication of the Racine American Legion Post 76. These must be rare because the March 1931 issue that this image comes from is the only one the author has ever seen.

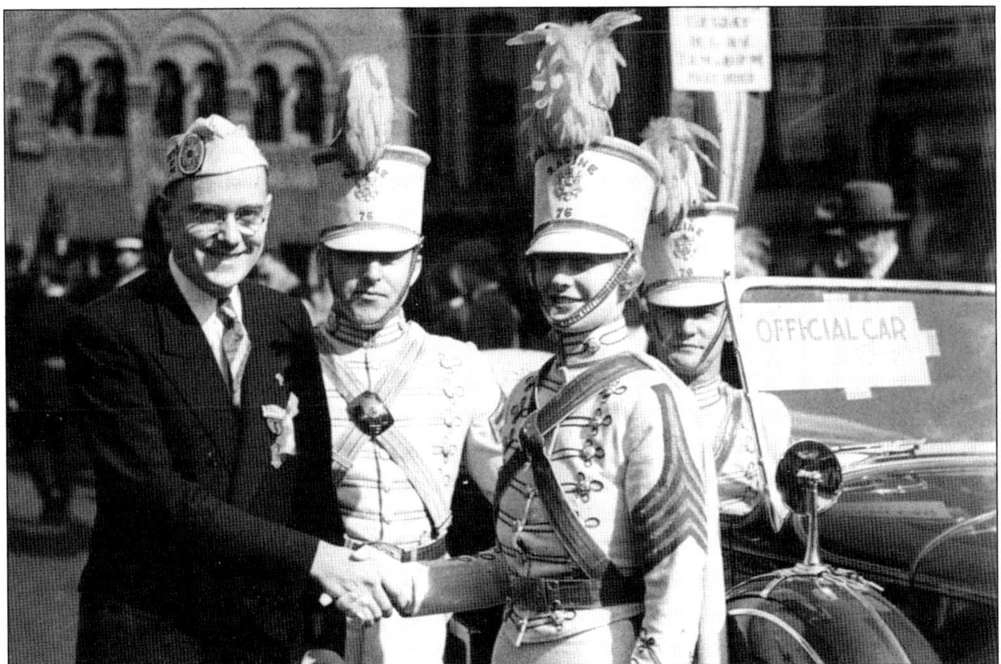

Every year, beginning in 1926 and continuing well into the 1930s, the Boys of 76 sponsored a dance in September. Female contestants were recruited to compete for the title of Miss 76. The beautiful young lady wearing a Boys of 76 uniform is Miss 76 Lillian Anderson, pictured here in Chicago in 1932 shaking hands with Dr. W. D. Gearen, commander of Racine Post 76. Immediately behind them is Ray Wilcox, left, adjutant of Racine Post 76, and Lloyd Jones, service officer for Racine Post 76. (Courtesy of RHM.)

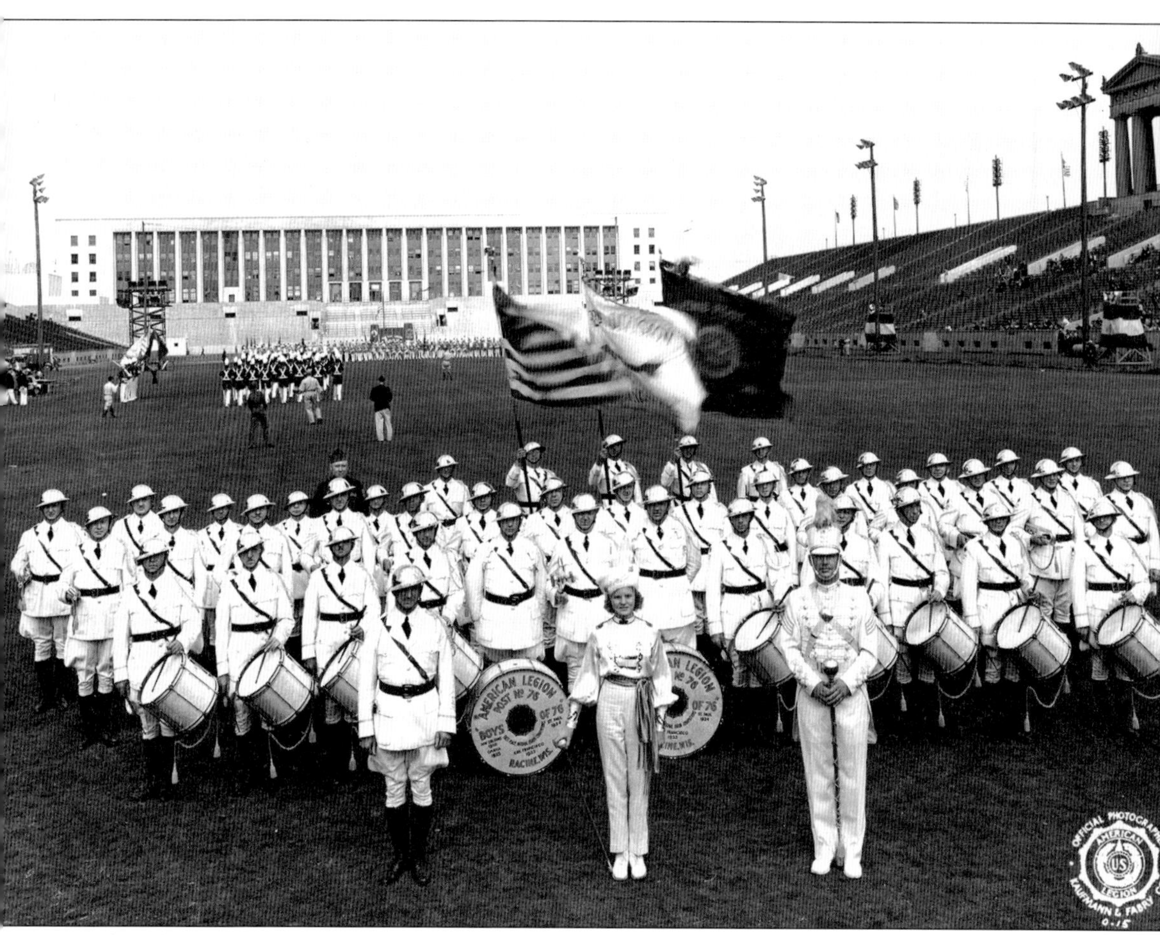

This photograph of the Racine Boys of 76 Drum and Bugle Corps was taken after the group's preliminary performance at the American Legion Drum and Bugle Corps National Championship at Chicago's Soldier Field on Monday, September 25, 1939. The group battled its way into the 12-corps finals by placing sixth in preliminary competition with 29 other drum corps. The Boys of 76 fell to 10th place at finals, held at Soldier Field that same night. (Courtesy of RHM.)

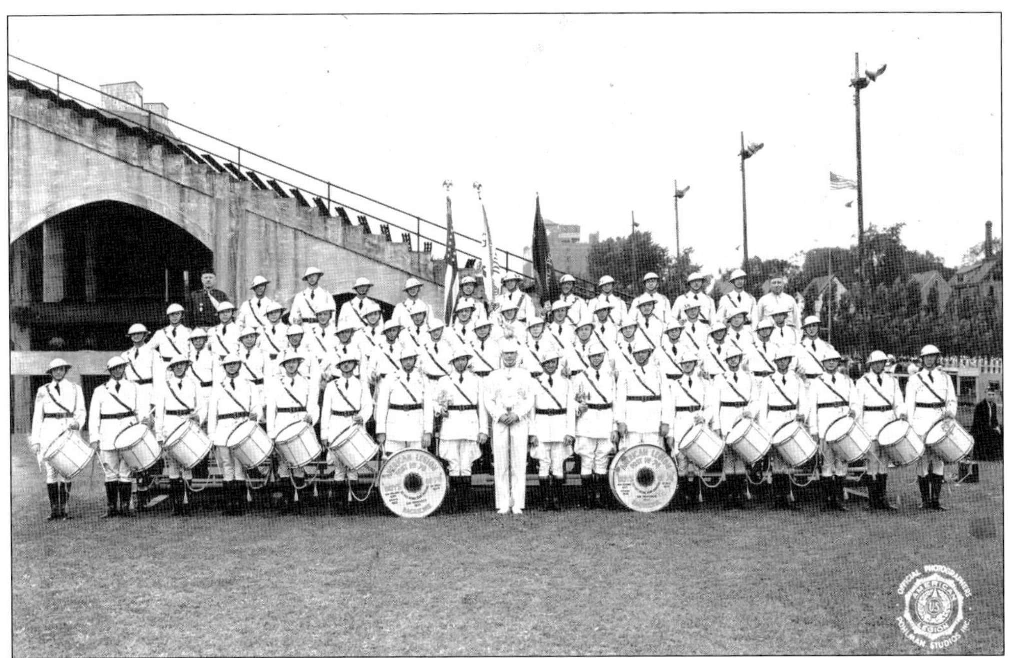

This formal portrait of the Boys of 76 Drum and Bugle Corps was taken in Milwaukee during the annual American Legion national convention held in 1941. In the drum and bugle corps competition held in conjunction with the 1941 American Legion national convention, the Boys of 76 earned a spot in the 12-corps finals contest by placing fifth in preliminary competition. They took seventh place at finals. (Courtesy of RHM.)

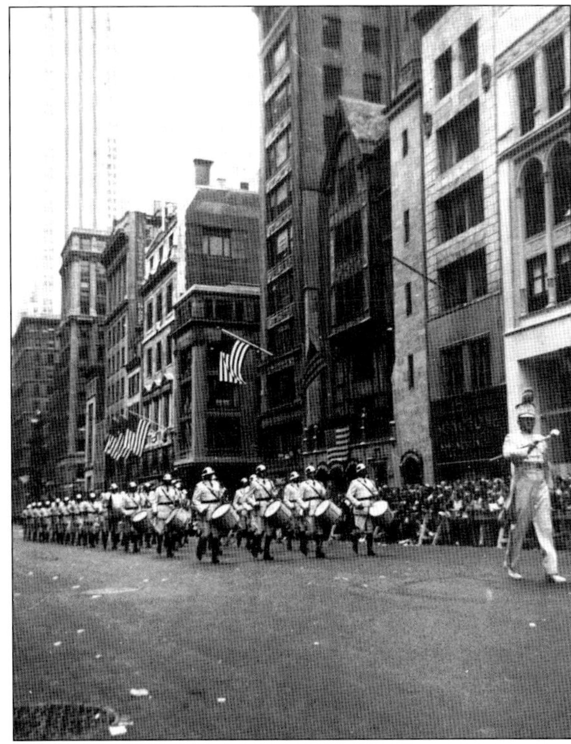

The Boys of 76 Drum and Bugle Corps is seen marching on Fifth Avenue in New York City during the 1947 American Legion national convention parade. In preliminary competition, 37 drum and bugle corps, including the Racine Boys of 76, vied for the 11 open spots in the finals of the national American Legion championship. Last year's champion drum corps automatically received the 12th finals spot. The Boys of 76 finished in a tie for 13th place, which did not qualify them for a spot in the finals. (Courtesy of RHM.)

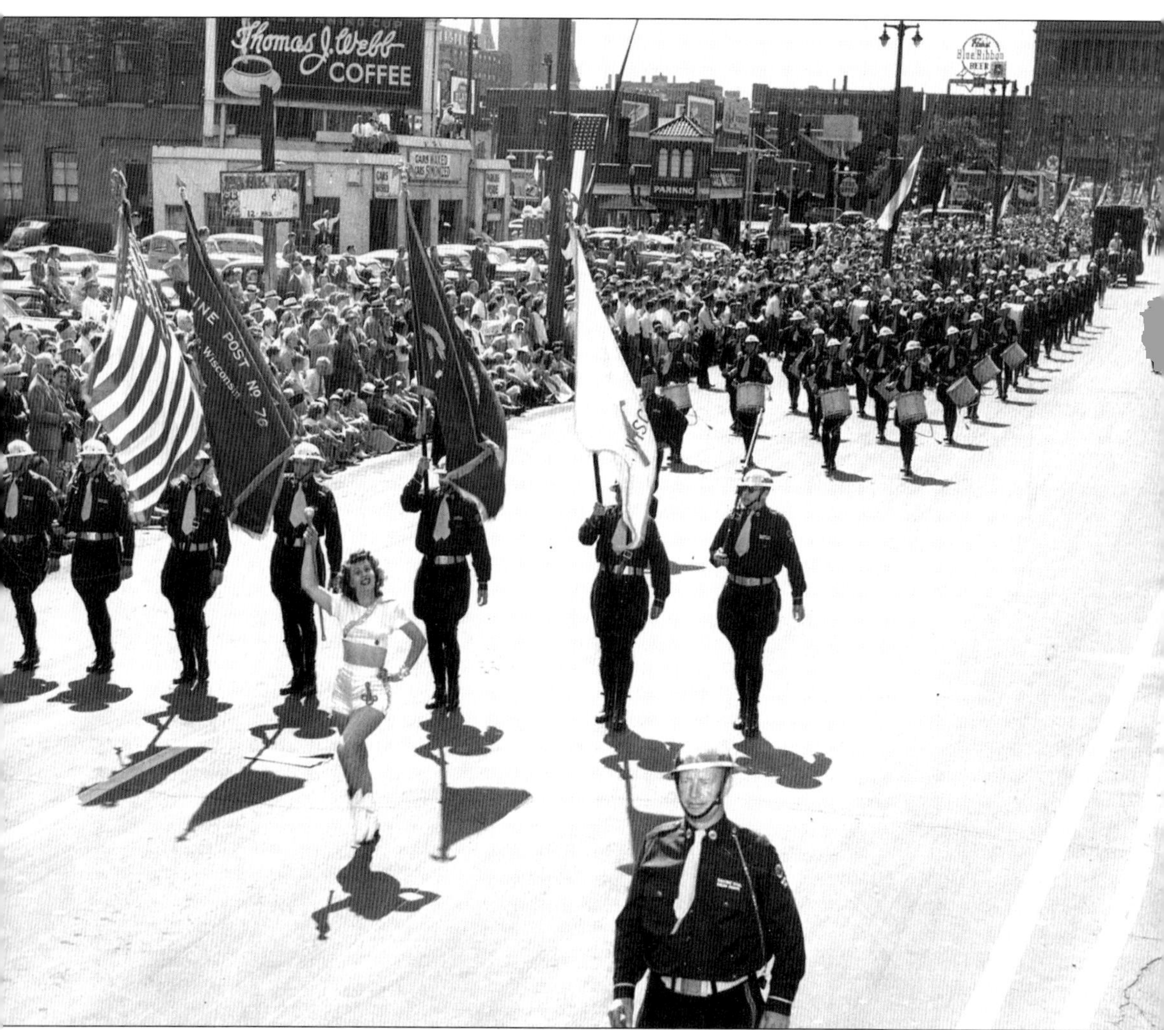

The Boys of 76 are being led by a baton-twirling majorette during the 1940s. Although all competitions at state and national American Legion conventions were suspended during World War II, the Boys of 76 still found numerous opportunities to participate in local parades. (Courtesy of RHM.)

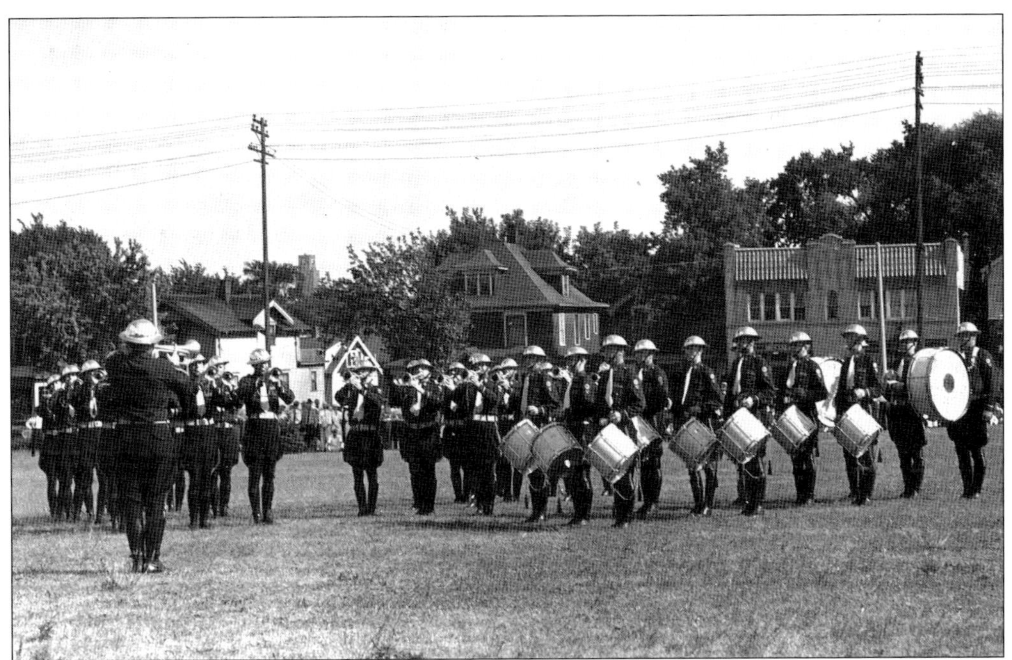

The Boys of 76 are performing at an unknown location in their navy blue uniforms, sometime in the 1940s. The group wore these uniforms for most appearances throughout the 1940s in an effort to save the wear and tear on its famous white uniforms. Its white uniforms were now only worn on special occasions and at state and national American Legion conventions. (Courtesy of RHM.)

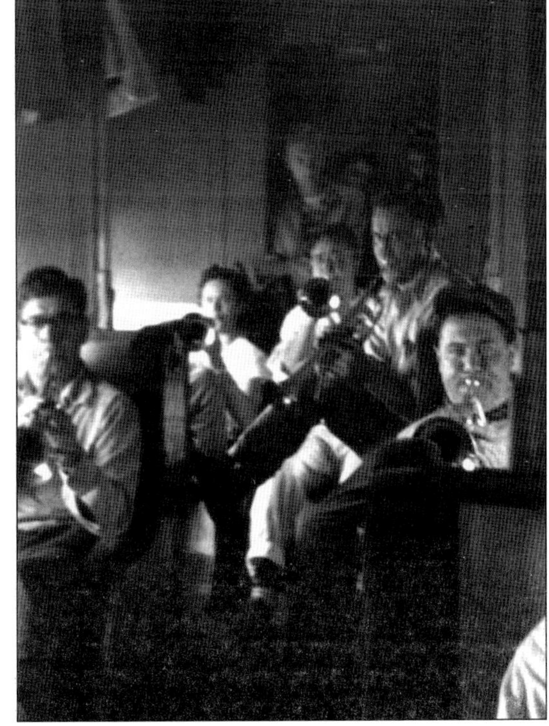

Traveling by train was quite common for drum and bugle corps prior to 1960. Most legionnaires, including members of American Legion drum and bugle corps, would take the train to state and national conventions. Here members of the Boys of 76 are practicing in the cramped quarters aboard a train. (Courtesy of RHM.)

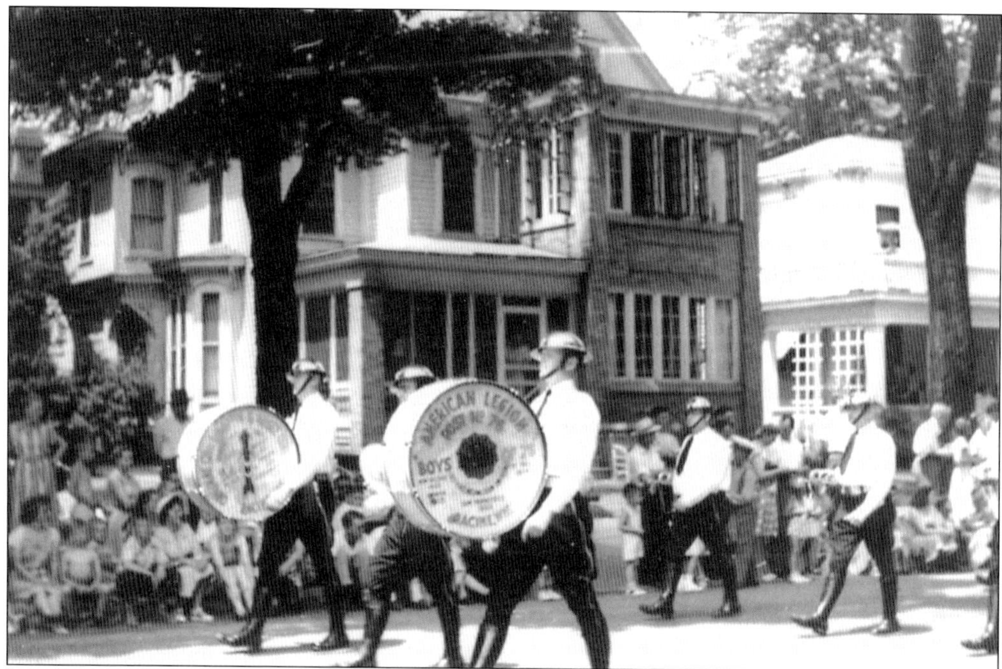

The Boys of 76 are parading south on Main Street in Racine's 1947 Fourth of July parade. By this time, many of the World War I veterans from Racine Post 76 had left the Boys of 76. So in 1947, the drum corps was opened up to World War II veterans in order to maintain the number of members needed to compete successfully on a national level. Harald Kahlert, the Boys of 76's bass drummer in the foreground, was one of the many World War II veterans to join the corps after the war. Originally joining the Kilties as a snare drummer, he became the first Kilties drum major in 1936.

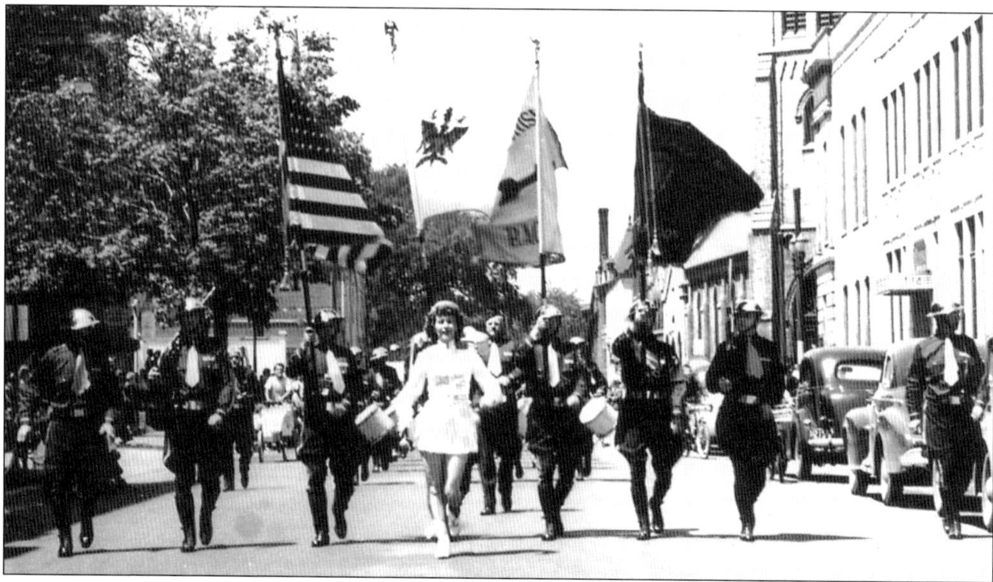

The Boys of 76 are marching east on Seventh Street just past Main Street in downtown Racine in Racine's Memorial Day parade, May 31, 1948. Racine's Memorial Day services were held at the lakefront then.

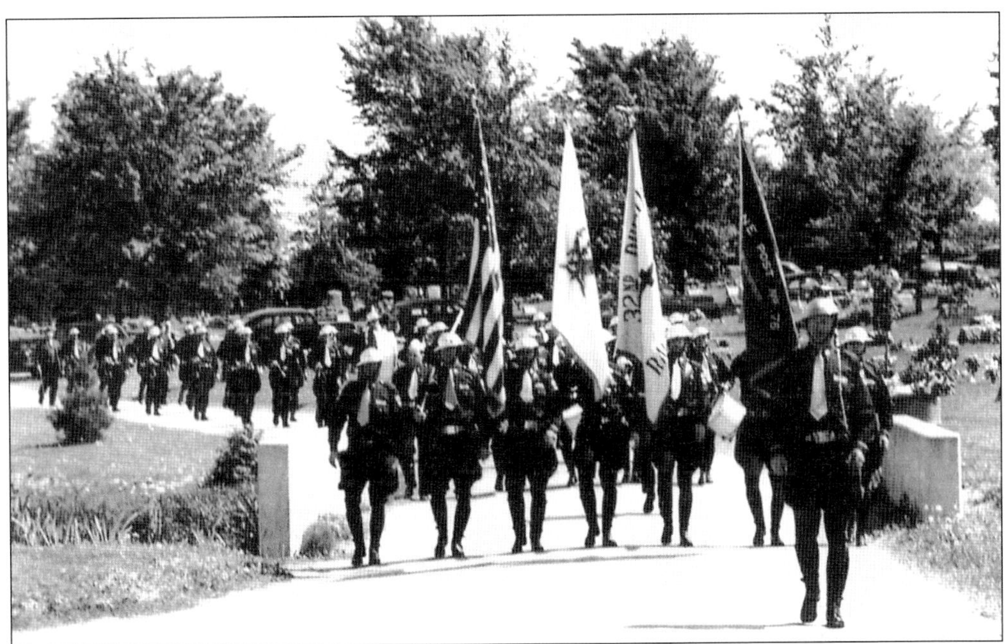

This photograph of the Boys of 76 marching into a local cemetery was also taken on Memorial Day, May 31, 1948. The highlight of the year for the Boys of 76 occurred in Miami, Florida, on October 18, 1948, when the group copped seventh place in the American Legion's national convention finals before 60,000 spectators in the Orange Bowl.

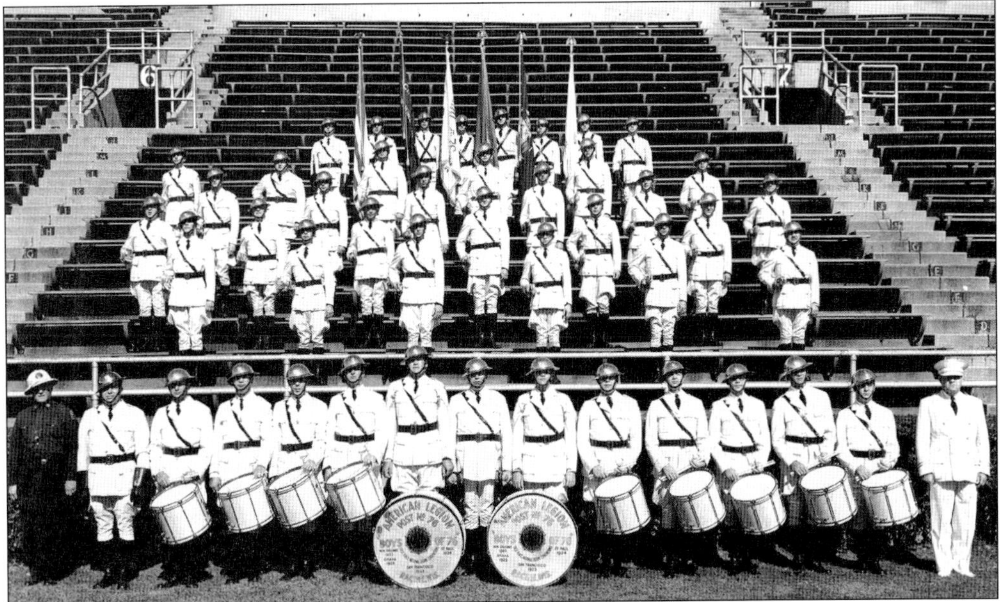

It was customary at many American Legion national conventions for the competing drum and bugle corps to pose for a group photograph after the group finished its preliminary performance. This photograph of the Boys of 76 was taken on Randall's Island in New York City at the 1952 American Legion national convention. There the Boys of 76 took 10th place in preliminary competition and finished in 9th place in finals at the 1952 American Legion Drum and Bugle Corps National Championship. (Courtesy of RHM.)

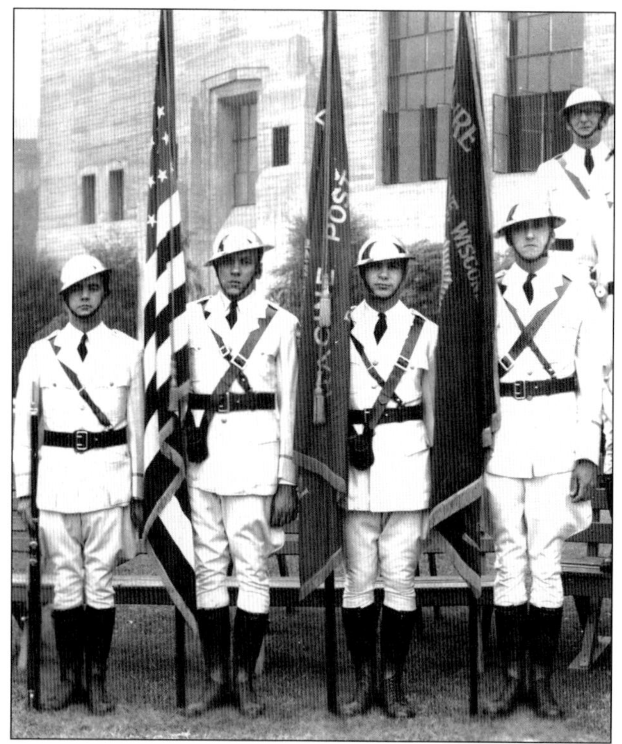

The four photographs on these two pages are four different portions of a large panoramic photograph that was taken of the Boys of 76 at the American Legion nationals in October 1950, in Los Angeles. The panoramic photograph was so wide that it took four sections to get the whole drum corps. This is the far left side of the panoramic photograph, which includes half of the Boys of 76's color guard.

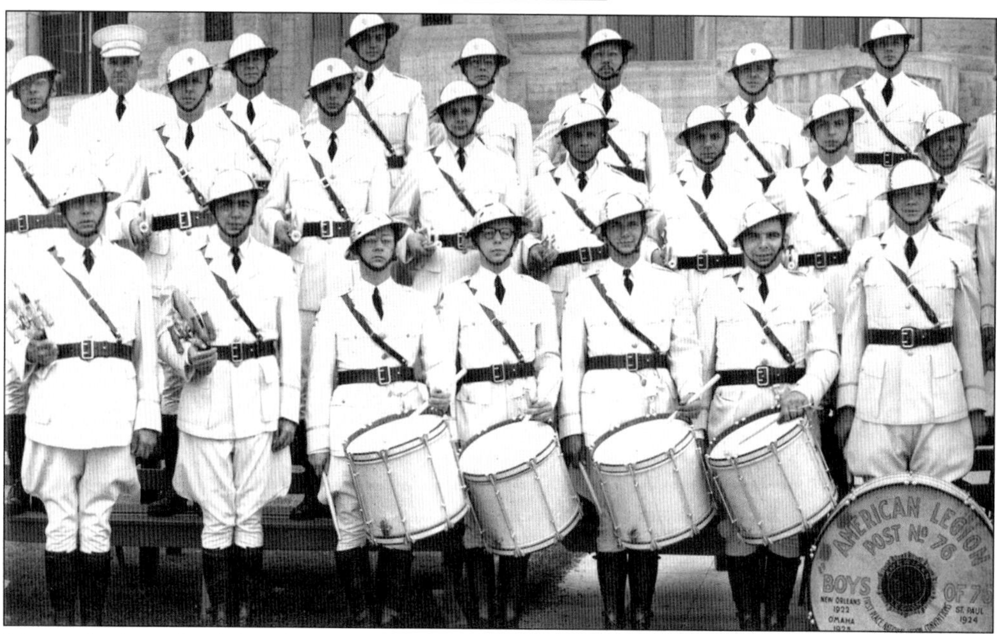

This is the left side of the playing members of the Boys of 76. By 1950, the character of the drum corps had changed significantly. Once it was comprised solely of the World War I veterans of Racine American Legion Post 76. By 1950, many of these legionnaires had dropped out over the years and were replaced by "outsiders," including many members from Racine's American Legion Post 310. During the summer of 1950, less than a dozen members of Racine's Post 76 were marching and playing in the drum corps.

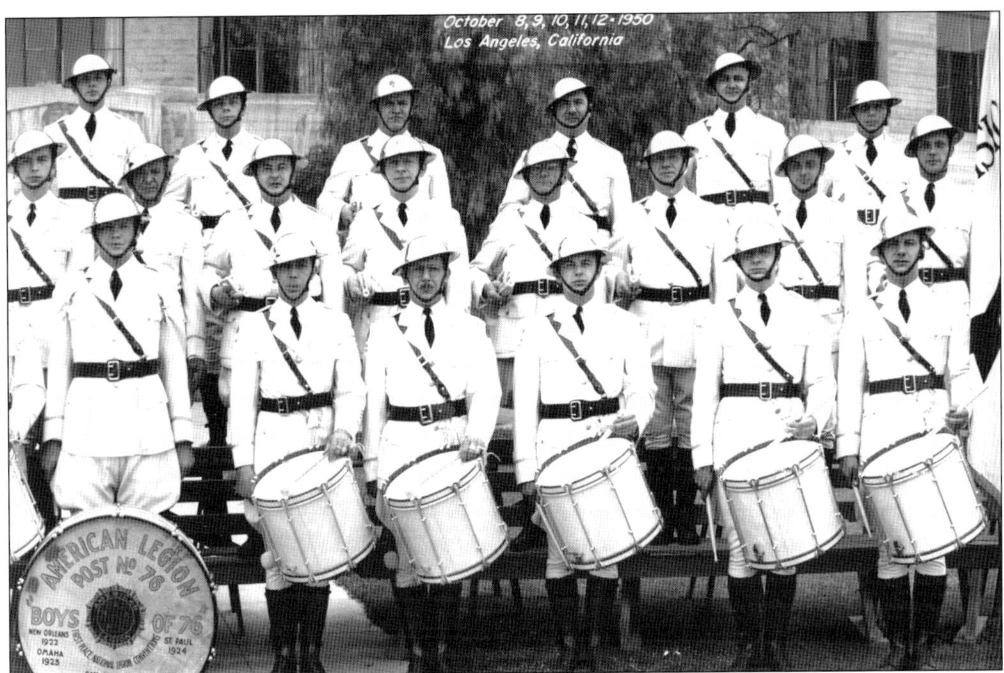

This is the right side of the playing members of the Boys of 76. The Boys of 76 took third place at finals at the 1950 American Legion Drum and Bugle Corps National Championship in Los Angeles.

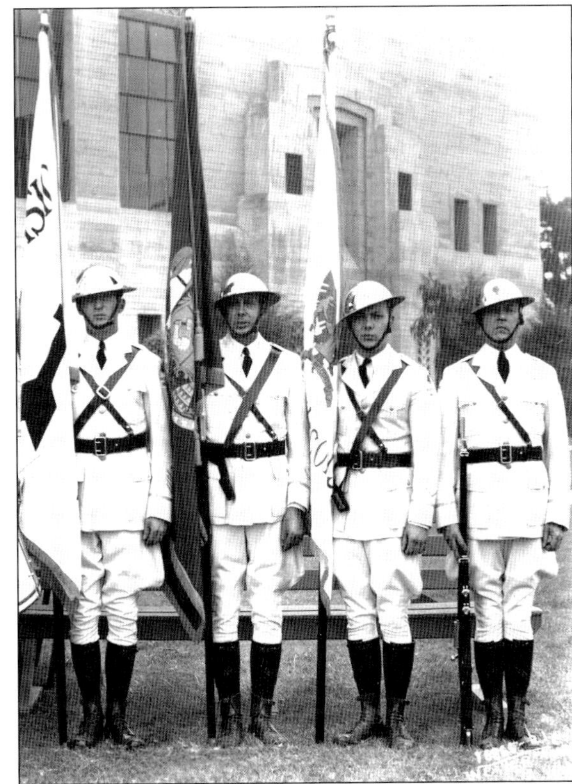

This is the far right side of the panoramic photograph and includes the other half of the Boys of 76's color guard. Four members of the color guard were located on each side of the main body of playing members of the drum corps when this photograph was taken.

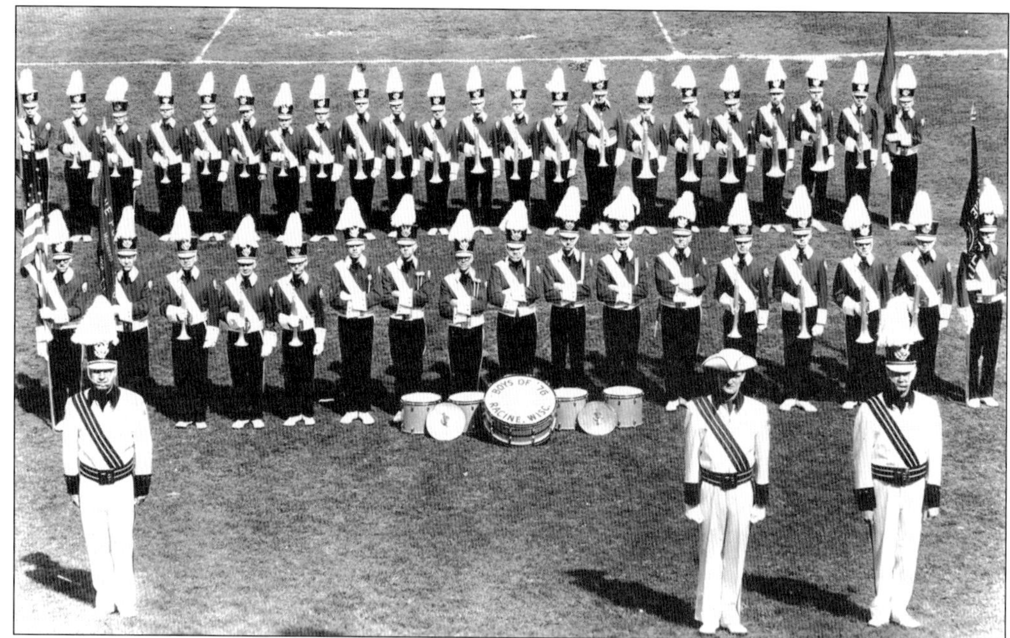

The Boys of 76 members are shown here in 1962 wearing their brand-new red, white, and blue uniforms. The year 1962 was the first time since 1955 that the Boys of 76's color guard did not compete for the American Legion's state color guard championship. From 1956 through 1961, the Boys of 76's color guard won six consecutive American Legion state color guard championships. (Courtesy of RKAA.)

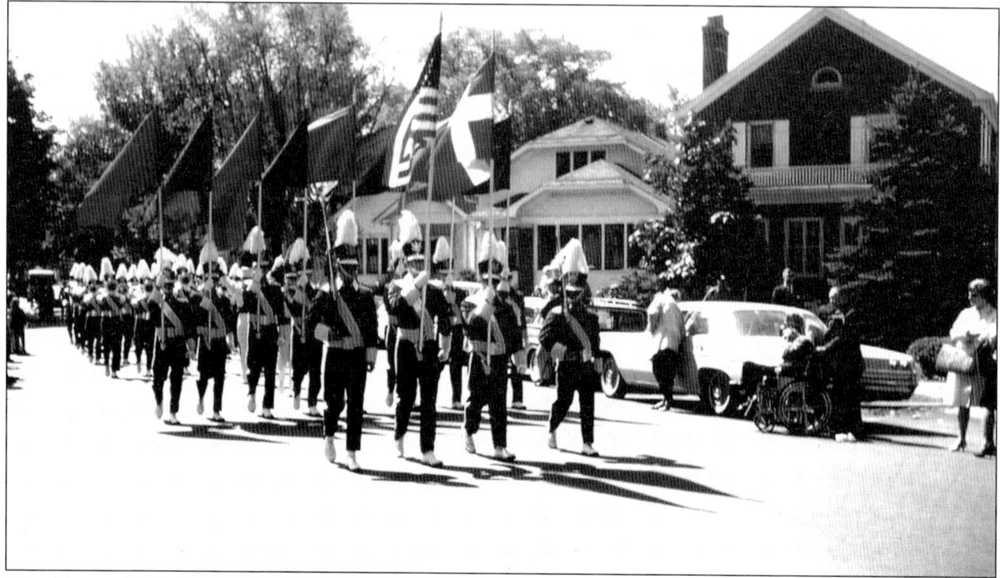

The Boys of 76 are seen in Racine's Memorial Day parade in 1966. This is the first time in the group's history that it was not marching through the streets of Racine as the American Legion state champions. The group had never lost in state competition until 1965, when it was defeated by the Kenosha Kingsmen and had to settle for second place. The Boys of 76 did turn the tables on the Kenosha Kingsmen in July 1966 and won the American Legion Drum and Bugle Corps State Championship. (Courtesy of RKAA.)

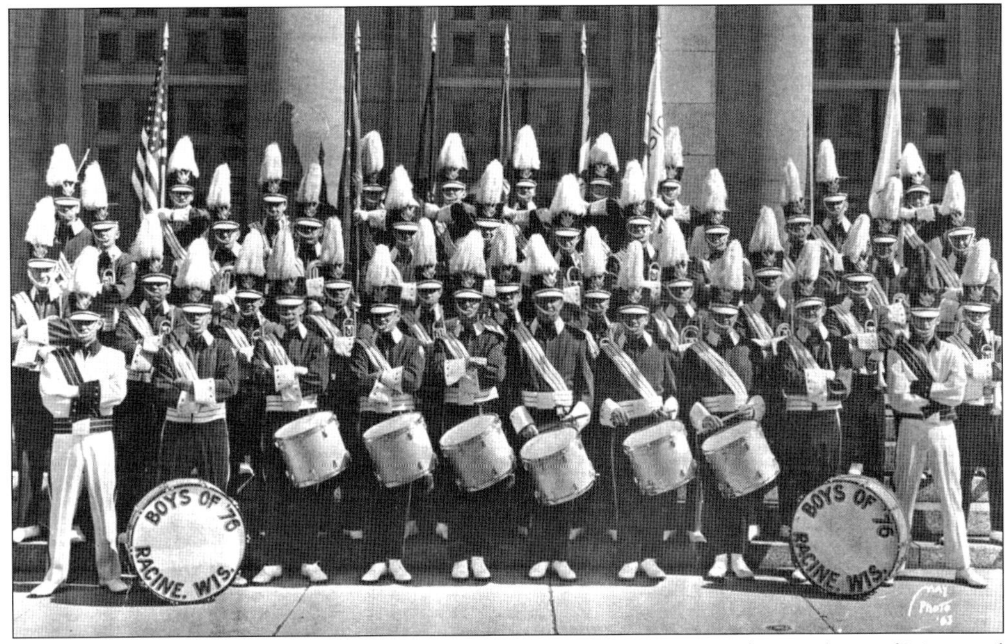

This is a 1963 photograph of the Boys of 76 Drum and Bugle Corps taken in front of Memorial Hall in Racine. The Boys of 76 won the Wisconsin American Legion Drum and Bugle Corps State Championship by besting three other corps in Madison for the title. The group traveled to Miami, Florida, for the 1963 American Legion Drum and Bugle Corps National Championship, where it took seventh place in finals, down one spot from its sixth-place finish at preliminaries. (Courtesy of RHM.)

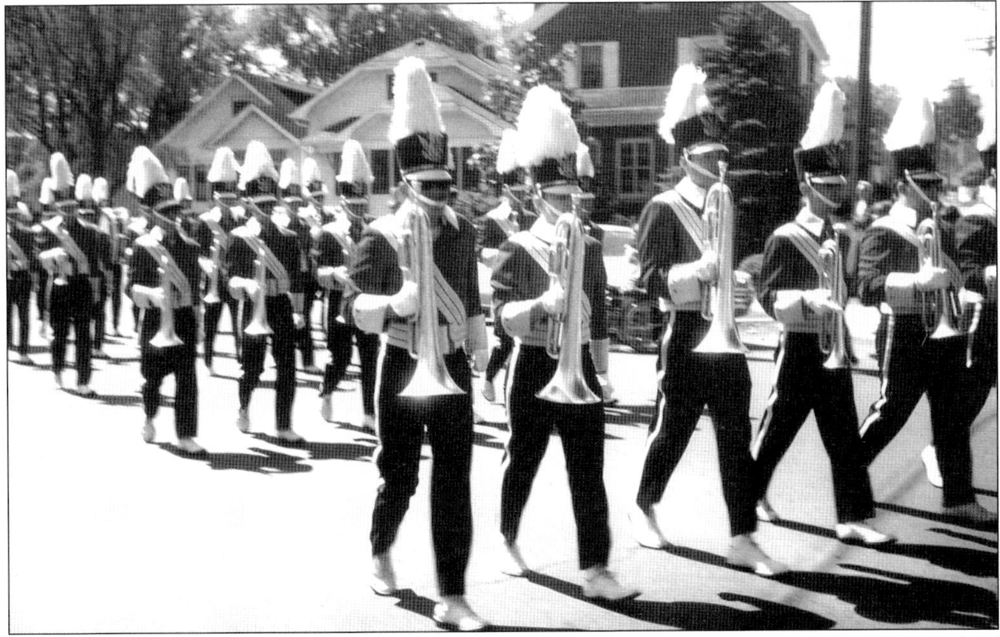

Larry Hansen is the bass horn bugler on the far left in the front row of this 1966 photograph of the Boys of 76 in Racine's Memorial Day parade. He also was the corps director of the Racine Ambassa"Dears," the all-girl drum and bugle corps at that time. (Courtesy of RKAA.)

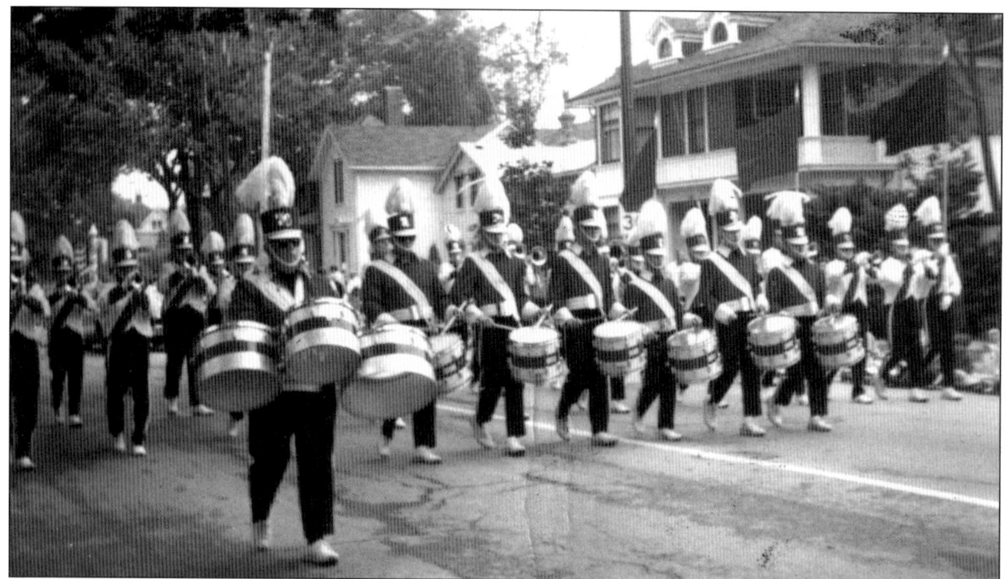

The Racine Boys of 76 Drum and Bugle Corps is on parade in 1969. The Boys of 76 reclaimed the American Legion Drum and Bugle Corps State Championship in 1969 in Milwaukee after coming in second place to the Kenosha Kingsmen the previous two years. Then, in 1970, the Boys of 76 made history when the group became the first Midwest senior corps to make finals at the Drum Corps Associates Championship in Rochester, New York. The group finished in ninth place in the 10-corps finals. (Courtesy of RHM.)

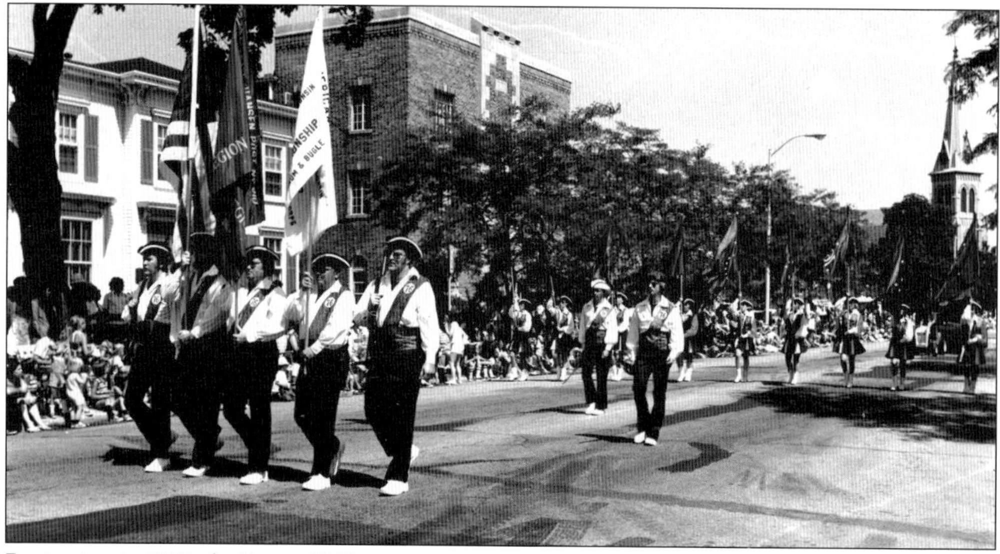

Beginning in 1973, the Boys of 76 began experiencing membership problems and started allowing women into the corps, but only into the color guard. This is a 1973 photograph of the Boys of 76 on parade in Racine. By 1975, the group changed its name to the Spirit of '76 to better reflect that women were now allowed in all sections of the corps. The group continued competing with some success through 1985. In 1977, it won its fifth and final American Legion Drum and Bugle Corps National Championship in Denver, Colorado, while in 1983 the group won the senior division at the Drum Corps Midwest Championship. (Photograph by Ruth Mainland, courtesy of RKAA.)

Two

RACINE SCOUTS

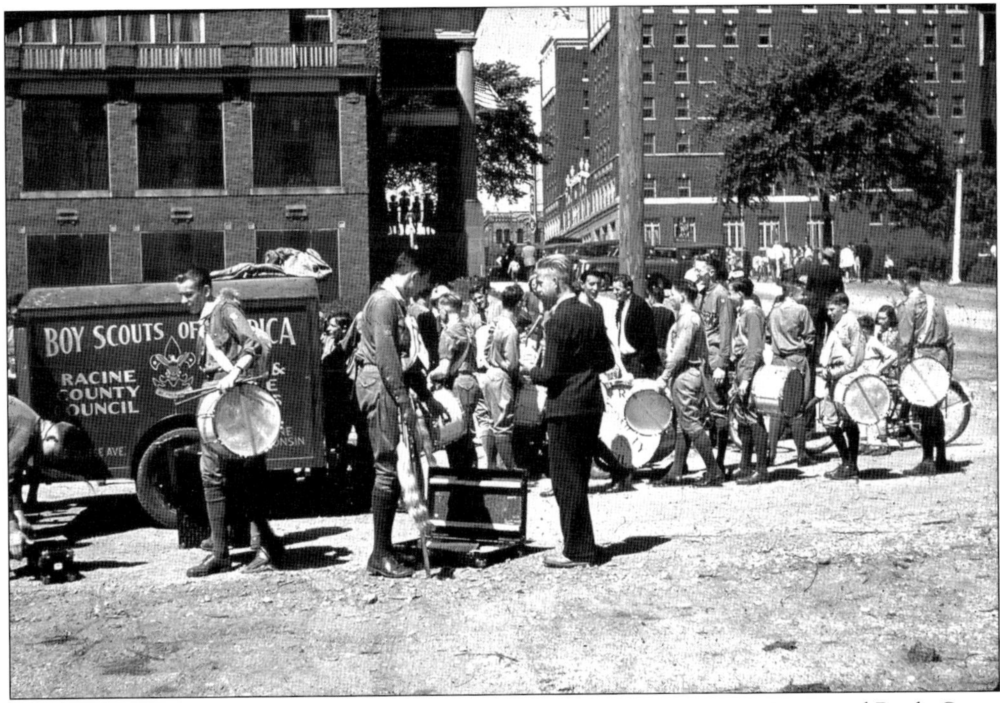

This is a very nice photograph of the Racine County Council Boy Scout Drum and Bugle Corps getting ready to march in a parade sometime in the 1930s. Today drum and bugle corps haul their equipment around in huge semitrailers; back then everything fit into a small trailer pulled behind an automobile. (Courtesy of RHM.)

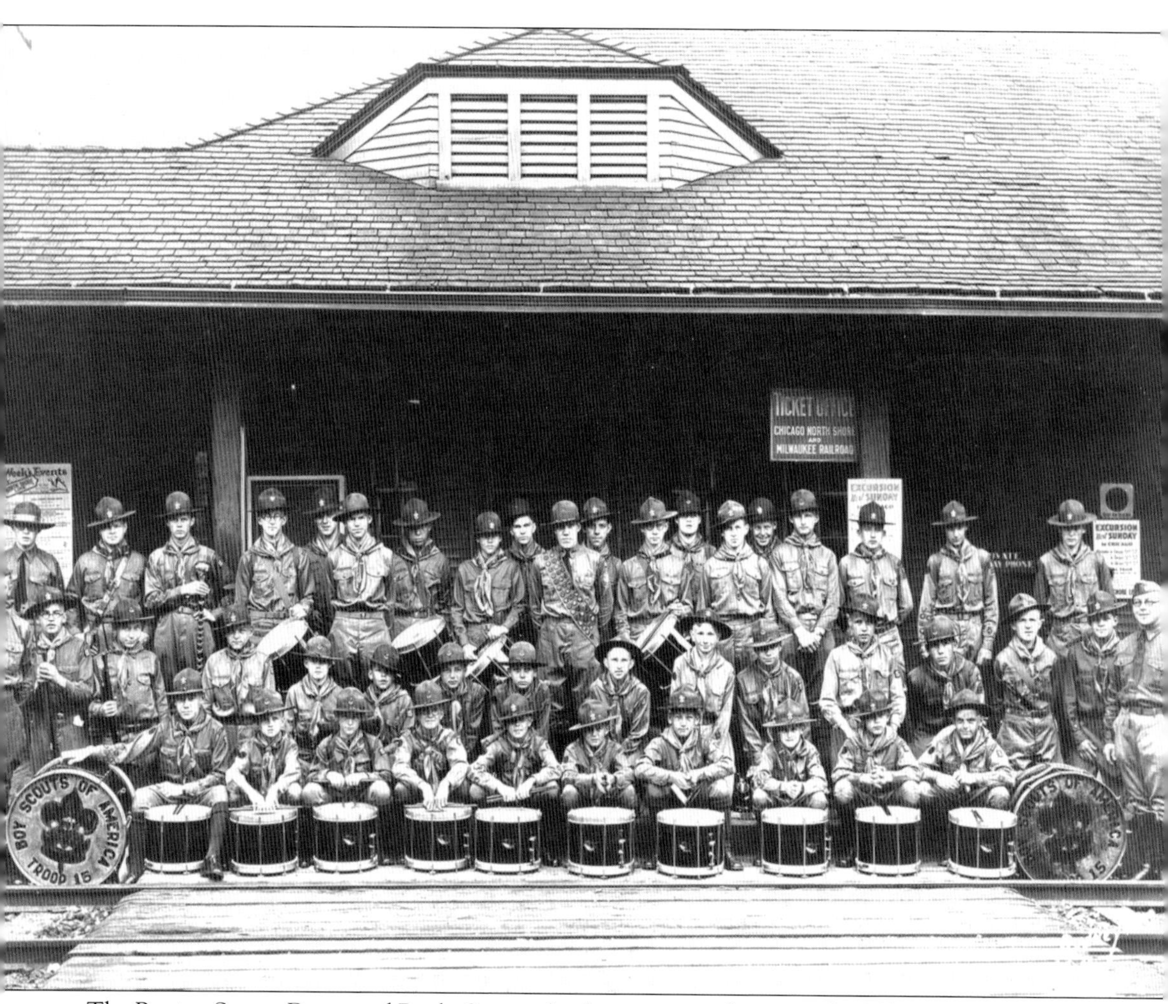

The Racine Scouts Drum and Bugle Corps of today came into being in the fall of 1927 as a troop activity for Boy Scout Troop No. 15 of the Church of Atonement. Here the Boy Scout Troop No. 15 Drum and Bugle Corps of Racine is seen at the North Shore train station in Racine on its way to compete in the first annual Chicagoland Music Festival drum and bulge corps contest. The contest was held on Saturday morning, August 23, 1930, at Grant Park in Chicago. In the junior drum and bugle corps contest, Racine's Boy Scout Troop No. 15 Drum and Bugle Corps took first place. (Courtesy of RHM.)

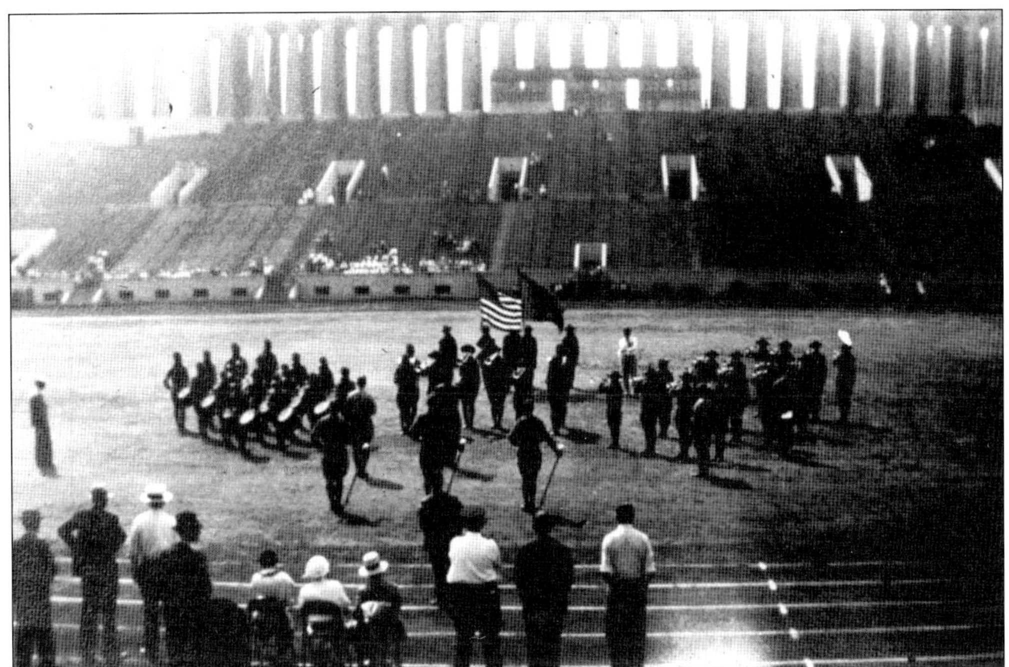

In October 1931, the Boy Scout Troop No. 15 Drum and Bugle Corps reorganized under the auspices of the Racine County Council so that Boy Scouts from any troop in the Racine County Council could join the corps. Here the Racine County Council Boy Scouts are seen on the field of competition at the Chicagoland Music Festival on Soldier Field on Saturday, August 18, 1934. The Racine County Council Boy Scouts came in third place. (Courtesy of RHM.)

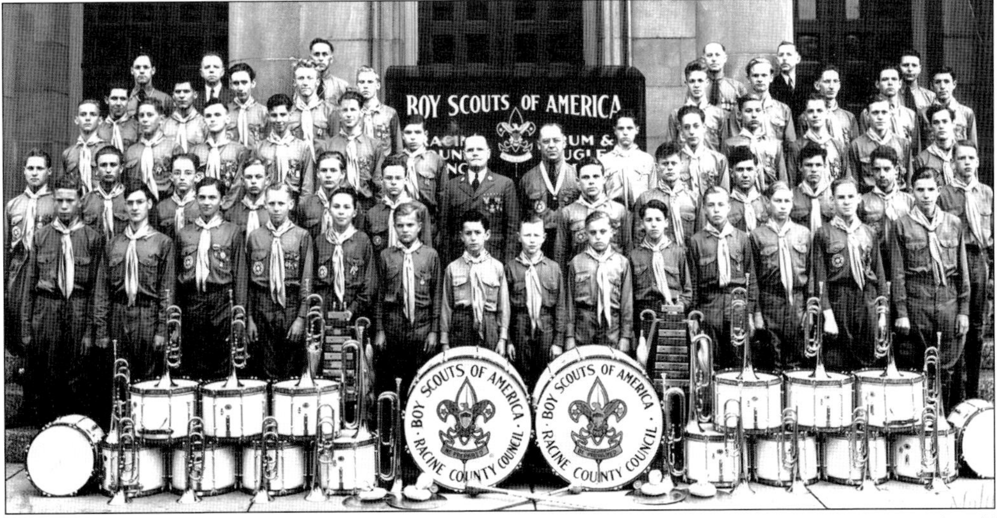

The Racine County Council Boy Scout Drum and Bugle Corps is seen in front of Memorial Hall in 1937. This year was the first time that the Racine Boy Scouts ever appeared at a Wisconsin American Legion convention. They only participated in the Wisconsin American Legion state convention's parade through downtown Milwaukee. Sponsored by American Legion Post 76, the Racine Boy Scouts won first prize as the best Scout drum and bugle corps entered in the parade, getting $25. However, the Racine Boy Scouts did not compete in the convention's annual drum and bugle corps contest. (Courtesy of RHM.)

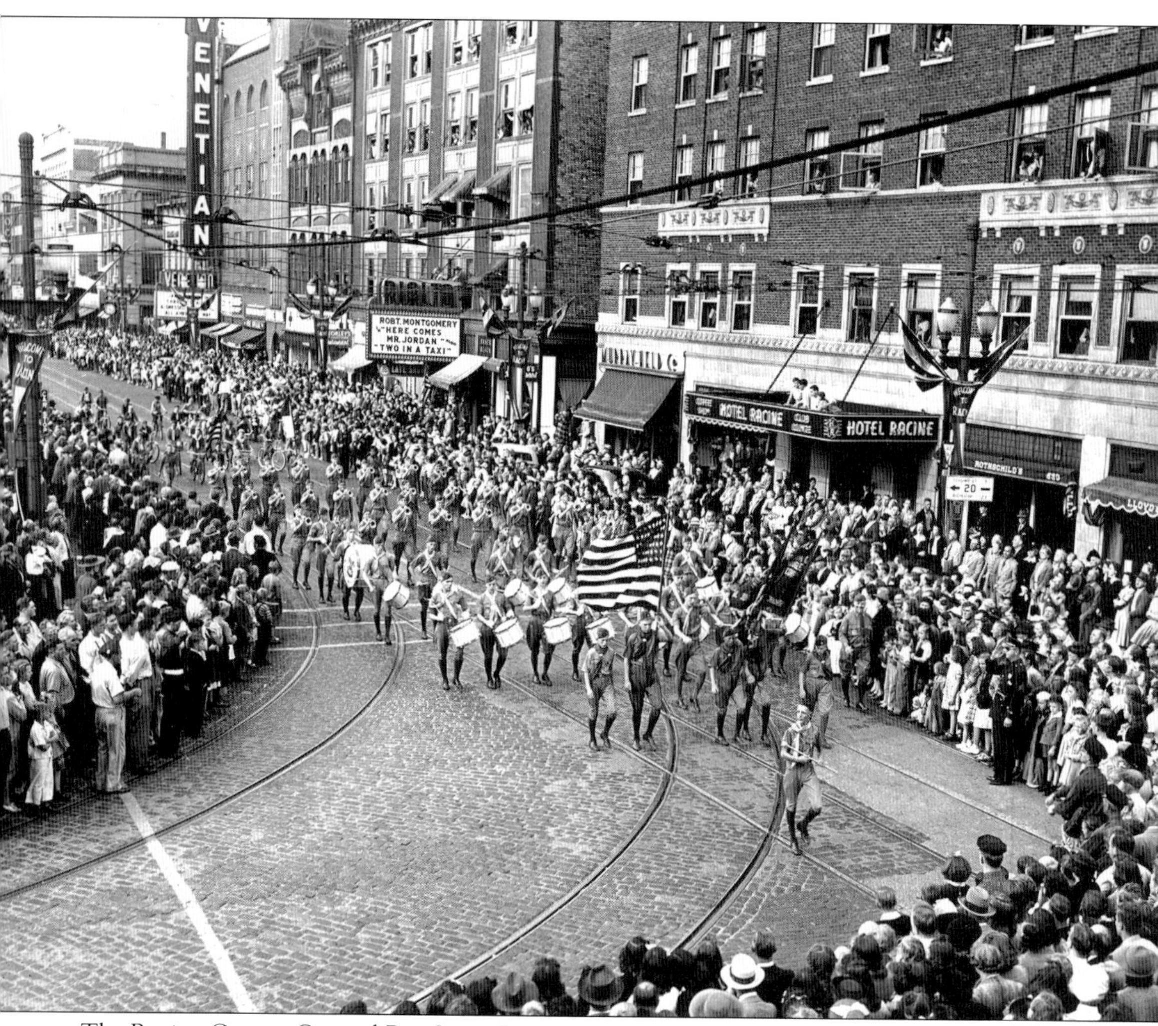

The Racine County Council Boy Scout Drum and Bugle Corps is seen in Racine's 1941 Fourth of July parade. The drum corps is marching south on Main Street just before it will follow the trolley tracks and head west on Sixth Street. (Courtesy of RHM.)

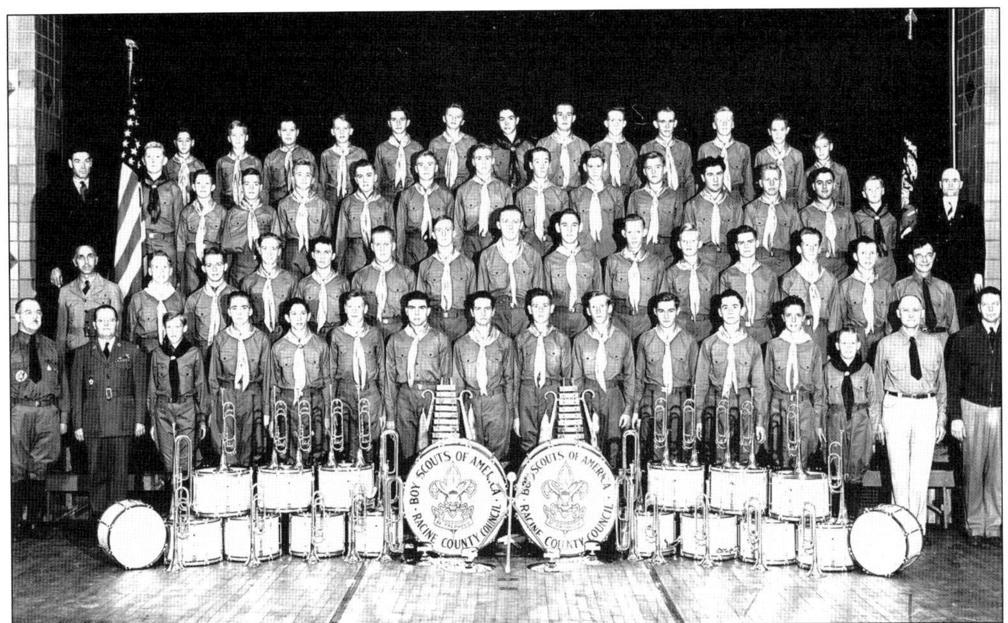

The Racine County Council Boy Scout Drum and Bugle Corps is seen at the McKinley Junior High School gymnasium in 1941. The Racine Scouts competed in a national competition for the first time in 1941. Sponsored by Racine's American Legion Post 76, the Racine Scouts placed seventh in the junior sponsored competition at the 1941 American Legion Drum and Bugle Corps National Championship held in the municipal stadium in Wauwatosa. (Courtesy of RHM.)

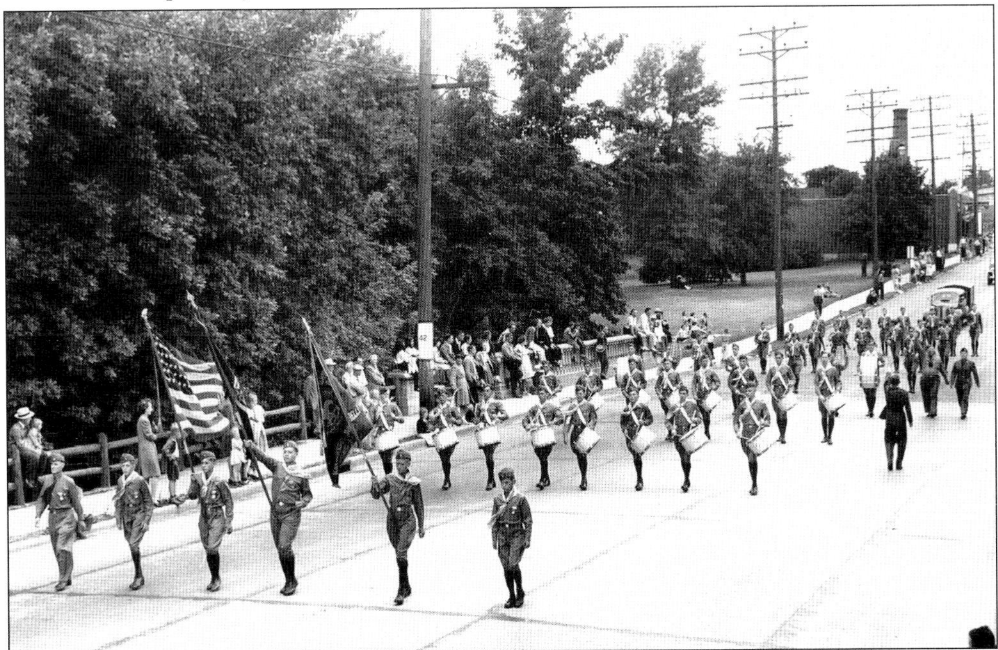

South Milwaukee's first annual Wisconsin Spectacle of Music was held on Saturday, August 10, 1946. The Racine County Council Boy Scout Drum and Bugle Corps is seen above marching in the afternoon parade. In the morning drum and bugle corps contest at Grant Park, the Racine County Council Boy Scouts came in third place. (Courtesy of RHM.)

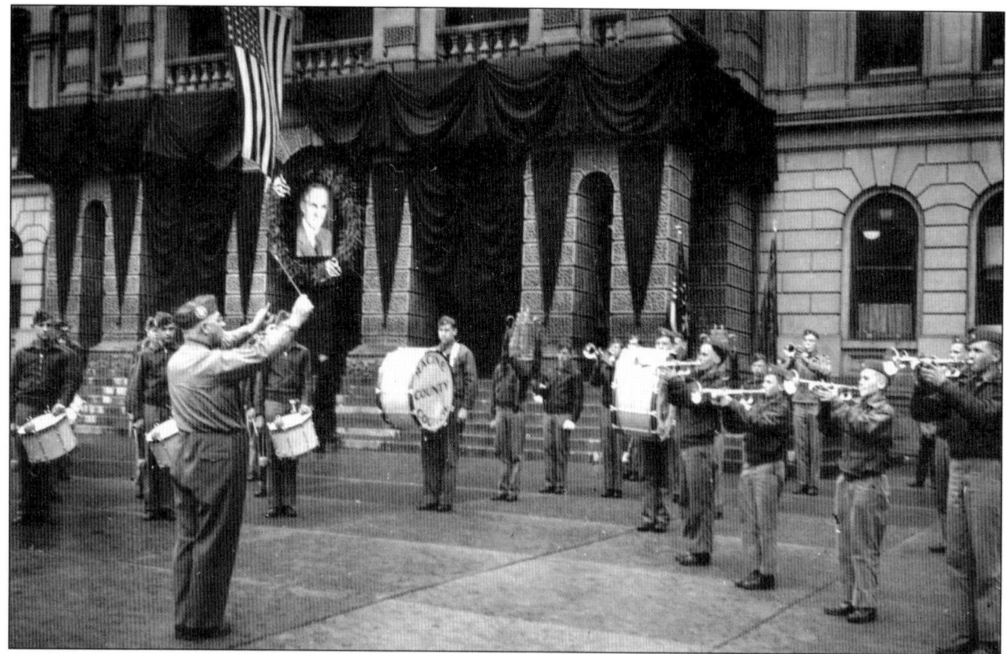

On Monday, April 7, 1947, just two days prior to the Racine Boy Scout Drum and Bugle Corps leaving on a six-day trip to Detroit, Henry Ford died suddenly at his home in Dearborn. On the courthouse grounds in Ann Arbor on Thursday, April 10, the Racine Boy Scouts played a noon hour concert. A wreath with a photograph of Ford was displayed at the courthouse in memory of him. This was a scheduled stop on their way to Detroit. (Courtesy of RHM.)

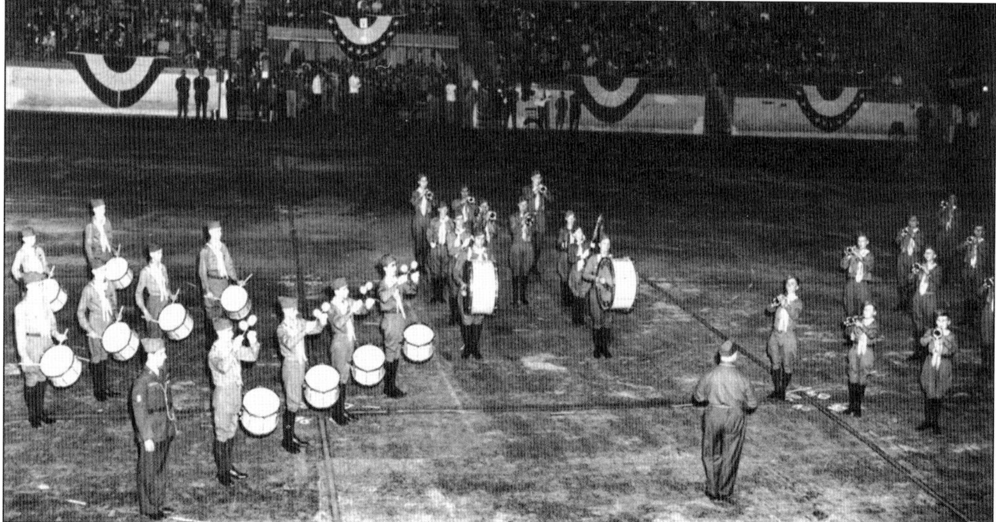

The Racine Boy Scout Drum and Bugle Corps is seen here at one of its two performances in the Detroit Coliseum during the six-day trip to Detroit in April 1947. The Racine Boy Scouts were the headline attraction in the Detroit Boy Scout Council's annual exposition, Tomorrow's Men, which was held at the coliseum, Detroit's largest auditorium at the time. The group performed as part of the main show on Friday and Saturday night, April 11 and 12. This six-day trip was jointly funded by the Detroit Boy Scout Council and the Drum Corps Mothers' Club. (Courtesy of RHM.)

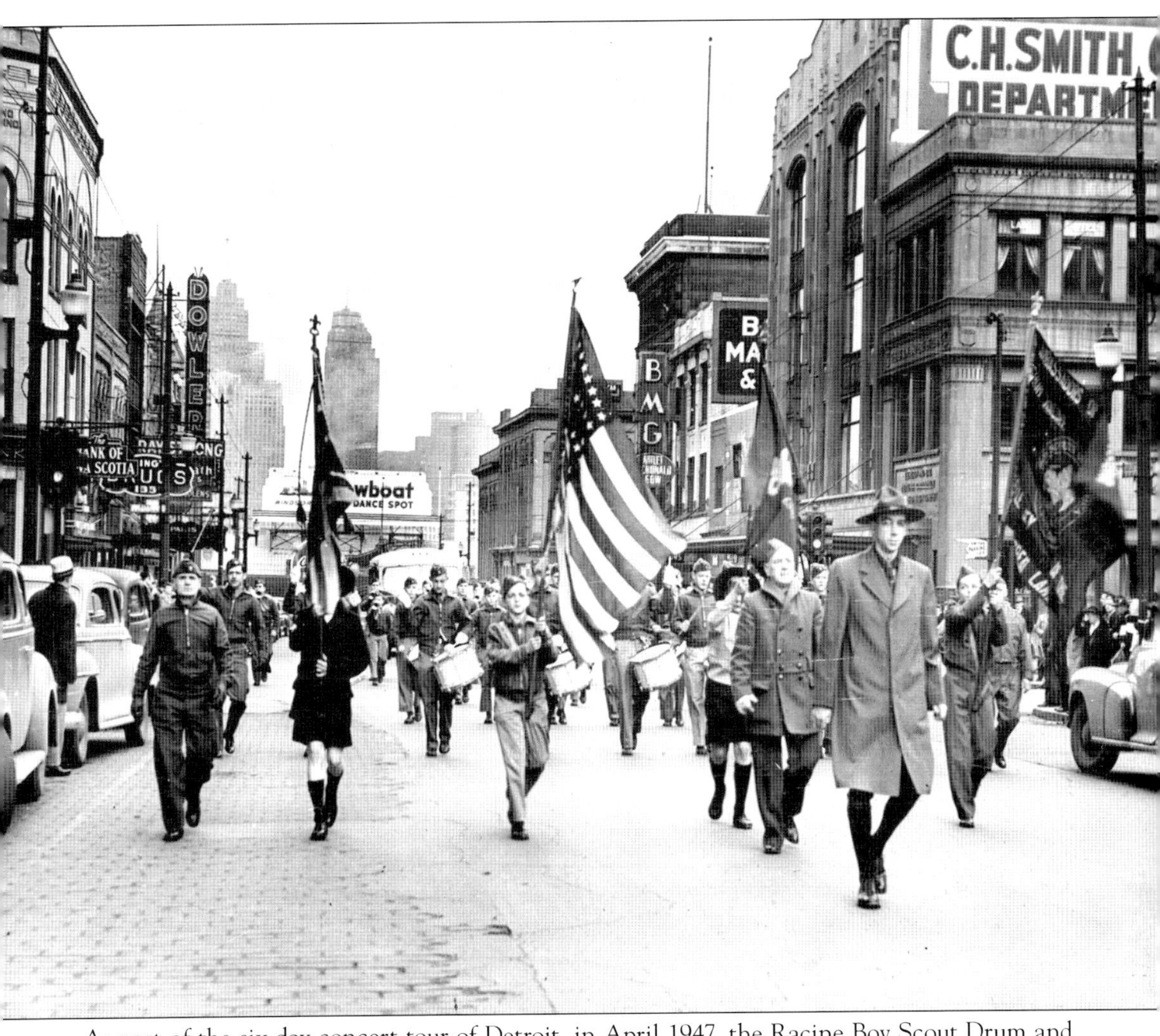

As part of the six-day concert tour of Detroit, in April 1947, the Racine Boy Scout Drum and Bugle Corps took a trip to Windsor, Ontario, Canada, on Saturday, April 12, by crossing the suspension bridge that joins Detroit and Windsor. The Racine Scouts are seen here on parade in Windsor that Saturday. They returned to Detroit early that evening through the tunnel that passes under the Detroit River. (Courtesy of RHM.)

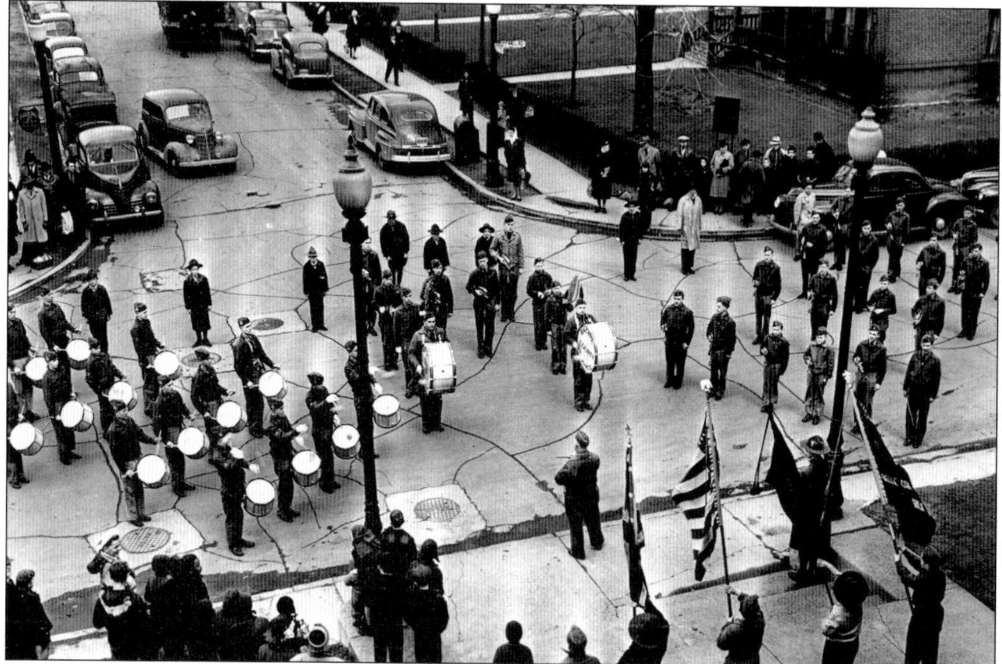

A concert is being given by the Racine Boy Scout Drum and Bugle Corps in Windsor, Ontario, Canada, on Saturday, April 12, 1947. On the trip to Windsor, the group was greeted at the Windsor City Hall by the mayor of Windsor and Canadian Scouts, for whom they played a short concert. (Courtesy of RHM.)

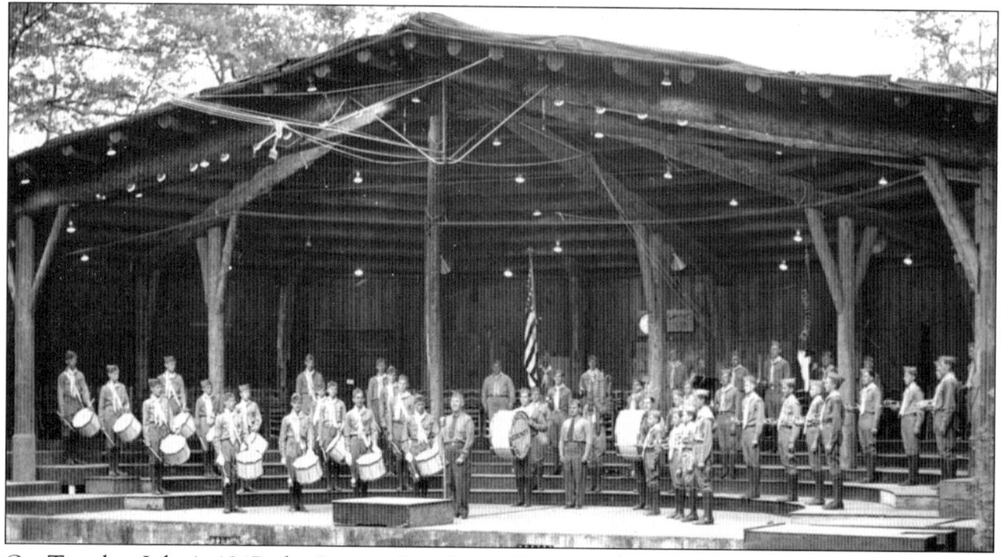

On Tuesday, July 1, 1947, the Racine Boy Scout Drum and Bugle Corps left Racine on its bus *Western* and a truck for a five-day trip to Michigan. In Milwaukee the group took the car ferry *City of Midland* for Traverse City, Michigan, where the boys would spend the next three days participating in the 100th anniversary celebration of Traverse City. On Friday, July 4, the drum corps spent the day at the National Music Camp in Interlochen, Michigan. This photograph of the Racine Boy Scout Drum and Bugle Corps was taken at the pavilion in Interlochen, where the corps gave its concert. (Courtesy of RHM.)

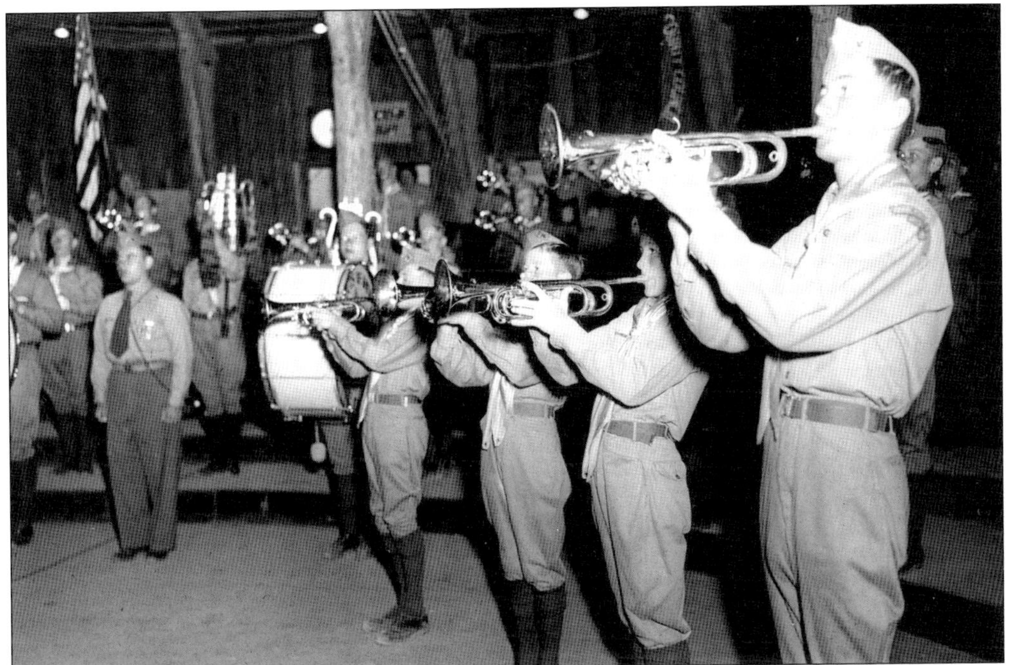

The Racine Boy Scout Drum and Bugle Corps is seen here performing a concert at the National Music Camp in Interlochen on Friday evening, July 4, 1947. This was the first time that an "outside" unit participated in the National Music Camp there. (Courtesy of RHM.)

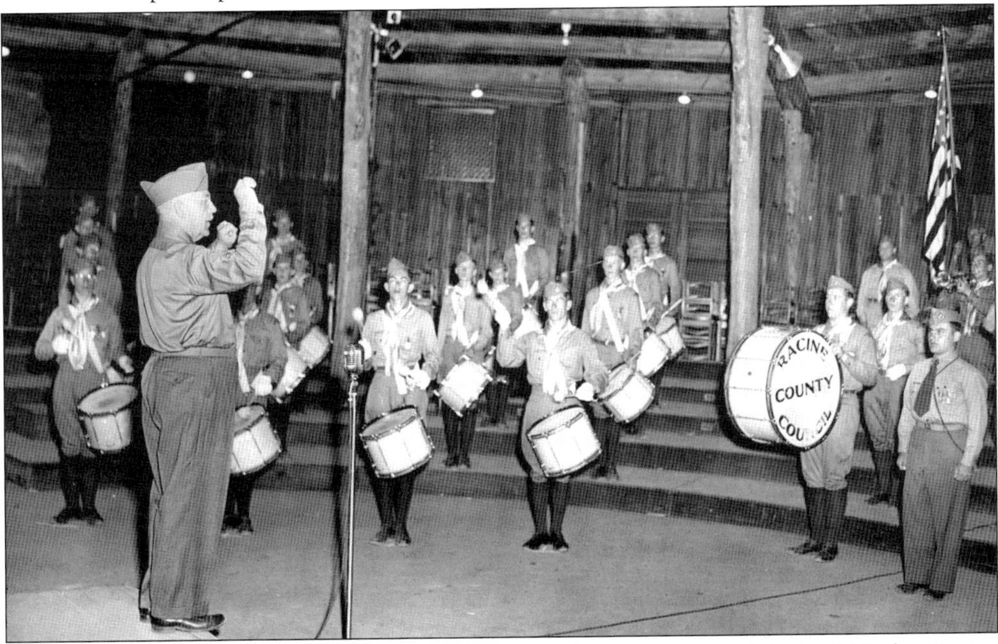

During the concert at the National Music Camp in Interlochen, on July 4, 1947, the Racine Boy Scout Drum and Bugle Corps played publicly for the first time a musical paraphrase of the fourth movement of Pyotr Ilich Tchaikovsky's Fifth Symphony. This piece was arranged for the group by Artha Marion Gruhl of Racine, a participant at the National Music Camp. (Courtesy of RHM.)

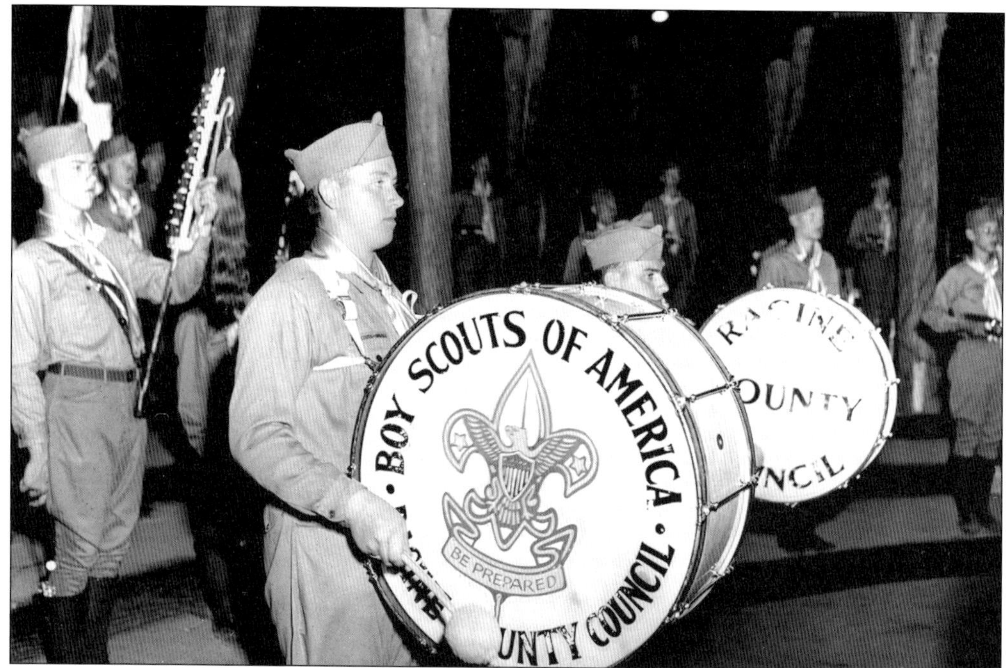

The July 1–5, 1947, trip to participate in the 100th anniversary celebration in Traverse City and at the National Music Camp in Interlochen, Michigan, meant that the Racine Boy Scout Drum and Bugle Corps would miss its own hometown's Fourth of July parade. Boy Scout corps director William L. Peterson obtained replacements for Racine's Fourth of July parade, the Kenosha American Legion Band and the Kenosha VFW Drum and Bugle Corps. This is another photograph of the Racine Boy Scout Drum and Bugle Corps in concert at the National Music Camp in Interlochen on July 4, 1947. (Courtesy of RHM.)

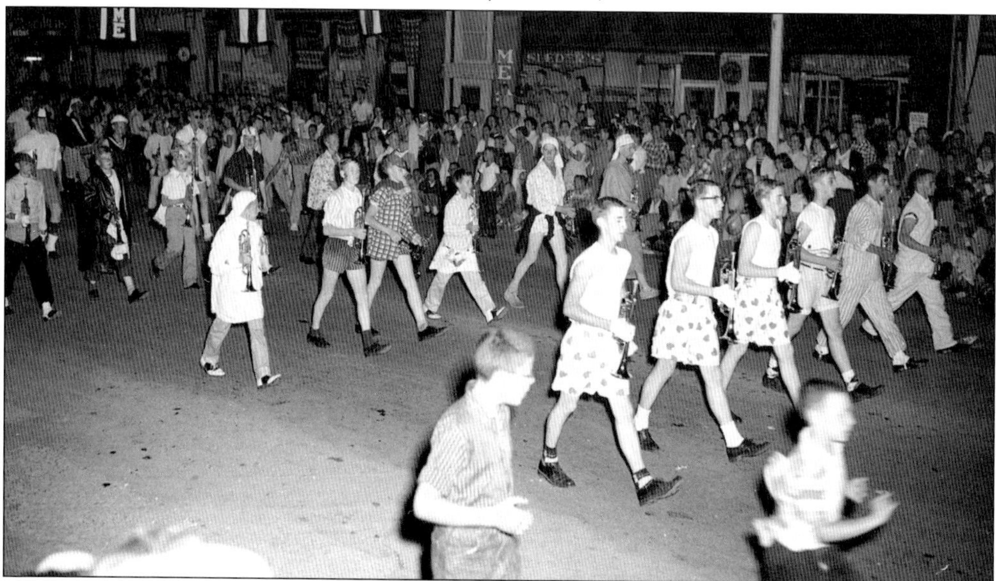

The Racine Boy Scout Drum and Bugle Corps is marching in a nighttime parade in their pajamas, swimsuits, and other unusual attire at the National Cherry Festival in Traverse City, Michigan, in July 1947. (Courtesy of RHM.)

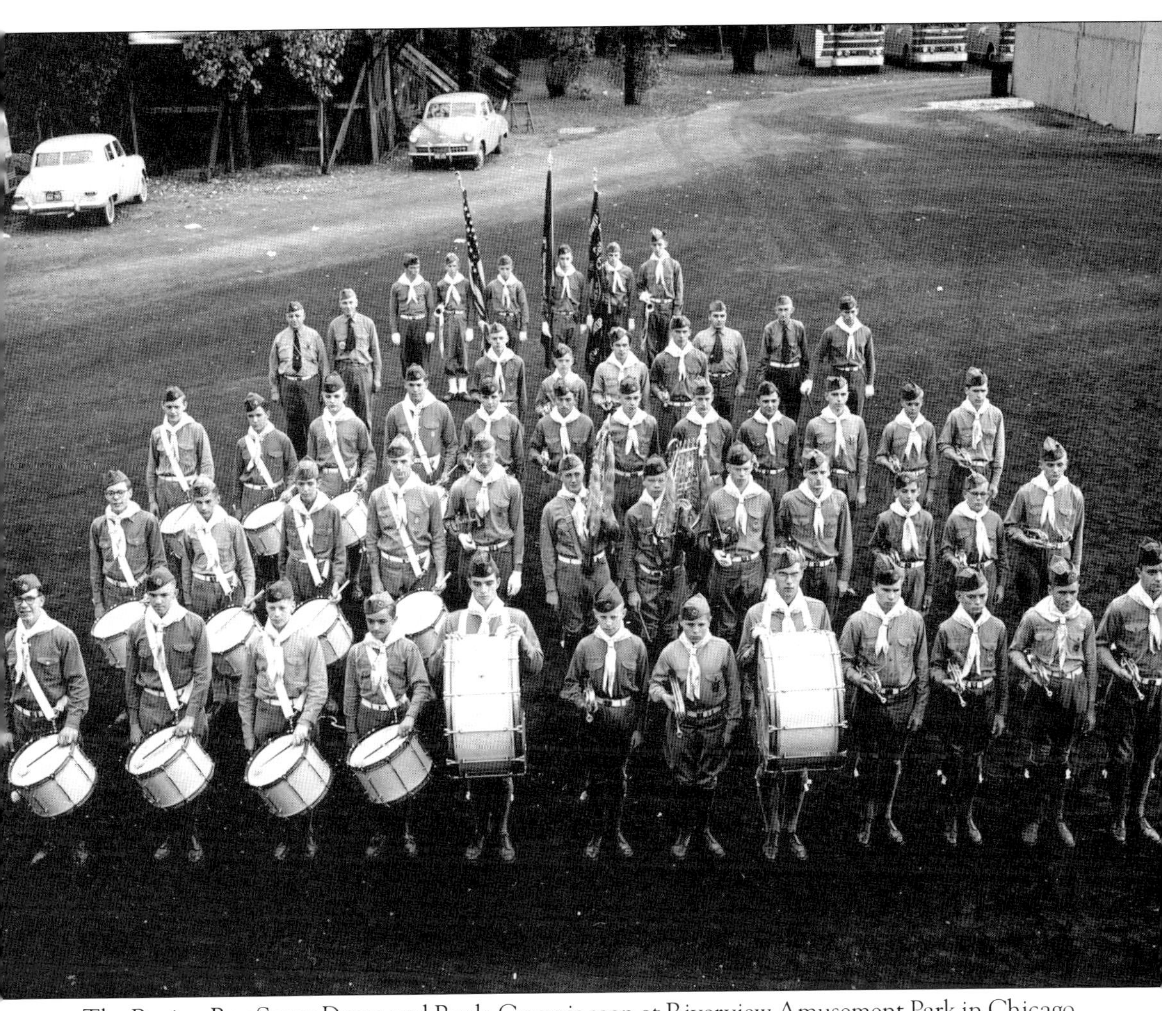

The Racine Boy Scout Drum and Bugle Corps is seen at Riverview Amusement Park in Chicago in 1947. The group took first place at Riverview's annual Tournament of Music competition in 1947. (Courtesy of RHM.)

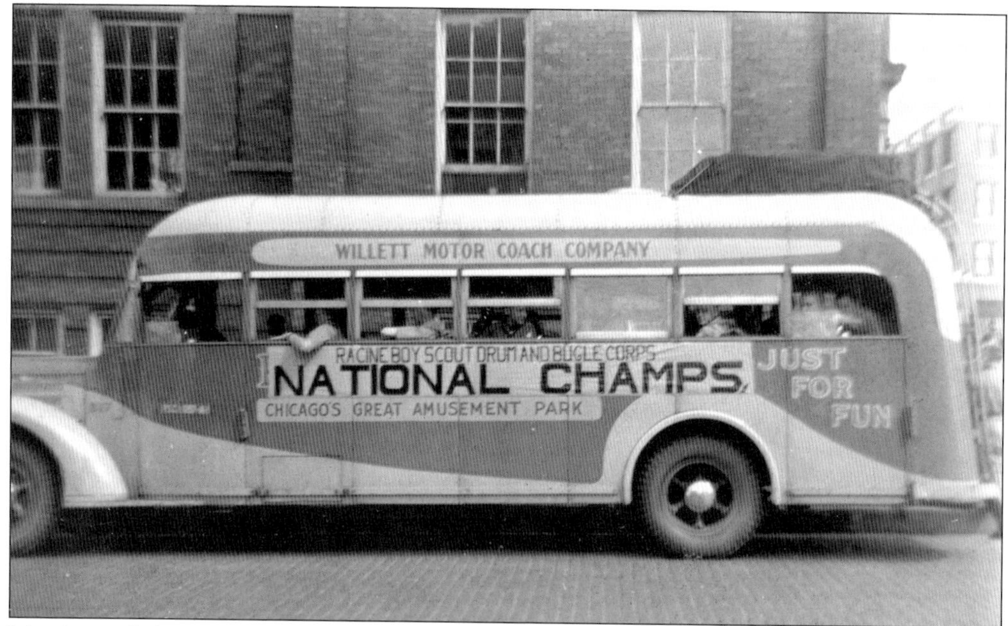

Members of the Racine Boy Scout Drum and Bugle Corps are on an outing to Riverview Amusement Park in Chicago in 1947. Today's drum and bugle corps tour in air-conditioned coaches with bathrooms on board. (Courtesy of RHM.)

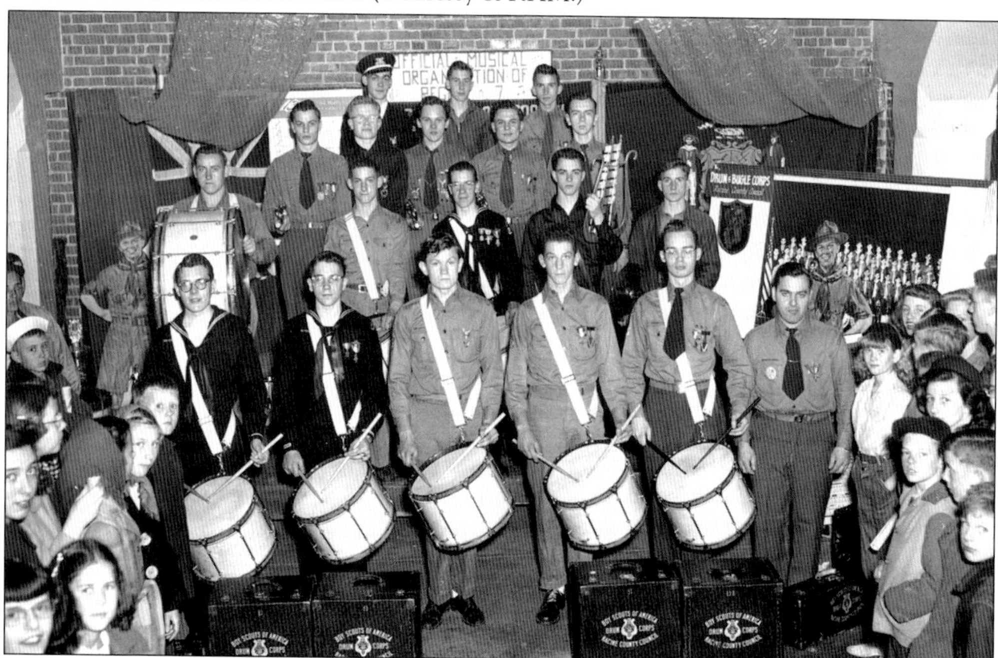
Some members of the Racine Boy Scout Drum and Bugle Corps at Scout-a-rama, April 1948, are seen in their booth. They are, from left to right, (first row) Donald Wordon, Edward Steberl, William Stenovich, James Shallbrock, Thomas Rognanoag, and John Batikis; (second row) Melvin Moyer, Lenard Moyer, John Frank, Richard Metz, and Richard Willis; (third row) Richard Lonergon, William Fawcett, Robert Koln, Dominic Frentadue, and William Buckley; (fourth row) Robert Aldert, James Barnes, and Robert Willis. (Courtesy of RHM.)

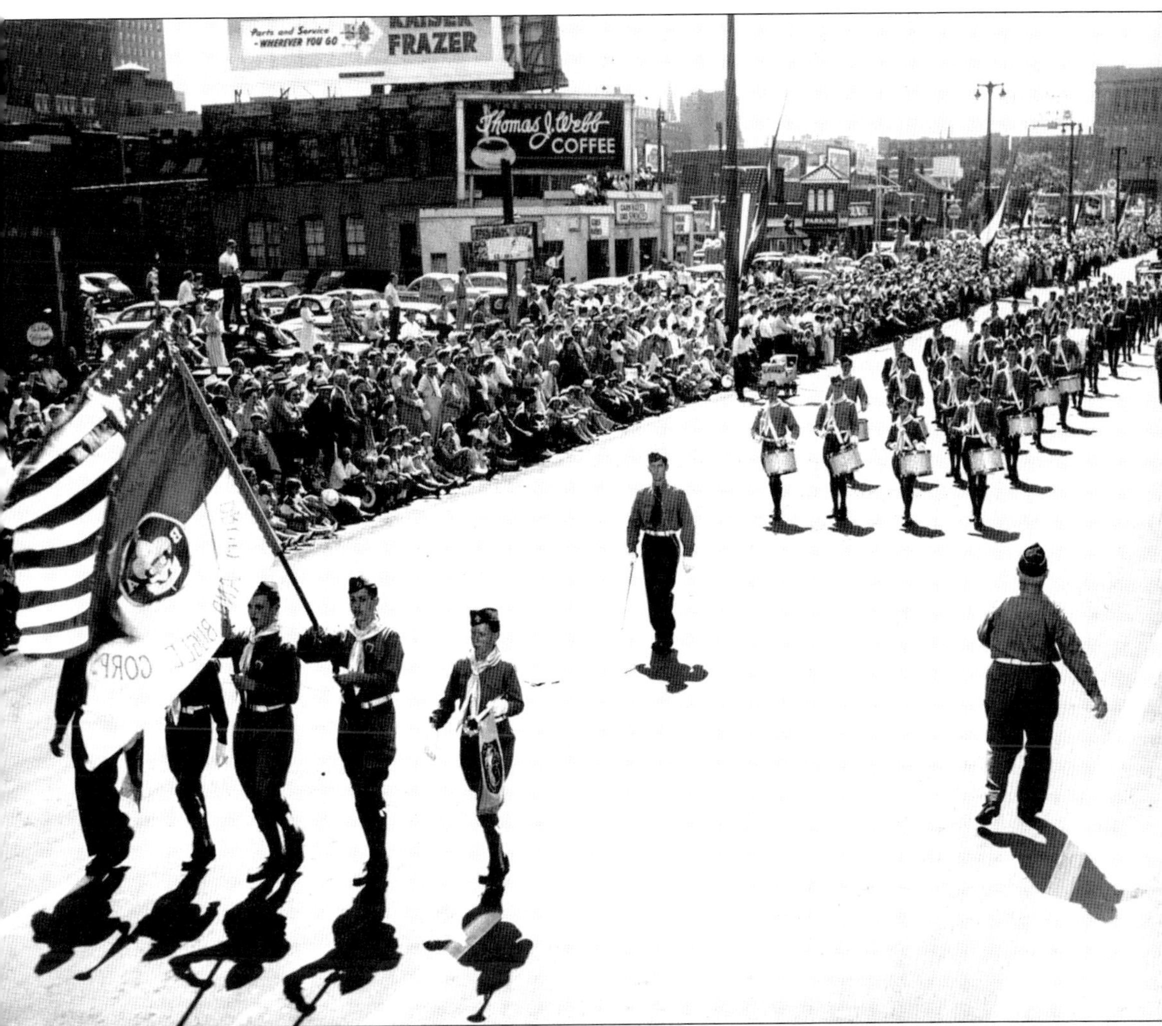

The Racine Boy Scout Drum and Bugle Corps is on parade in Milwaukee in the 1948 Wisconsin American Legion state convention parade. The Wisconsin American Legion state convention's annual Tournament of Music was held in Marquette University's stadium in Milwaukee. The Racine Boy Scouts, sponsored by Racine's Harvey R. Hansen American Legion Post 310, took first place at this contest in the junior sponsored competition. This was their first American Legion Drum and Bugle Corps State Championship. (Courtesy of RHM.)

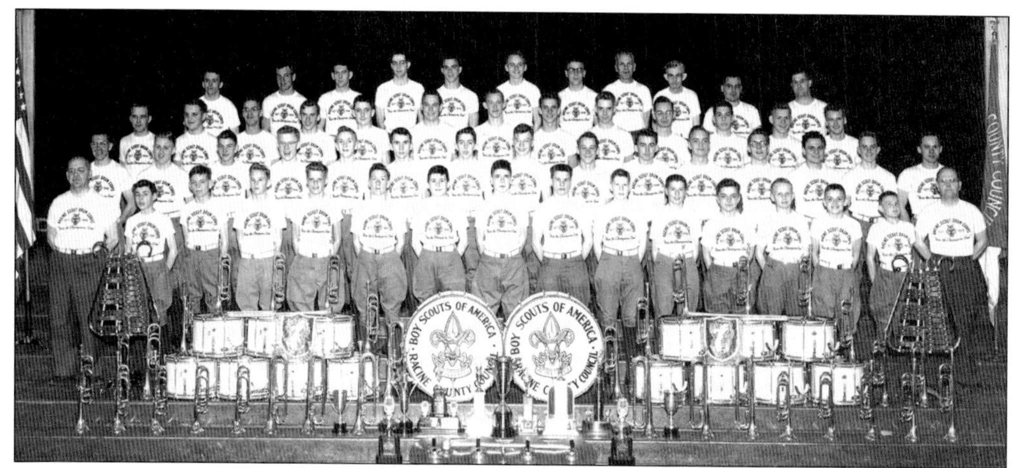

This is the Racine Boy Scout Drum and Bugle Corps full corps photograph in 1948. During 1948, the Racine Boy Scouts set a new record for themselves by winning three firsts in one day. Saturday afternoon, August 14, 1948, before 10,000 people in the grandstand at the Wisconsin Centennial Exposition in West Allis, the corps won first place in the V-J Day and Peace Parade. The award was a two-foot-high gold trophy. Then the corps drove to Elkhorn and won first place for being the best-appearing musical organization in a V-J Day parade there and then won first place in the drum corps competition. (Courtesy of RHM.)

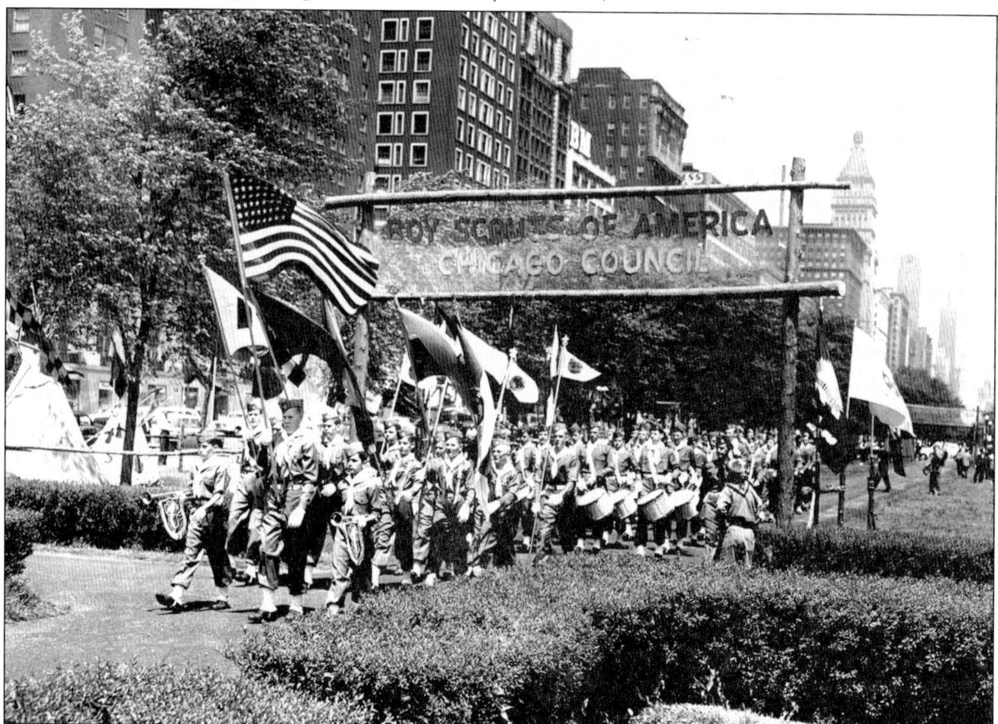

In 1951, the Racine Boy Scout Drum and Bugle Corps was again very successful competitively, winning both the Wisconsin American Legion Drum and Bugle Corps State Championship and the Wisconsin State Fair championship. Also among its honors in 1951, the Racine Boy Scouts opened the sessions of the National Council of the Boy Scouts of America in Chicago, as pictured above. (Courtesy of RHM.)

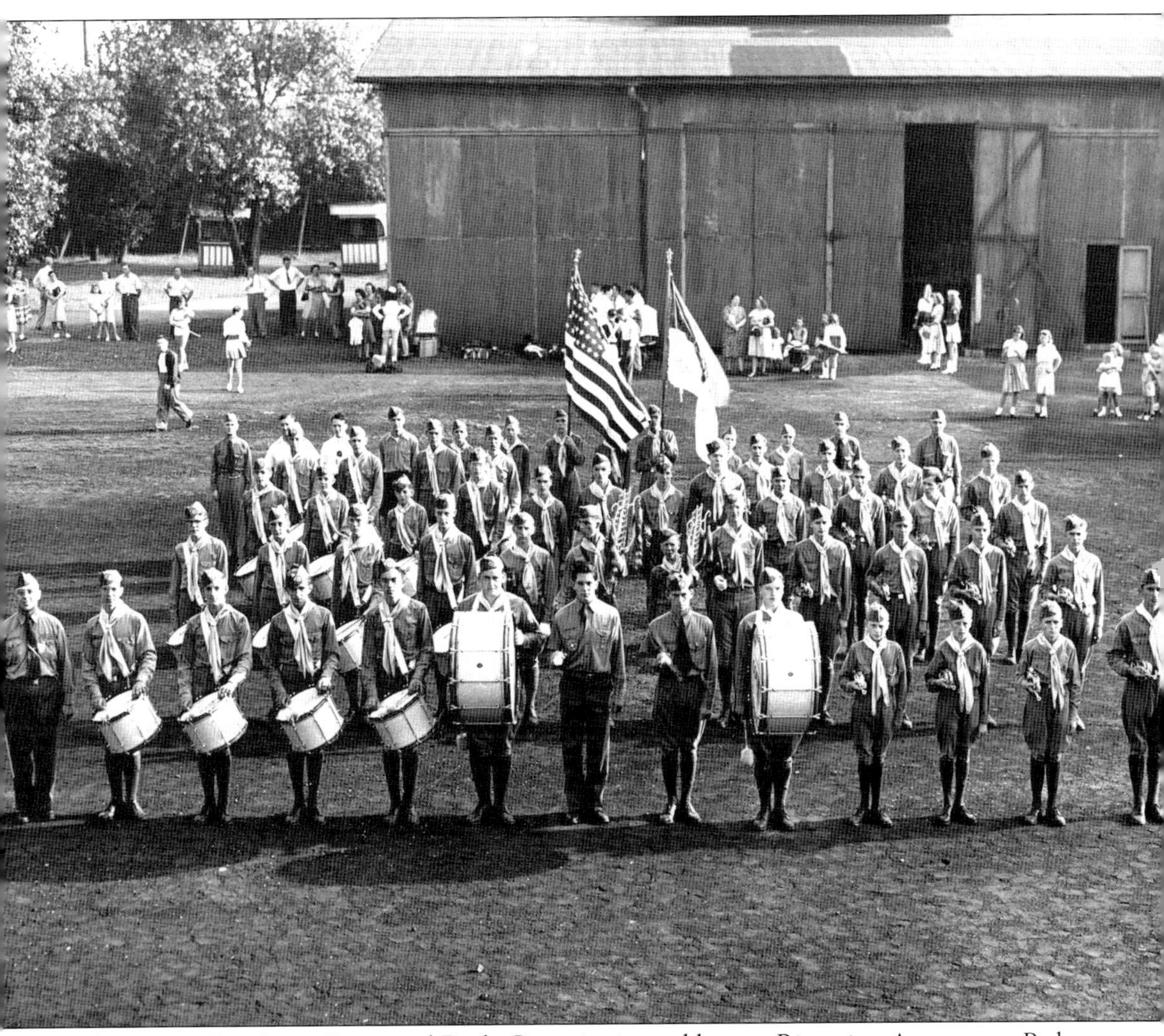

The Racine Boy Scout Drum and Bugle Corps is pictured here at Riverview Amusement Park in Chicago in 1949 where the group again took first place at the annual Tournament of Music competition. In 1949, the up-and-coming Racine Kilties Drum and Bugle Corps had arrived, so to speak. As a result of the Kilties winning preliminaries and their 3rd-place finish in finals at the prestigious Spectacle of Music in South Milwaukee, after having placed 14th out of 15 corps there in preliminaries in 1948, everyone in Racine was anticipating the first meeting of the 1949 season between the Kilties and the Racine Boy Scouts. The two Racine corps finally met at the American Legion Drum and Bugle Corps State Championship in Milwaukee on Friday, August 12. The Racine Boy Scouts won the junior sponsored competition at the 1949 American Legion Drum and Bugle Corps State Championship for the second year in a row. The Kilties took second. This settled the argument for 1949, but the rivalry between these two corps continued for decades. (Courtesy of RHM.)

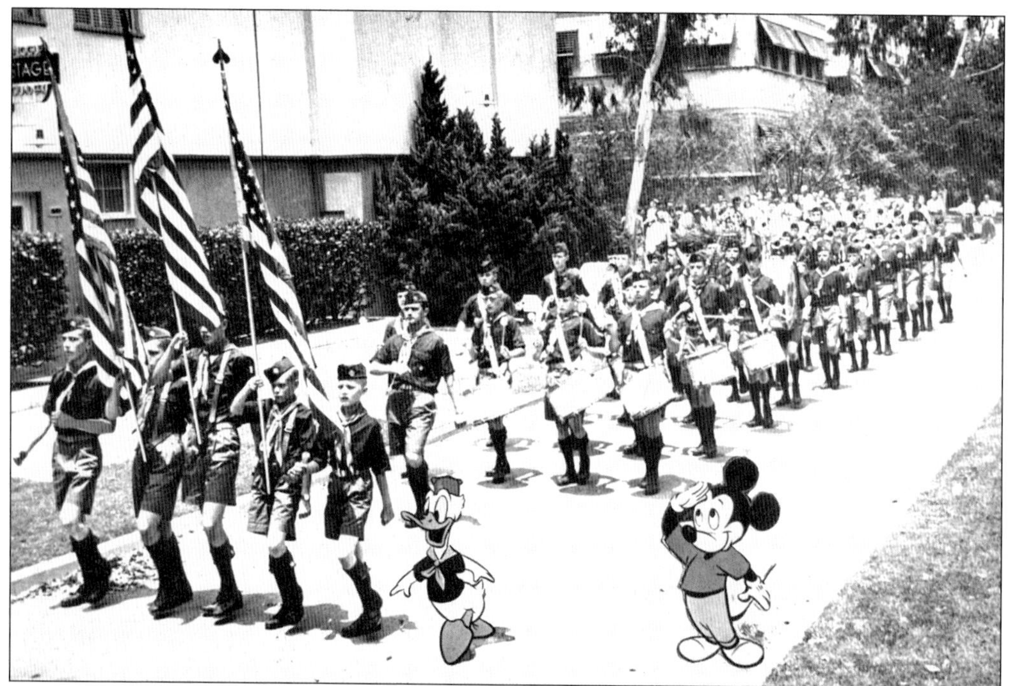

In 1953, the Racine Boy Scout Drum and Bugle Corps attended the national jamboree in Irvine Park, California. While there, the corps played at the opening of Disneyland, as seen above, and played a concert at Los Angeles's famous intersection Hollywood Boulevard and Vine Street. (Courtesy of RHM.)

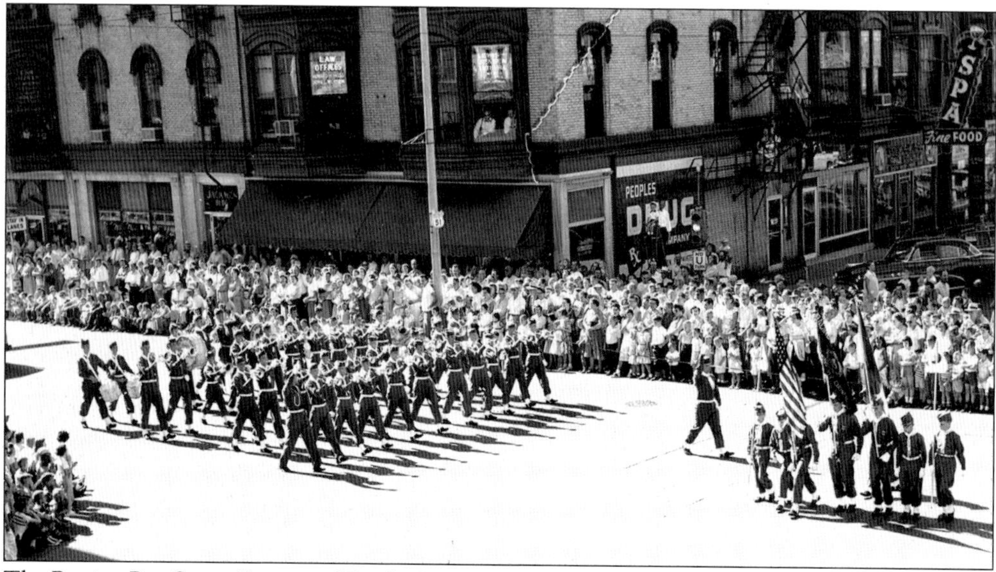

The Racine Boy Scout Drum and Bugle Corps is marching in a 1950s Tournament of Champions parade in Janesville. Originated by Janesville's now defunct Indian Trails Council Boy Scout Drum and Bugle Corps in cooperation with the Janesville Labor Temple Association, the Tournament of Champions was first held on September 1, 1952. Held annually for decades on Labor Day in Janesville, it included an afternoon parade followed by an evening drum and bugle corps competition at Monterey Stadium. (Courtesy of RHM.)

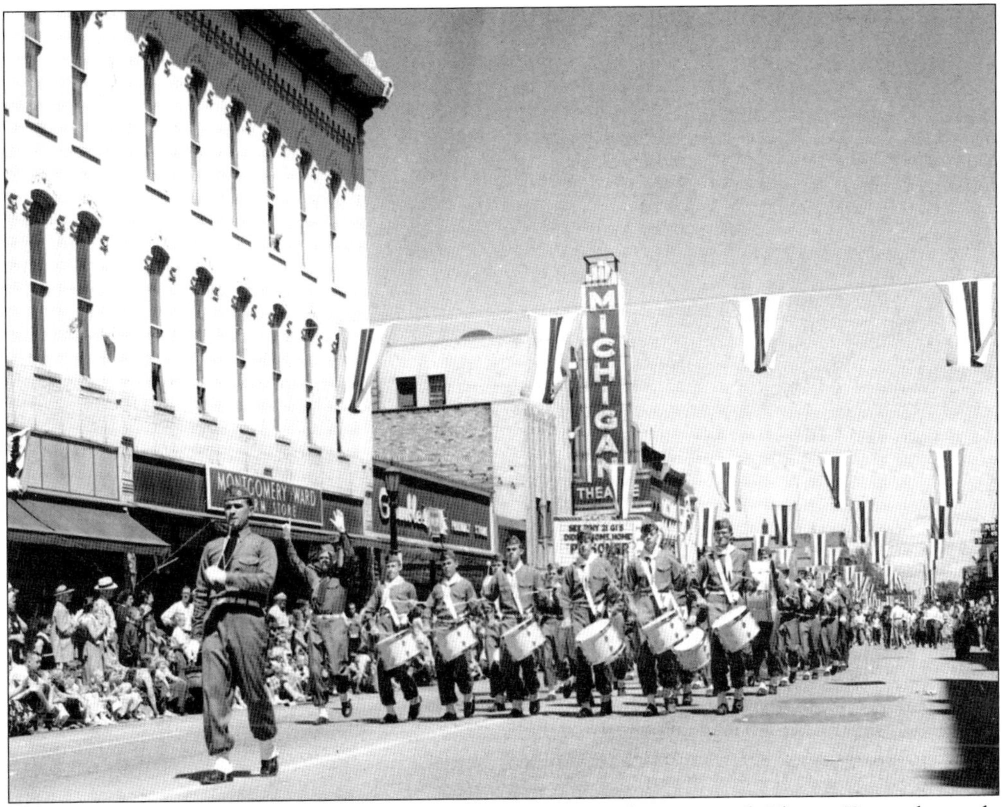

The Racine Boy Scout Drum and Bugle Corps is seen at the National Cherry Festival parade in Traverse City, Michigan. The year is unknown; however, the Racine Boy Scouts attended the National Cherry Festival often during the 1940s and 1950s. Peter Barry is leading the corps while Roland Olson is giving hand signals. Since 1925, parades have been a featured attraction of the National Cherry Festival. (Courtesy of RHM.)

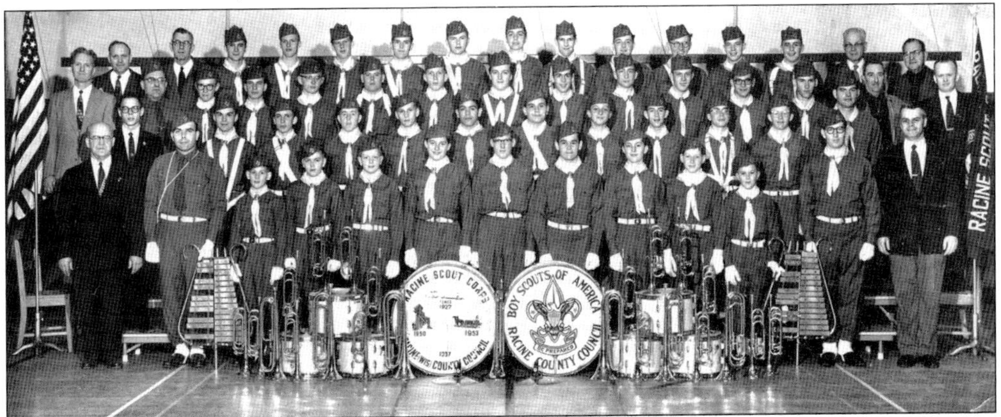

This is the 1954 Racine Boy Scout Drum and Bugle Corps. On August 21, 1954, special recognition was given to the Racine Boy Scout Drum and Bugle Corps at the 25th anniversary of the Chicagoland Music Festival, honoring it as one of the corps that competed in the music festival's first competition in 1930. Before an estimated 80,000 spectators, the Racine corps opened the festival with a 10-minute concert. As the corps did in 1930, the 1954 edition left the field marching in the formation of a Christian cross and playing "Onward, Christian Soldiers."

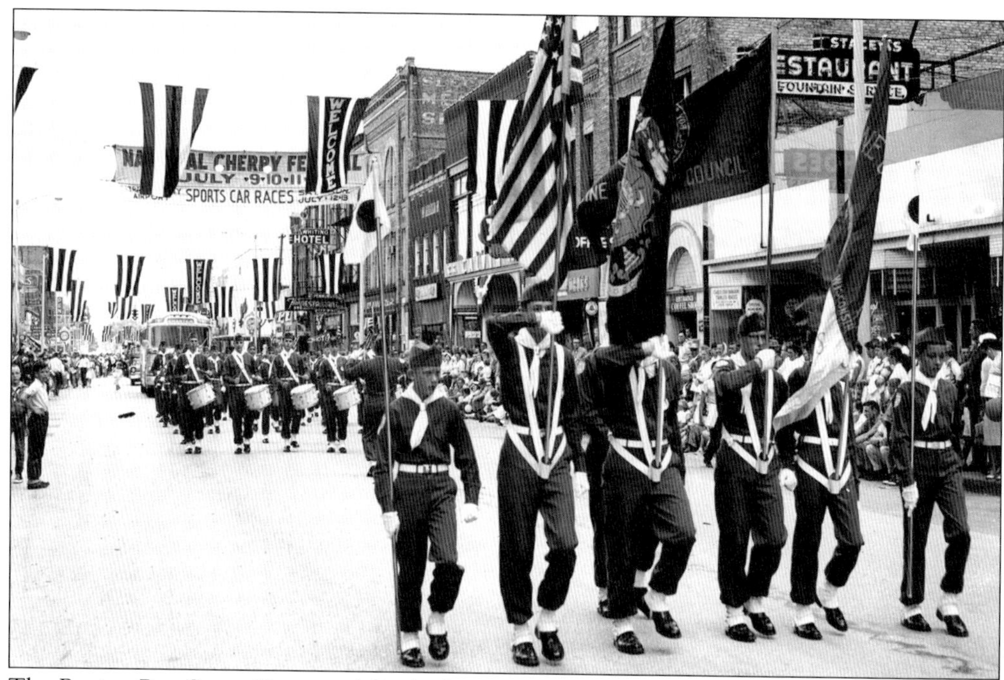

The Racine Boy Scout Drum and Bugle Corps is seen in the National Cherry Festival parade in Traverse City, Michigan, in 1959. Competitive during 1959, the group's best finishes in competition were at Edgerton, Wisconsin Rapids, and Appleton and at Menominee, Michigan, where it came in second place. The group also took third place at the Wisconsin American Legion Drum and Bugle Corps State Championship. (Courtesy of RHM.)

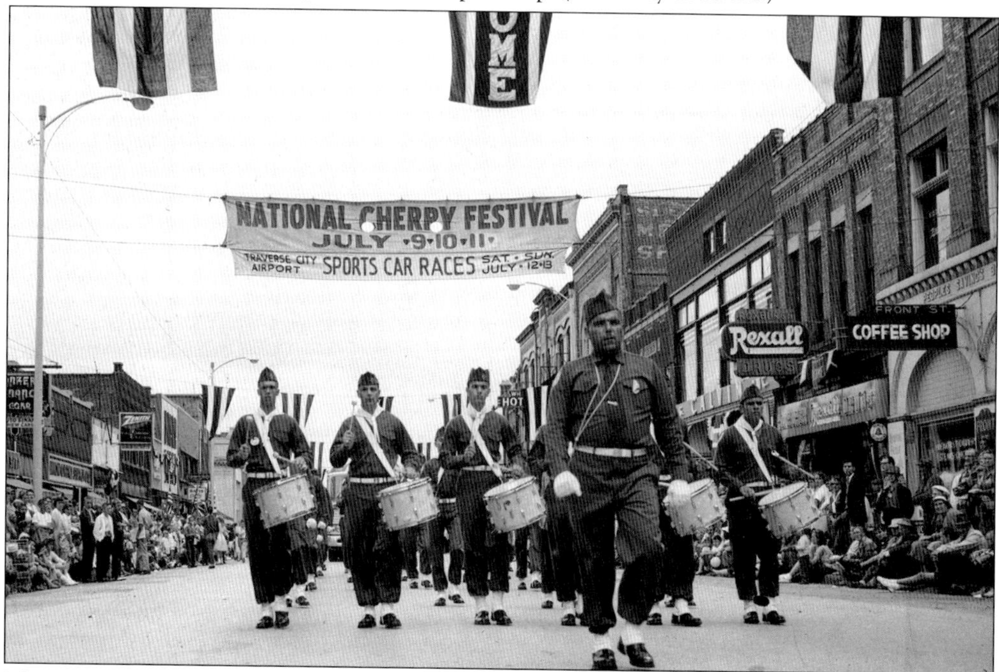

This is another great shot of the Racine Boy Scout Drum and Bugle Corps on parade in Traverse City, Michigan, in the annual National Cherry Festival parade in 1959. (Courtesy of RHM.)

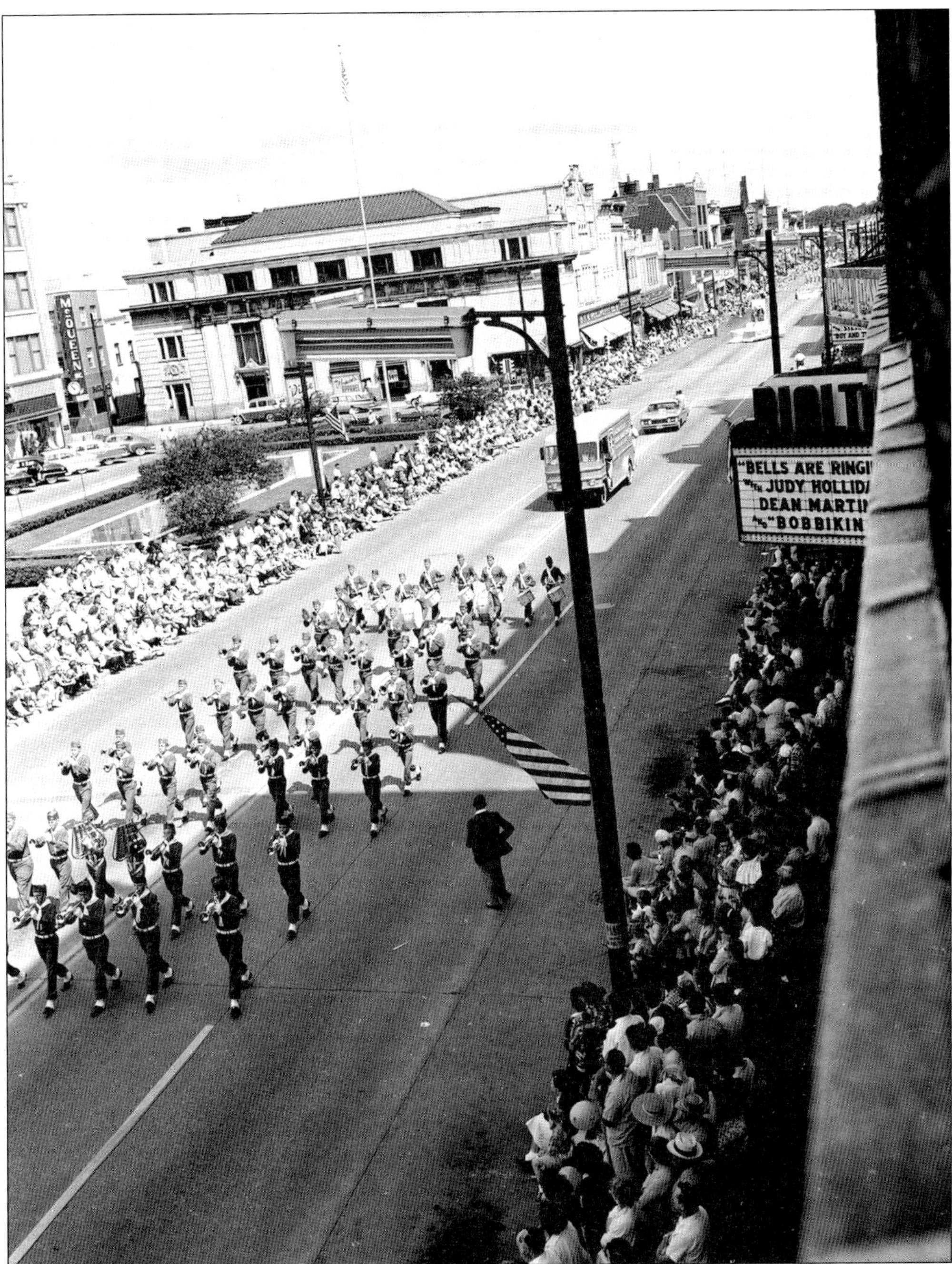

The Racine Boy Scout Drum and Bugle Corps is seen in the Fourth of July parade in Racine in 1960. In August 1960, the Racine Boy Scouts attended the Boy Scout National Jamboree, which was held in Colorado Springs, Colorado. On Saturday night, August 30, the Racine Boy Scouts appeared on a nationwide television program, *World Wide 60*, which told the story of the Boy Scout National Jamboree held in Colorado the previous week. They were selected to appear from the many corps attending the jamboree. (Courtesy of RHM.)

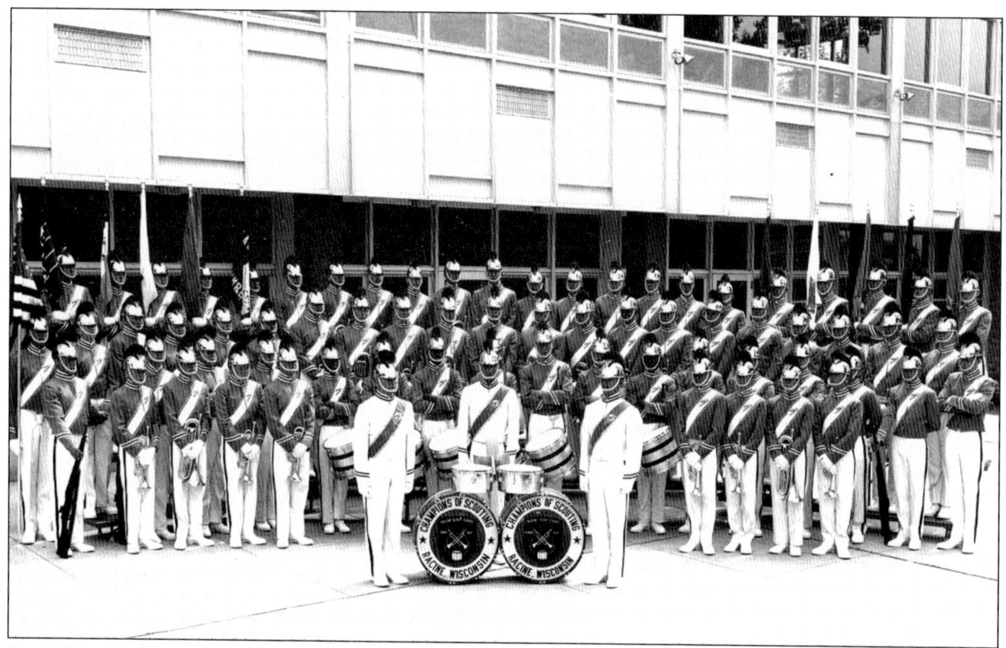

In 1964, the Racine Boy Scout Drum and Bugle Corps entered a new era by reorganizing the drum corps into the then-new national program of Explorer Scouting. When the musical Explorer Scout post was formed, the boys doffed their official Boy Scout fatigue green uniforms for the red, white, and blue uniforms pictured in this photograph. As a result of this reorganization, the group officially became the Racine Explorer Scout Drum and Bugle Corps. Because of the members' new chrome helmets, they were immediately given the nickname Chrome Domes. (Courtesy of RHM.)

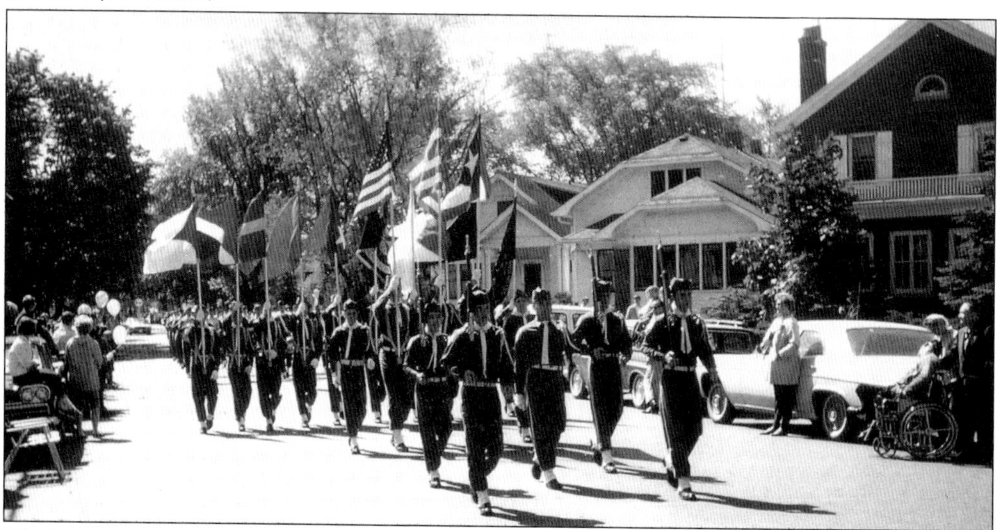

The best year that the Racine Explorer Scout Drum and Bugle Corps experienced in over a decade was 1966. Important victories for the Racine Explorer Scouts in 1966 came at the Badgerland Association Championship, the Wisconsin VFW Drum and Bugle Corps State Championship, and the Wisconsin American Legion Drum and Bugle Corps State Championship. The color guard also won the championship at all three of these contests. Pictured above are the Racine Explorer Scouts on parade in Racine's 1966 Memorial Day parade.

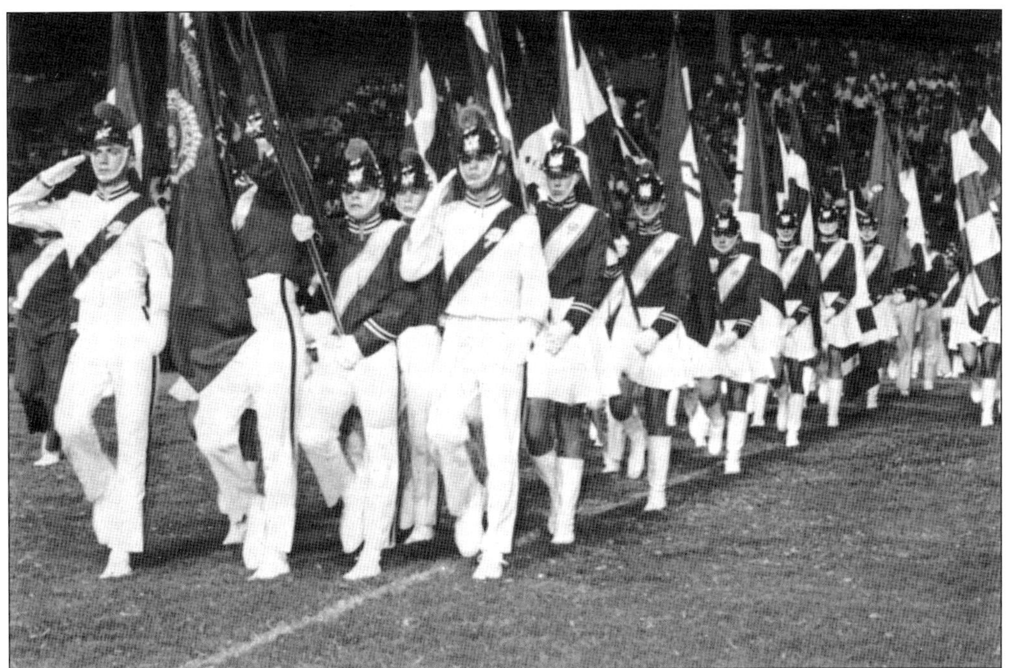

Above are the 1969 Racine Explorer Scouts. The biggest news to hit Racine's drum corps came out in January 1969 when it was announced that the Racine Explorer Scouts had opened up their color guard to girls, 15 years of age and older. Some highlights for the Racine Explorer Scouts during 1969 include capturing first place at Madison's Zor Shrine Drums on Parade and the Kiltie Kontest in Burlington. (Courtesy of RKAA.)

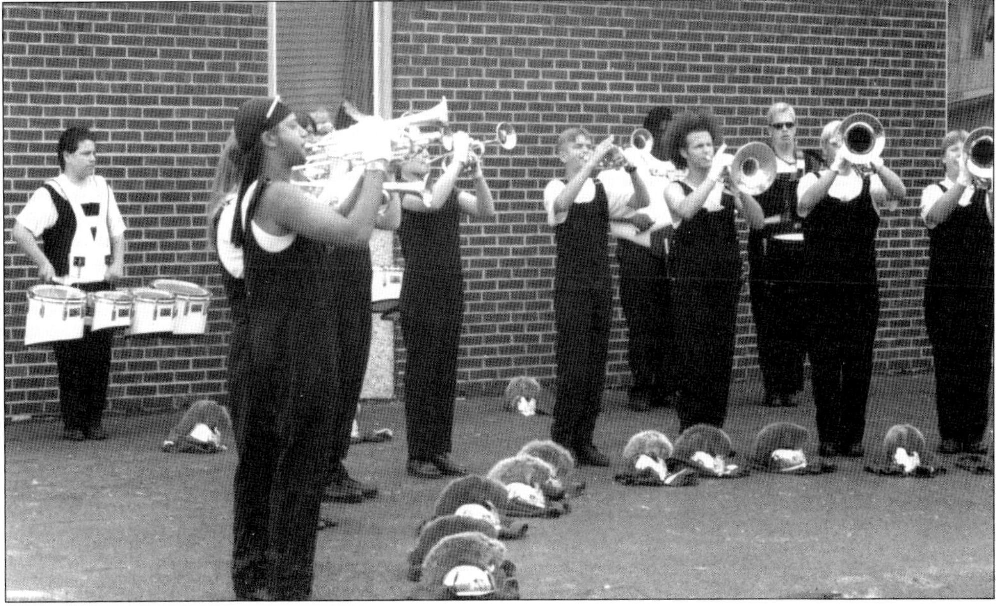

The Racine Scouts Drum and Bugle Corps is seen warming up before Racine's Memorial Day parade in 1999. In 1974, the Racine Explorer Scout Drum and Bugle Corps experienced a large loss of personnel and had a hard time recruiting new ones. The corps decided to continue on, despite its small membership.

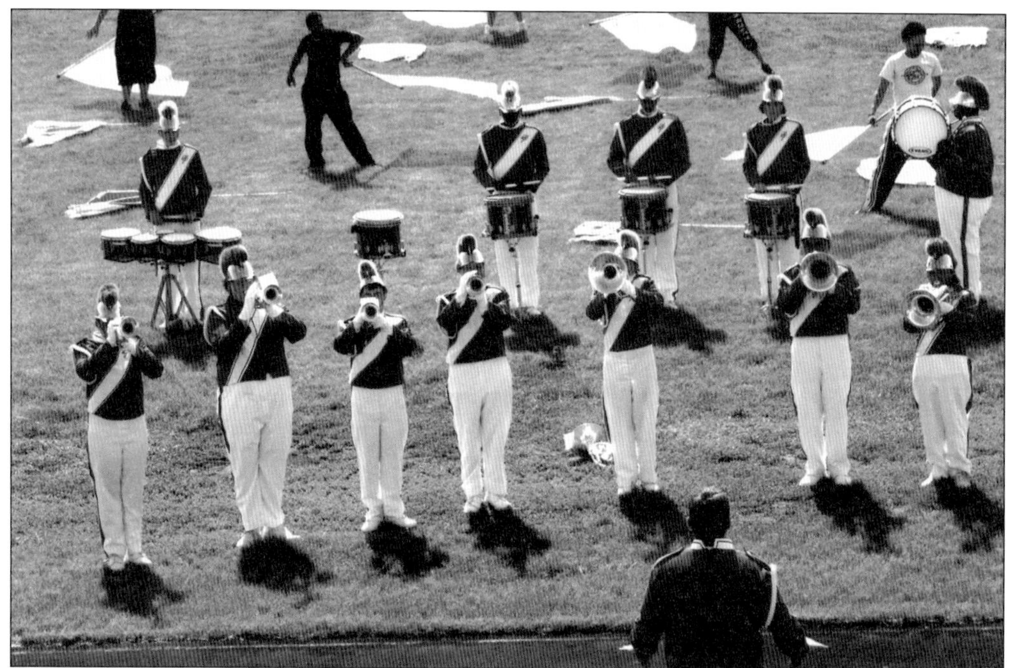

The Racine Scouts Drum and Bugle Corps is performing at its 80th anniversary celebration at J. I. Case High School's Hammes Field in Racine in 2007. The Racine Scouts still wear their famous Chrome Dome helmets, which were introduced in 1964, but with an updated uniform. It is a thriving Open Class corps that travels extensively to competitions throughout the United States and Canada.

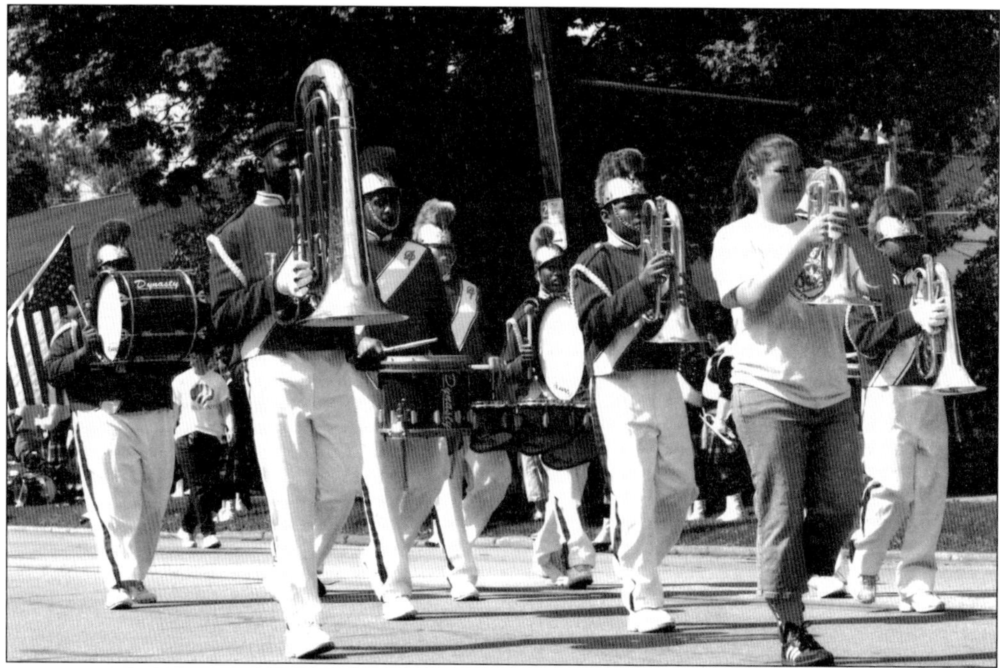

The Racine Scouts are seen smartly marching in Racine's 2007 Memorial Day parade. Today still finds the Racine Scouts entertaining people throughout North America.

Three

Racine Junior Scouts

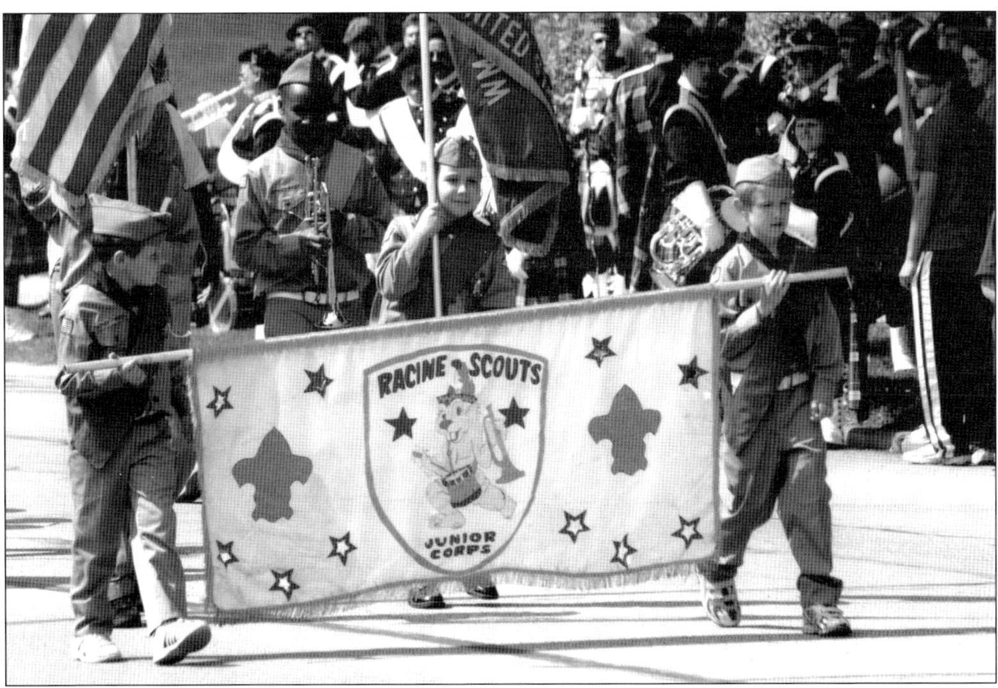

Under the watchful eyes of the Racine Kilties Senior Drum and Bugle Corps, the Racine Scouts Junior Drum and Bugle Corps steps off in Racine's Memorial Day parade in 2007. The Racine Boy Scout Junior Drum and Bugle Corps was organized 50 years prior in October 1957, for the purpose of training younger Boy Scouts for the Racine Boy Scout Drum and Bugle Corps. Its first public appearance was in the 1958 Memorial Day parade in Racine.

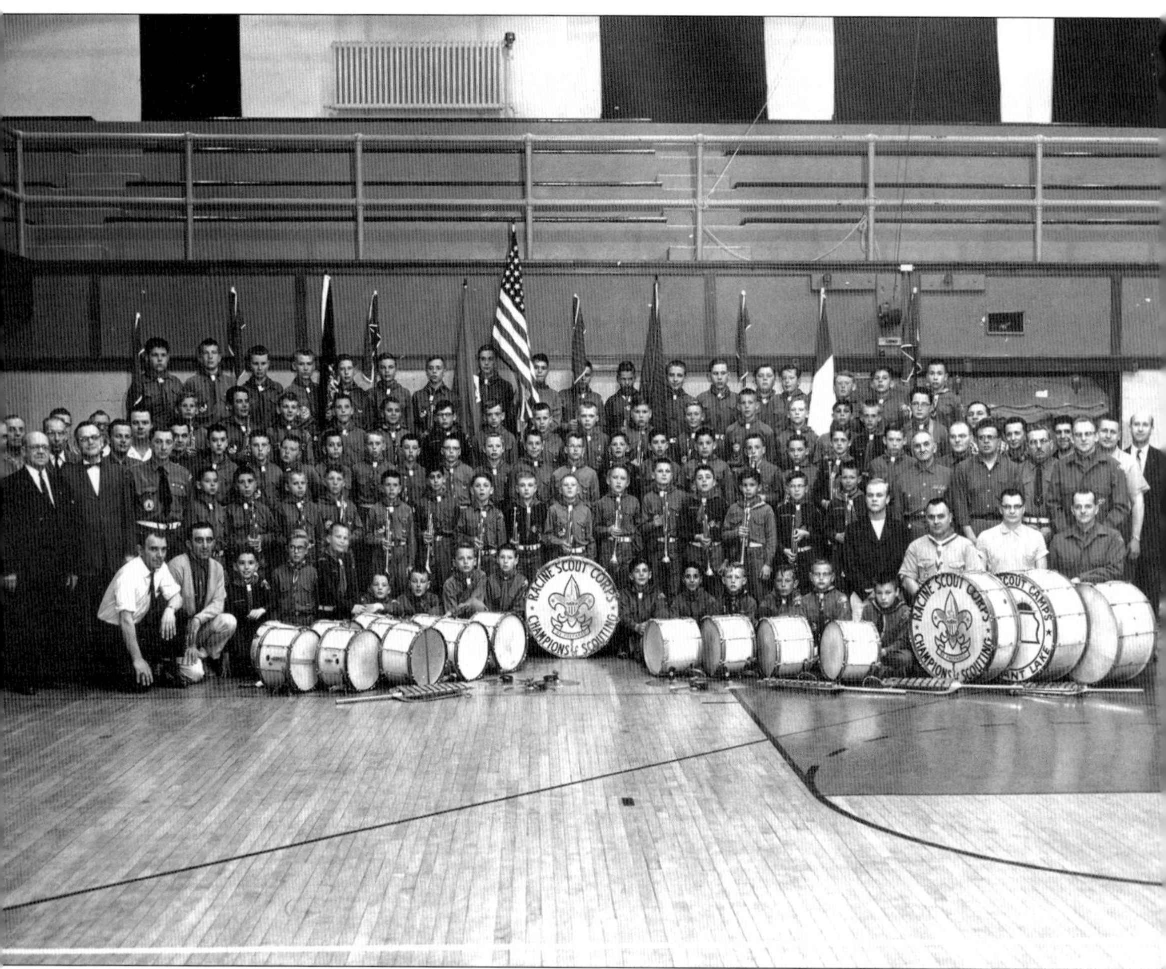

This is a photograph of the 1959 Racine Boy Scout Junior Drum and Bugle Corps. The Junior Boy Scouts' equipment originally was purchased in 1935 by the Drum Corps Mothers' Club. In several instances, Junior Boy Scouts of the late 1950s were playing on the same instruments that were issued to and played by their fathers. (Courtesy of RHM.)

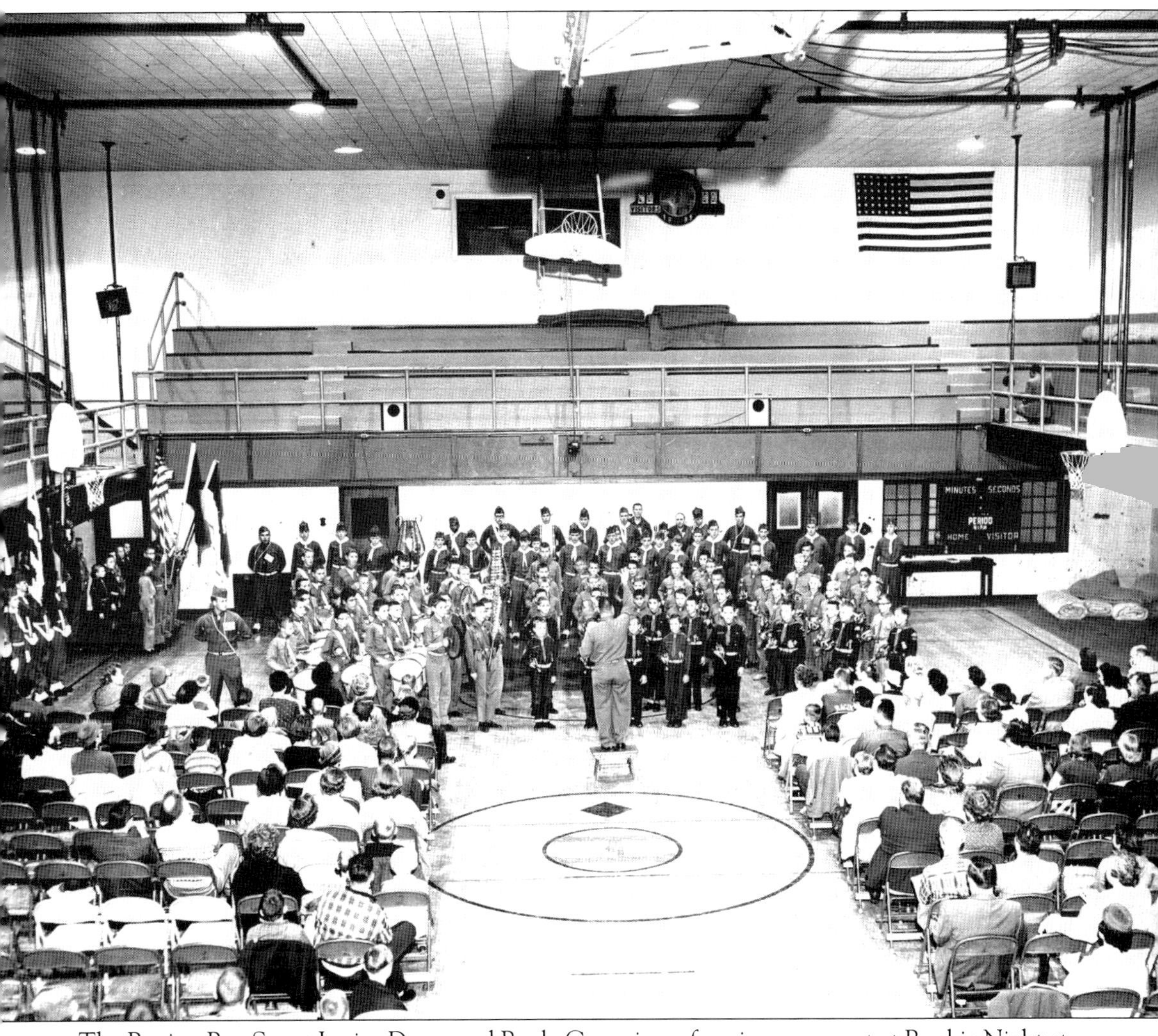

The Racine Boy Scout Junior Drum and Bugle Corps is performing a concert at Rookie Night at the Horlick High School gymnasium, probably in the late 1950s. The Racine Boy Scout Drum and Bugle Corps is in the background behind the Junior Boy Scouts; both color guards are on the left side. (Courtesy of RHM.)

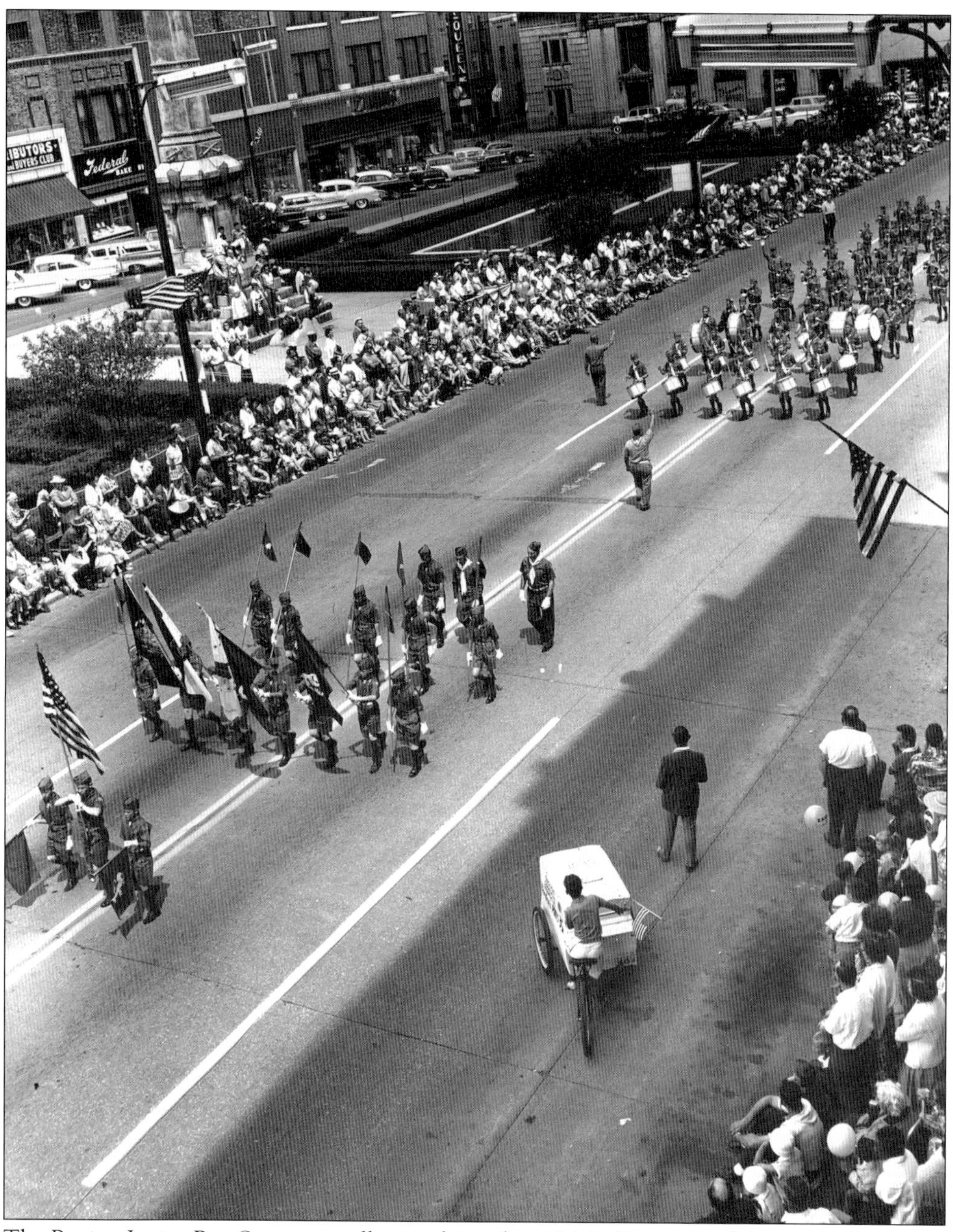

The Racine Junior Boy Scouts proudly march south on Main Street past Monument Square in Racine's 1960 Fourth of July parade. (Courtesy of RHM.)

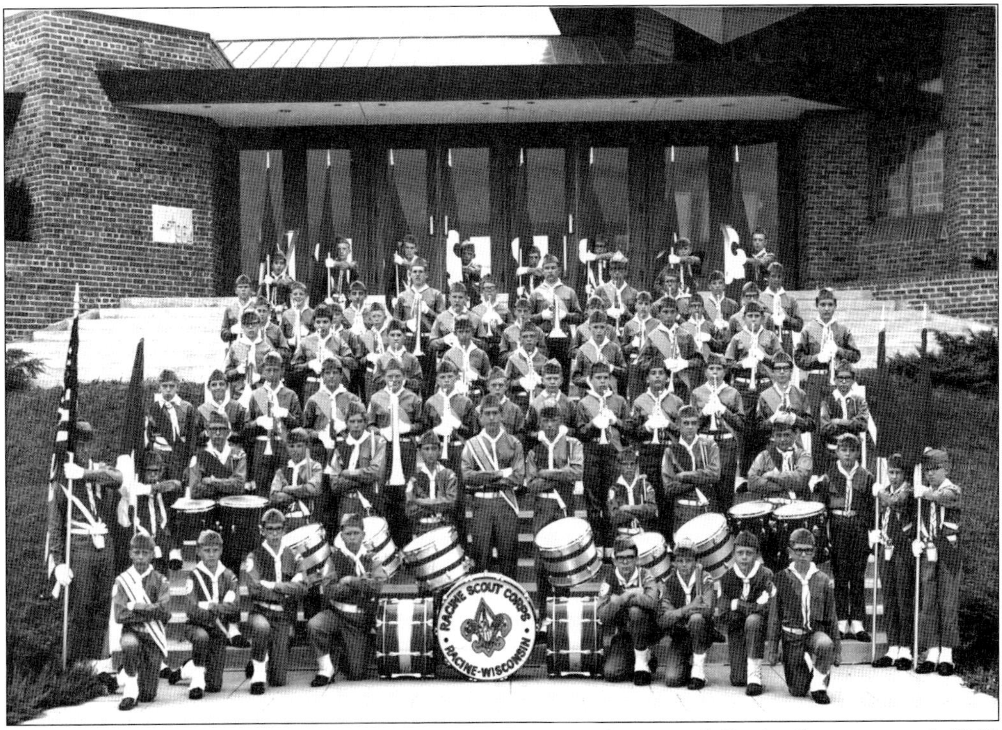

This is a photograph of the Racine Boy Scout Junior Drum and Bugle Corps around 1967. During 1967, the Racine Junior Boy Scouts took third place in Class C at the Wisconsin VFW Drum and Bugle Corps State Championship and took second place in Class B at the Kenosha Music Round-Up. (Courtesy of RHM.)

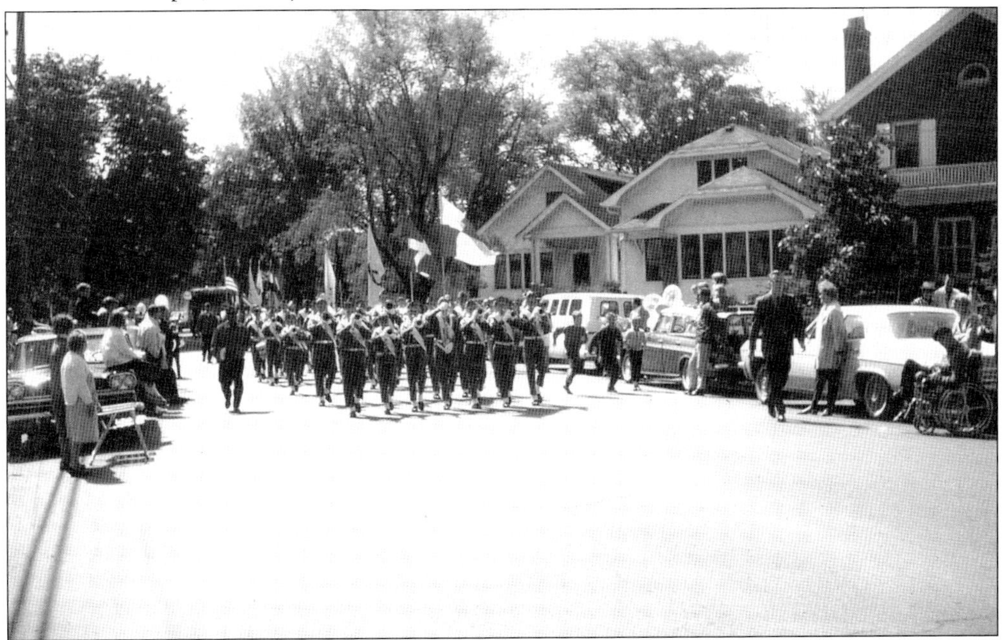

The Racine Junior Boy Scouts are heading west on Osbourne Boulevard in Racine's 1966 Memorial Day parade. (Courtesy of RKAA.)

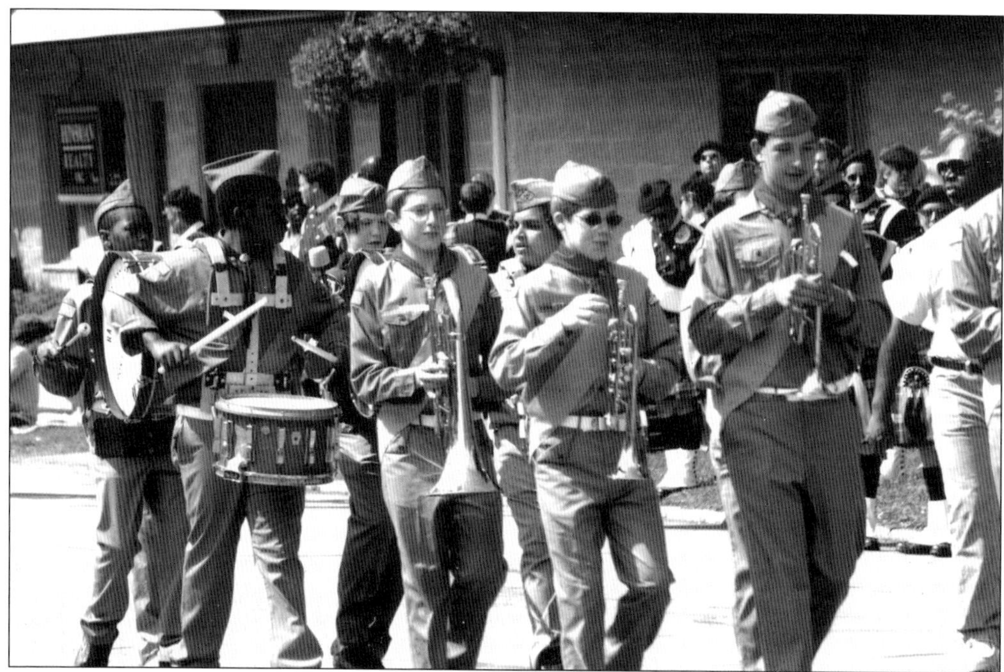

The Racine Junior Scouts step off in Racine's 2007 Memorial Day parade. Some 50 years after their founding, the Racine Junior Scouts can still be seen marching in area parades.

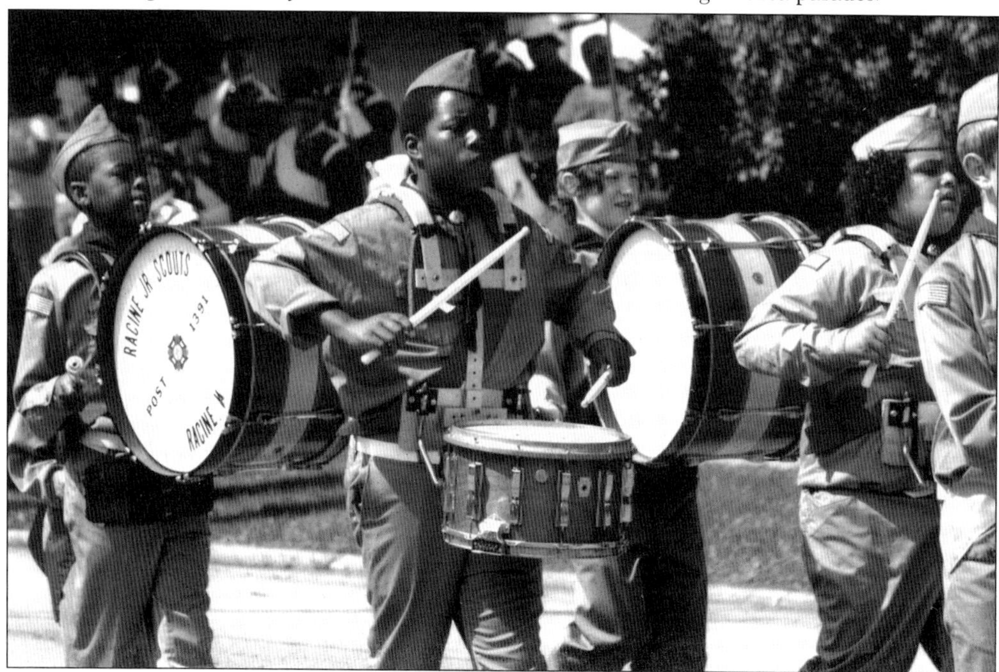

Although the Racine Junior Scouts are no longer a competing drum and bugle corps, the members are still proud of their parade corps and take it seriously, as indicated in this photograph of the corps in 2007. The Racine Scouts Junior Drum and Bugle Corps of today still serves its intended purpose as a training corps by providing expert instruction and a rewarding, positive experience for its young members.

Four

Racine Kilties

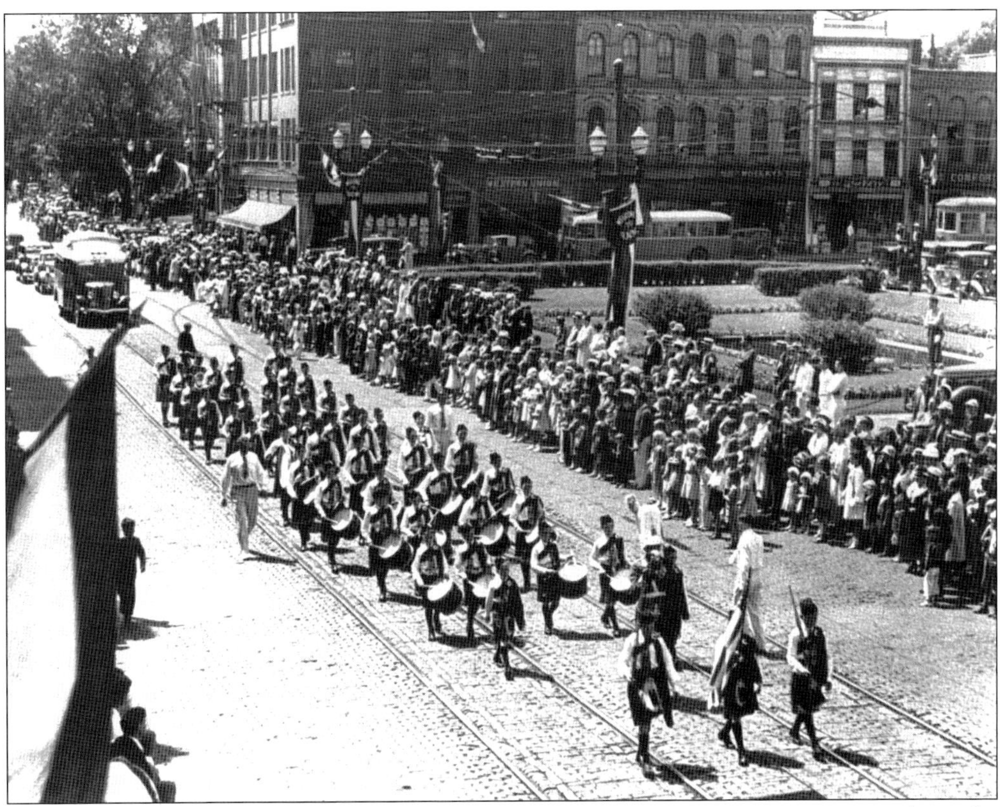

This is the Kilties' first public appearance in their Kiltie uniforms. They are on parade in the 500 block of Main Street in Racine's 1936 Fourth of July parade. In 1936, the parade still proceeded north on Main Street, not south like it does today. The Kilties received the award for the best-appearing unit in the parade. In the spring of 1936, the Racine Kiwanis Club donated money that was needed for the Kilties' uniforms. As a sign of appreciation on the part of the parents of the boys, it was decided to name the group the Kiwanis Kilties. On the bass drums, the emblems of both the Kiwanis Club and that of the YMCA were painted. (Courtesy of RKAA.)

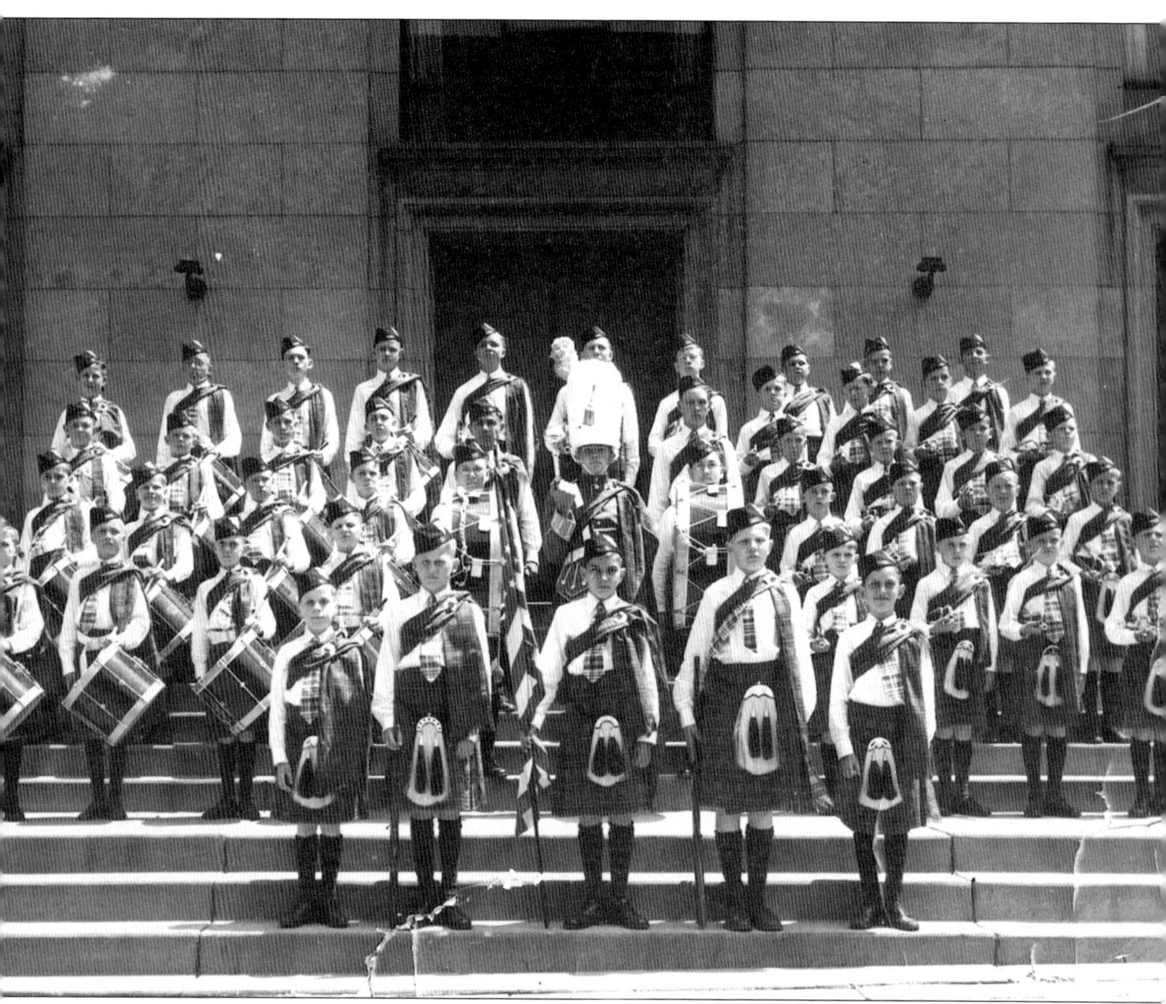

The Kilties Drum and Bugle Corps traces its origin to the summer of 1934 at Camp Anokijig, a boys' summer camp located about 90 miles north of Racine on Little Elkhart Lake. American Legion Week was held there from July 27 to August 30. During this week, the American Legion had many experts as instructors at the camp, including J. E. Asplund, who taught the boys drumming, and Chester Nelson, who taught the boys bugling. Their intention was to train some boys at Camp Anokijig in drumming and bugling so that they could help with the different flag ceremonies. A large number of boys turned out, and a credible drum and bugle corps was developed in only a few days. It was at this time that plans for organizing a YMCA drum and bugle corps were first discussed. Scotty McCreadie, also a member of the Racine American Legion Post 76 drum and bugle corps at Camp Anokijig for American Legion Week, said definitively, "Let's put 'em in kilts!" The Racine YMCA received so many continuing requests from both parents and boys to organize a Y boys' drum and bugle corps that all boys from 10 to 14 years old interested in forming such a "kiltie outfit" were invited to a meeting on October 15, 1934. Twenty-eight boys showed up at this first meeting, and the Kilties Drum and Bugle Corps was born. This photograph of the Kilties was taken after their first public appearance in Racine's 1936 Fourth of July parade at Memorial Hall. (Courtesy of RKAA.)

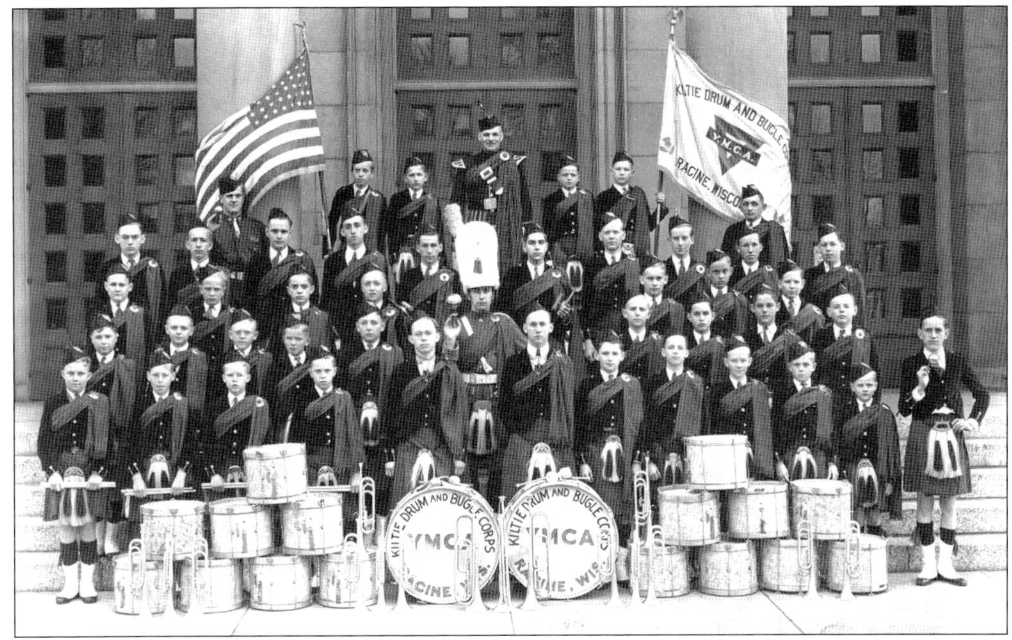

This photograph of the Kilties is from around 1942. One of the highlights for the Kilties during 1942 was their four-day trip to Camp Anokijig, the Racine YMCA camp in Sheboygan County. This trip over Labor Day weekend found the Kilties leading the entry parade on both Saturday and Sunday afternoons at the Sheboygan County Fair in Plymouth. On Labor Day afternoon, the group led a parade through the business district of Plymouth. (Courtesy of RKAA.)

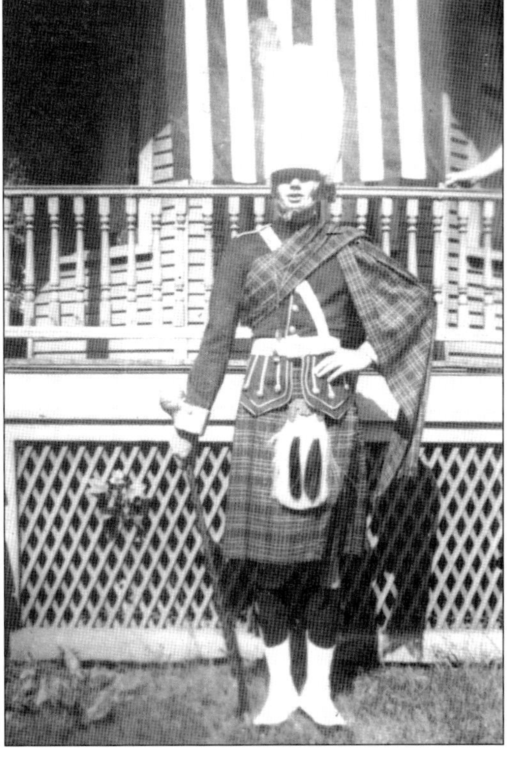

Harald Kahlert, in front of his home at 1224 Racine Street in 1936, became the Racine Kilties' first drum major. After serving in the U.S. Army in various capacities during World War II, Kahlert joined Racine's Boys of 76 Drum and Bugle Corps. During the 1950s, he also was an All-America judge. Kahlert is now 90 years old, lives in Kenosha, and is still active with the Racine VFW Firing Squad. (Courtesy of RKAA.)

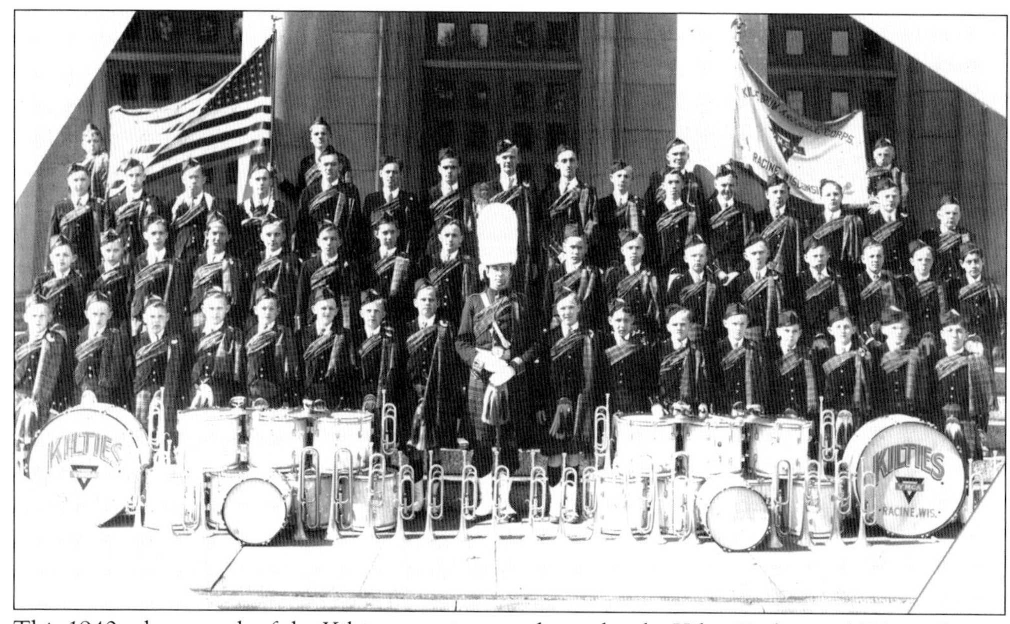

This 1940s photograph of the Kilties was given to the author by Kiltie Kadets and Kilties alumni Richard Hinderholtz. He said that he got it from Kilties alumni Thomas Sorensen, who rescued it from the garbage back in the 1970s when the Kilties moved out of Kiltie Hall.

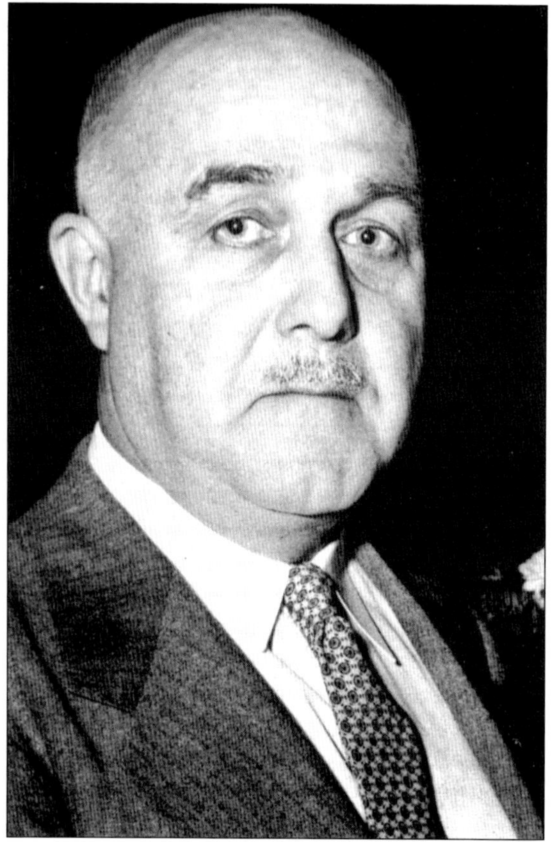

This is a 1963 photograph of Raymond C. Vance, who originally organized the Racine Kilties Drum and Bugle Corps. He was camp director of Camp Anokijig, the Racine YMCA's summer camp, when a drum and bugle corps was organized there during American Legion Week in July 1934. The drum and bugle corps was discontinued after this American Legion Week was over. After months of continuing requests from both parents and boys to form a Y drum and bugle corps, the YMCA finally gave in. In October 1934, the Kilties Drum and Bugle Corps was organized by Vance, who was also the youth director at the Racine YMCA at the time. (Courtesy of RKAA.)

Marching south in the 600 block of South Main Street in downtown Racine in the 1945 Memorial Day parade are the Kilties. This was the last year the Kilties were invited to participate in Racine's Memorial Day parade. The parade committee decided the group should no longer take part because it was not a "military organization." (Courtesy of RKAA.)

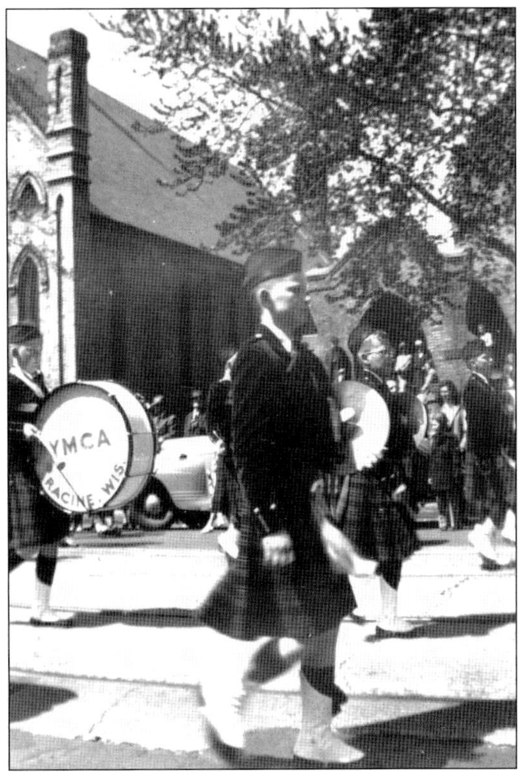

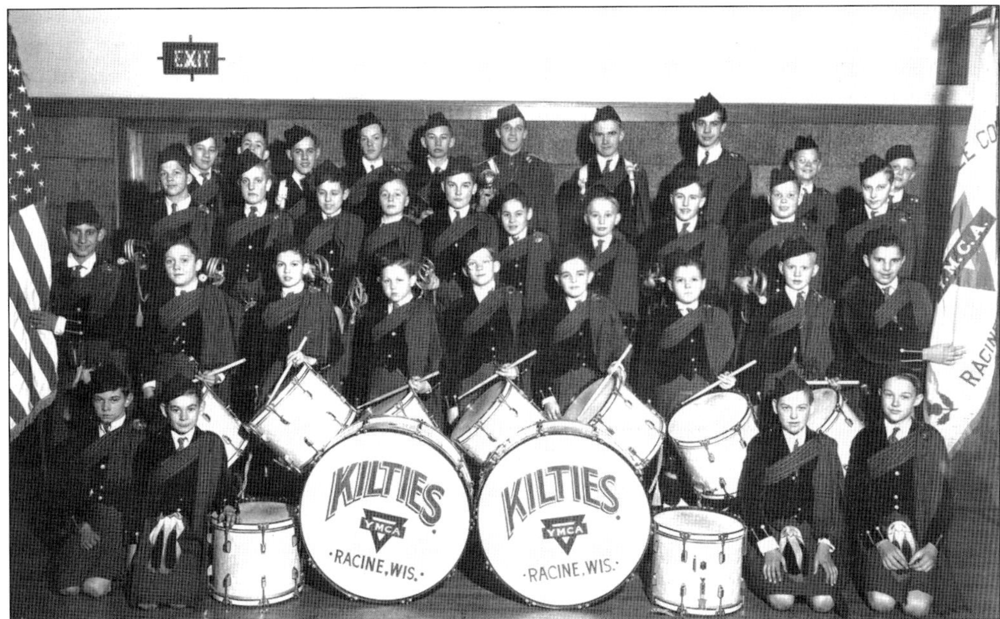

This is believed to be a 1944 or 1945 photograph of the Kilties Drum and Bugle Corps, but it could possibly be from as early as 1940. Occasionally during this era, the Kilties could be found performing at a Racine Belles women's professional baseball game at Horlick Field. The movie *A League of Their Own* was a story about two sisters playing in the women's professional baseball league on the Racine Belles baseball team. (Courtesy of RHM.)

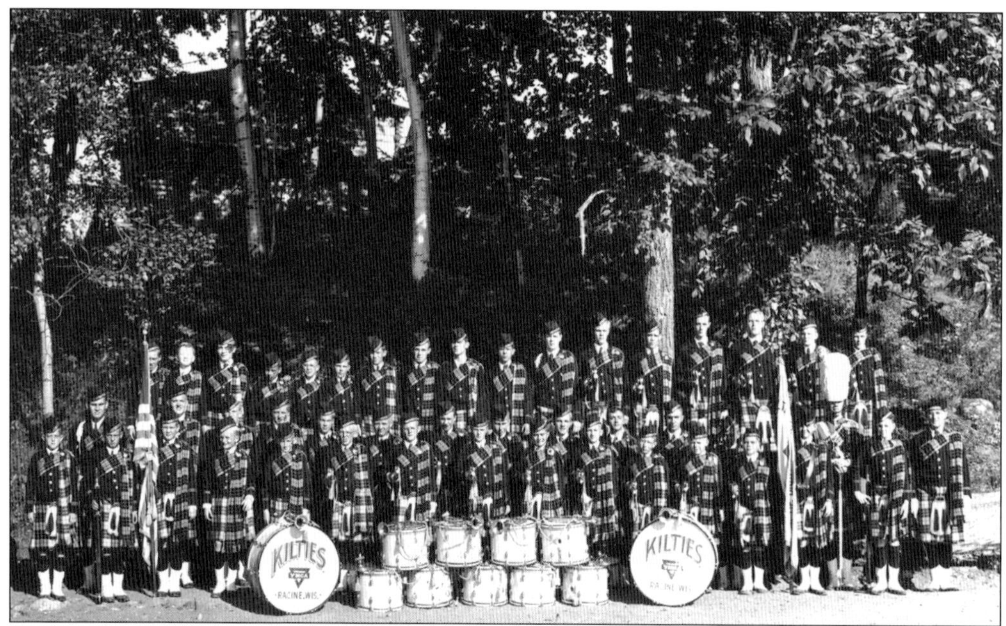

This is the 1949 Kilties Drum and Bugle Corps wearing the new McLeod plaid kilts and tartans. The green battle jacket, new in 1948, was still worn with the new McLeod plaid uniforms. The Kilties experienced their best season so far. The group received second place four times and third place once in the five competitions that it entered for 1949. (Courtesy of RHM.)

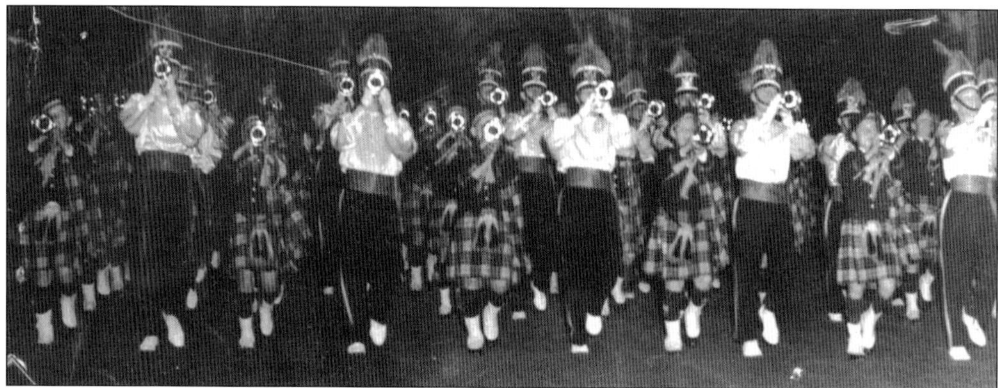

During the summer of 1950, the Chicago Gladstone Sons of the American Legion (SAL) and the Kilties Drum and Bugle Corps would often combine the corps whenever they were both at the same event. Then while marching in alternating columns they would play their identical arrangement of "Moonlight and Roses" together. Both corps combined in this manner on Sunday, August 14, 1950, and marched together playing "Moonlight and Roses" in Elkhorn's V-J Day parade. (Courtesy of RKAA.)

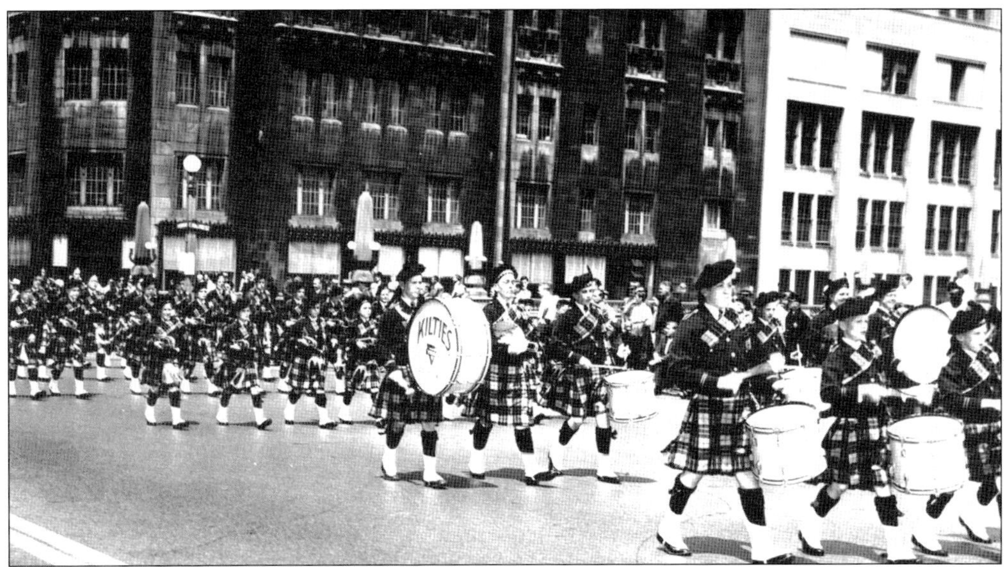

The Kilties are seen here on parade in Chicago's 1950 Memorial Day parade. Again the group was not invited to participate in Racine's parade. Even noted *Racine Journal-Times* columnist Tex Reynolds got involved in this controversy to no avail in his June 1, 1949, column. It would take until 1953 for an invite to finally be extended to the Kilties to participate in Racine's Memorial Day parade. (Courtesy of RKAA.)

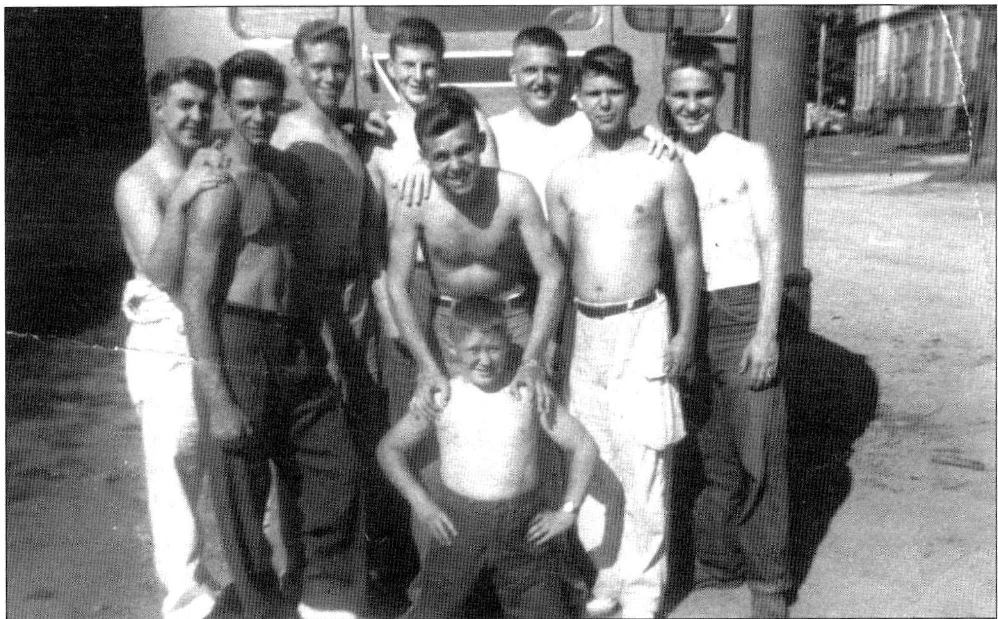

These young men are all members of the Kilties. Ten-year-old Thomas Clunie is the little guy kneeling in front. The corps was taking it easy between the parade and the competition at Cedarburg on Sunday, June 25, 1950. The Kilties took second place. The Gladstone SAL from Chicago won the contest. At the close of the evening, the Gladstone SAL serenaded the Kilties with "I Love You Truly" and then presented its first-place trophy to the Kilties because the members of the Gladstone SAL were so impressed with how good these young Kilties were. (Courtesy of RKAA.)

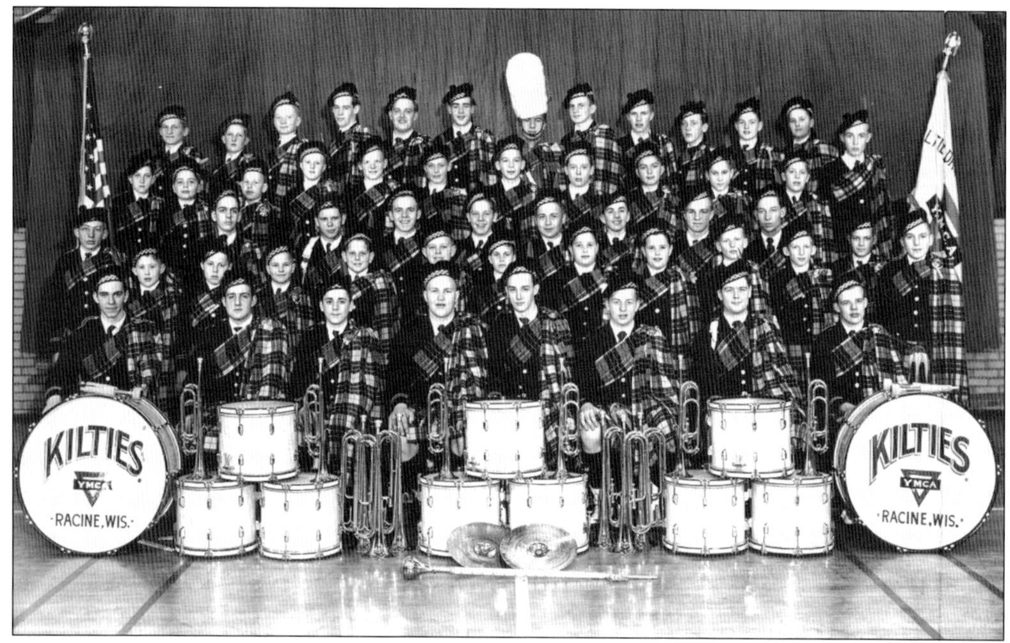

Pictured are the 1951 Kilties. During the summer of 1951, the Kilties traveled over 3,700 miles and participated in 30 events. The Kilties' rise to prominence continued during 1951 when the group won its first Wisconsin VFW Drum and Bugle Corps State Championship in Manitowoc. (Courtesy of RKAA.)

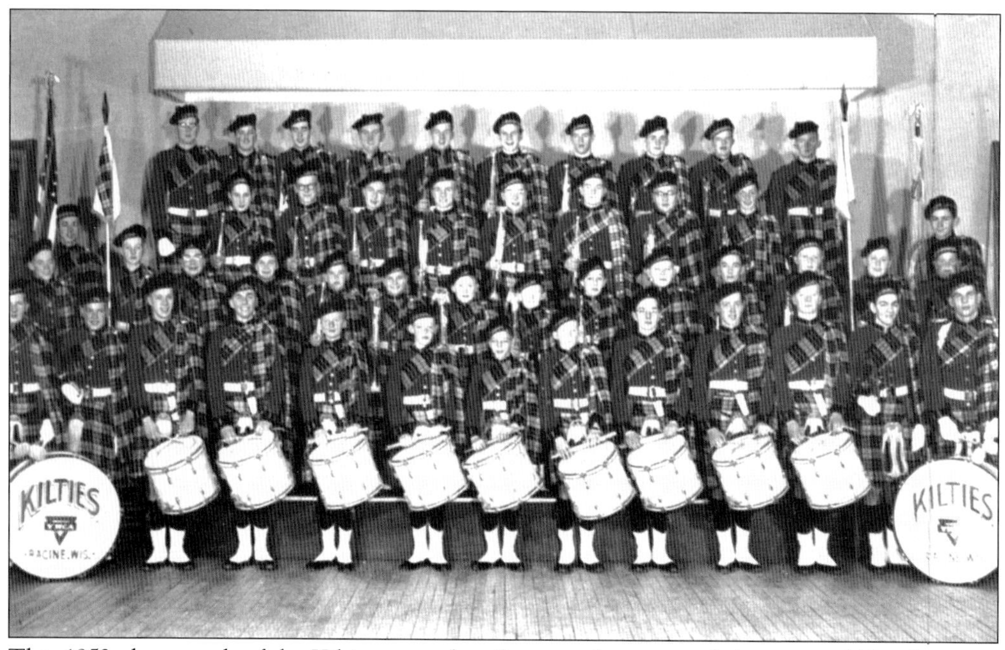

This 1952 photograph of the Kilties was taken from a color postcard that was sold by the corps as a fund-raiser. The year 1952 was another great year for the Kilties. In nine competitions the Kilties won four times, including winning their second consecutive Wisconsin VFW Drum and Bugle Corps State Championship in Wisconsin Rapids. (Courtesy of RKAA.)

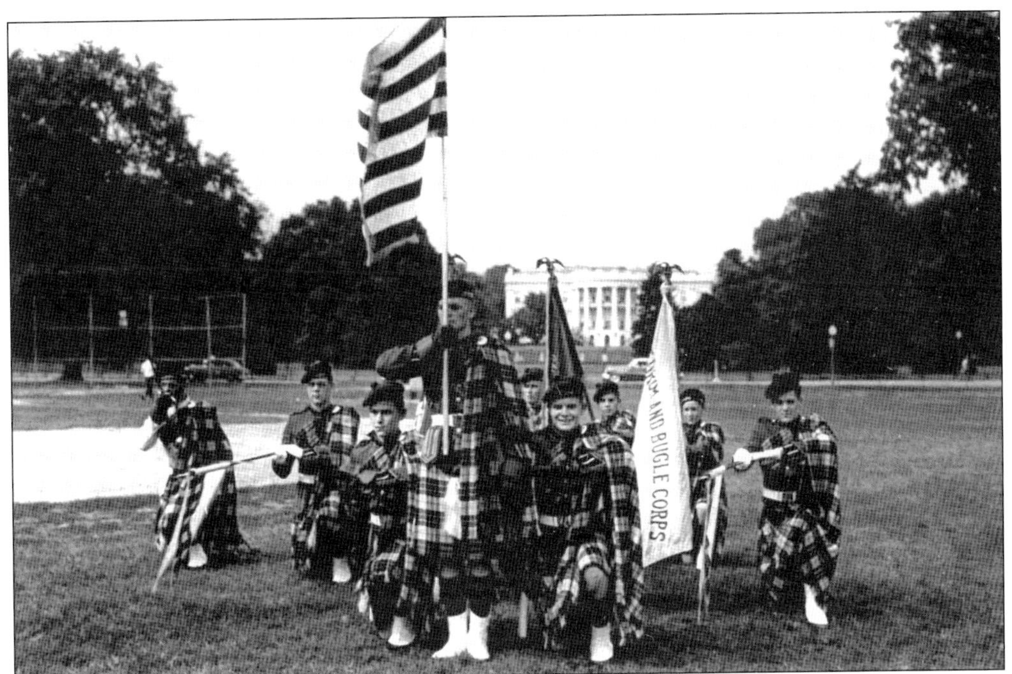

The 1954 Kilties color guard, sponsored by Racine's Harvey R. Hansen Post 310 of the American Legion, won the junior color guard national championship at the American Legion national championships in Washington, D.C. This was the first national championship of any kind won by the Kilties. The members of the color guard were Sgt. Jack Eschmann, rifle carriers Ronald Anderson and Donald Davis, guide-on carriers William Dawson and Robert Cormack, and flag carriers Robert Steberl, Kenneth Mascari, Robert Teska, and Thomas Schmitt. (Courtesy of RKAA.)

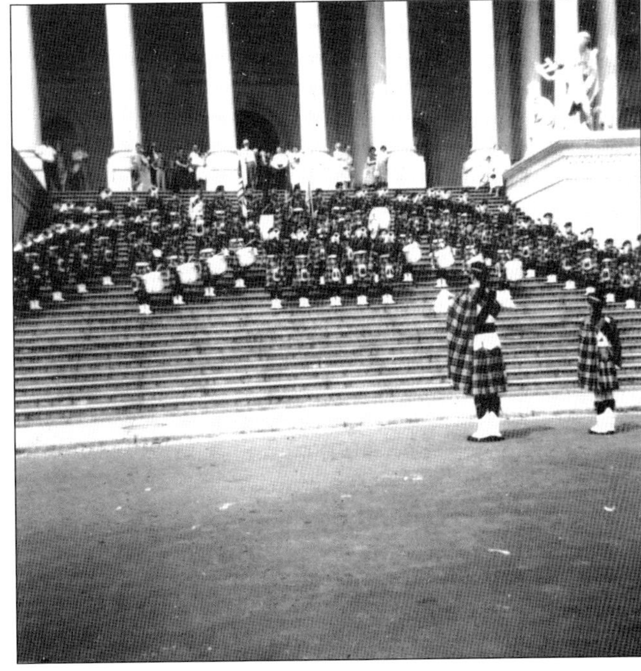

Playing a scheduled concert at noon on Monday, August 30, 1954, on the steps of the United States Capitol in Washington, D.C., are the Kilties. After the concert, members of the Kilties enjoyed free time and took sightseeing tours. (Courtesy of RKAA.)

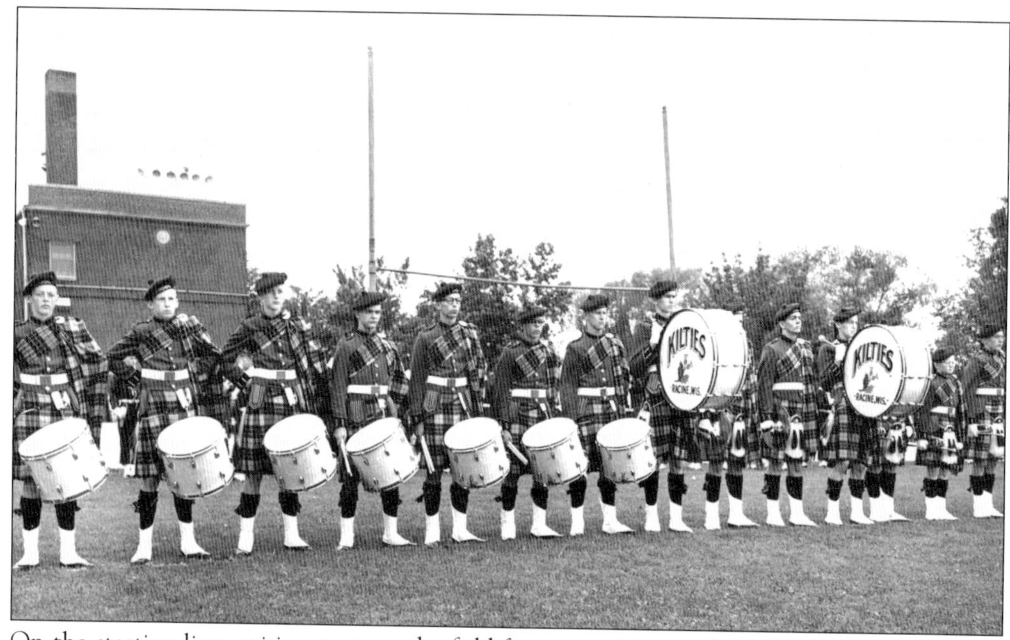

On the starting line waiting to enter the field for competition at the 1954 Spectacle of Music sponsored by the City of South Milwaukee are the Racine Kilties. "The Kilties will roar in 1954" was the corps motto as the group practiced throughout the winter and spring of 1954. And roar they did! The Kilties came out like a lion and won the first three contests of the season in 1954, firmly establishing themselves as the corps to beat in the Midwest. For the rest of the season in the Midwest, the Kilties took four more firsts, three seconds, a third, and a fourth. (Courtesy of RKAA.)

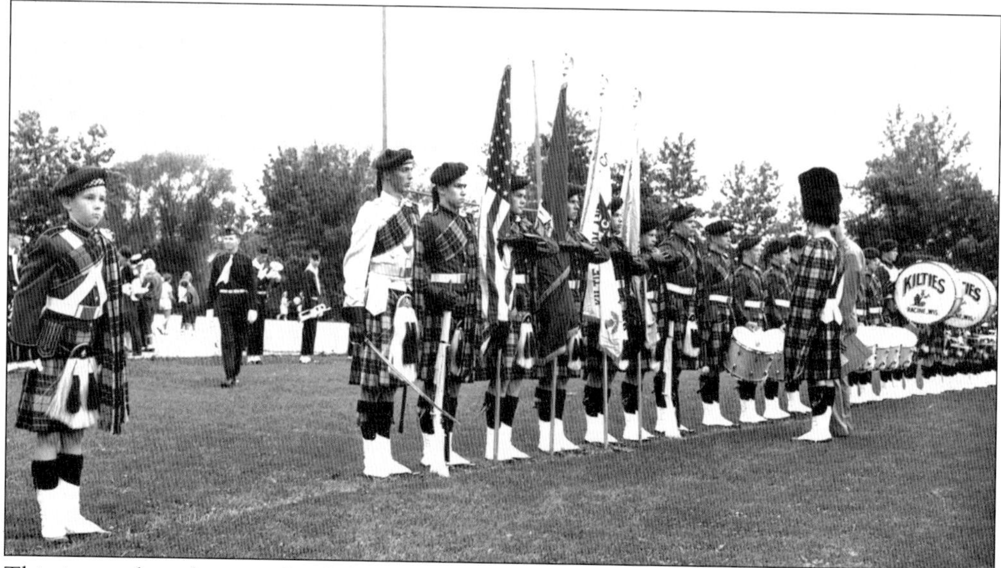

This is another photograph of the Kilties waiting on the starting line to enter the field for competition at the 1954 Spectacle of Music in South Milwaukee. Nationally the Kilties went out East in 1954 where the group finished in eighth place at the American Legion Drum and Bugle Corps National Championship in Washington, D.C., and then took fourth place at the National Dream contest at Roosevelt Field in Jersey City, New Jersey. (Courtesy of RKAA.)

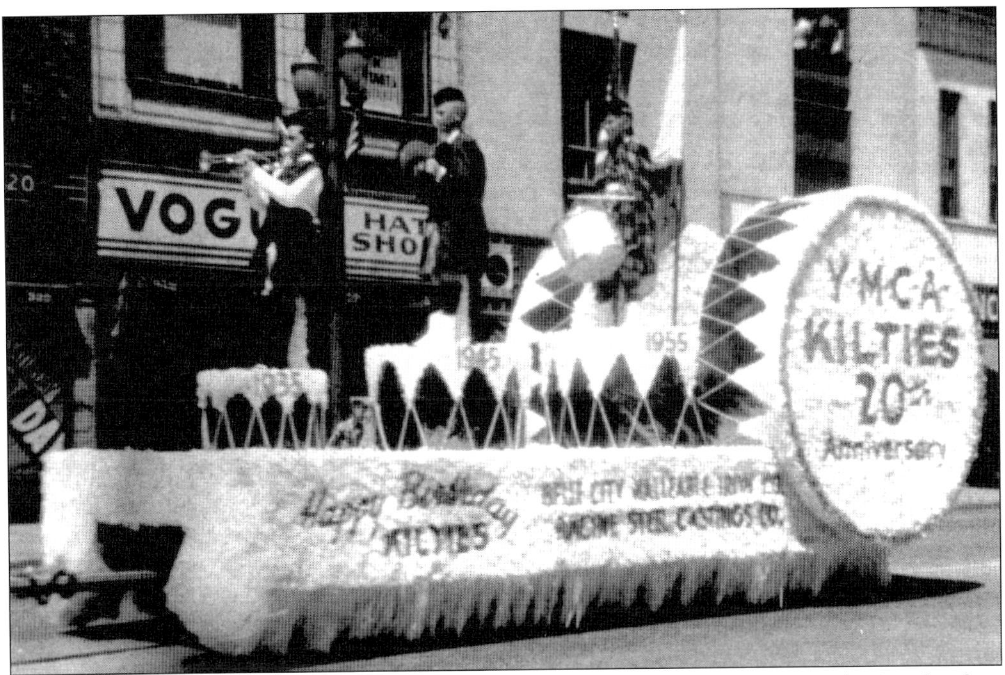

This is the Kilties' 20th anniversary float in Racine's 1955 Fourth of July parade. On the float are three boys: a bugler wearing a Kilties uniform from 1935, a cymbal player wearing a Kilties uniform from 1945, and a drummer wearing a Kilties uniform from 1955. (Courtesy of RKAA.)

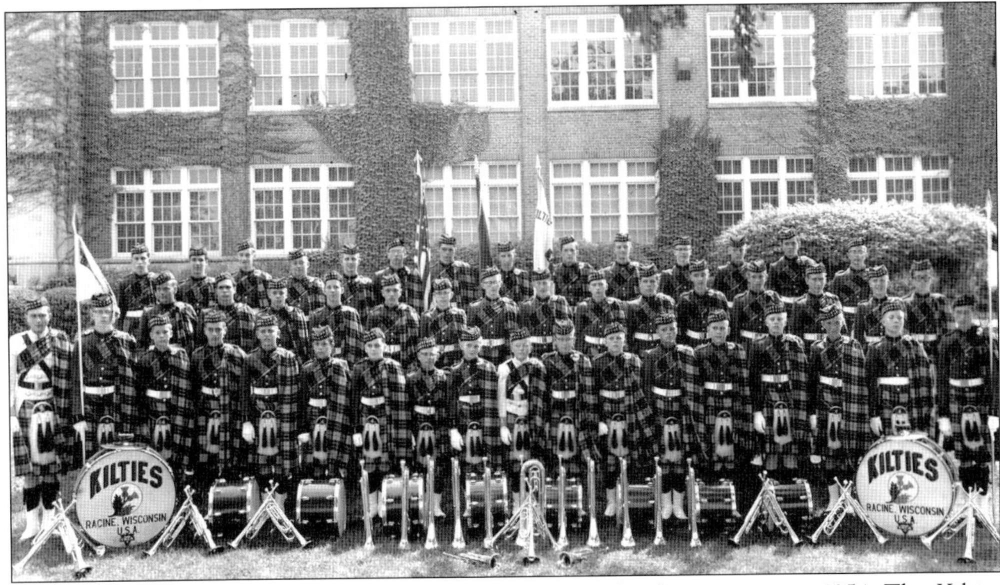

The Kilties reentered national competition in 1958 for the first time since 1954. The Kilties attended the VFW Drum and Bugle Corps National Championship in New York and placed 14th in preliminaries, not making the top 10 that advanced to the finals. The Kilties then competed at the American Legion Drum and Bugle Corps National Championship in Chicago and finished in 11th place. The 1958 Kilties members are seen above still wearing their yellow and black McLeod plaid kilts and tartans with their red jackets. The new Anderson plaid uniforms were introduced at the July 3rd Spectacular in Racine in 1958.

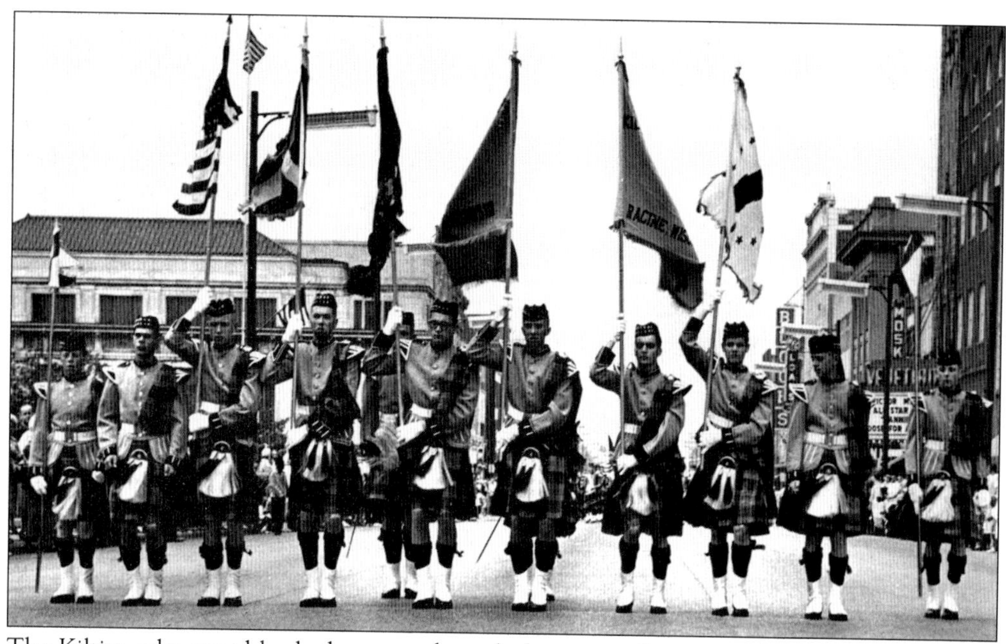

The Kilties color guard leads the corps through downtown Racine in the 1958 Fourth of July parade wearing its new Anderson plaid kilts and tartans with matching blue jackets. The Kilties color guard would only wear these Anderson plaid uniforms from July 3, 1958, through the 1961 season. In 1962, the color guard switched back to the old red jacket but still wore its Anderson plaid kilts and tartans. Then in 1963, the color guard switched back to the old yellow and black McLeod plaid with red jackets. (Courtesy of RHM.)

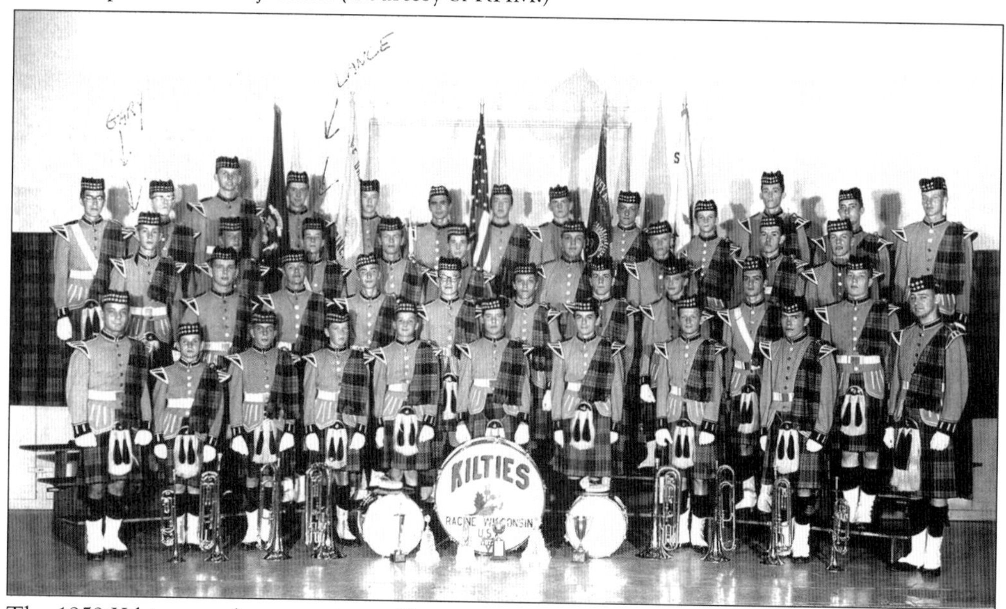

The 1959 Kilties members are pictured here wearing their new Anderson plaid kilts and tartans with matching blue jackets. During 1959, the Kilties placed second to the Madison Scouts at both the VFW and American Legion Drum and Bugle Corps State Championships. At the 1959 American Legion Drum and Bugle Corps National Championship in Minneapolis, the Kilties placed ninth. (Courtesy of RKAA.)

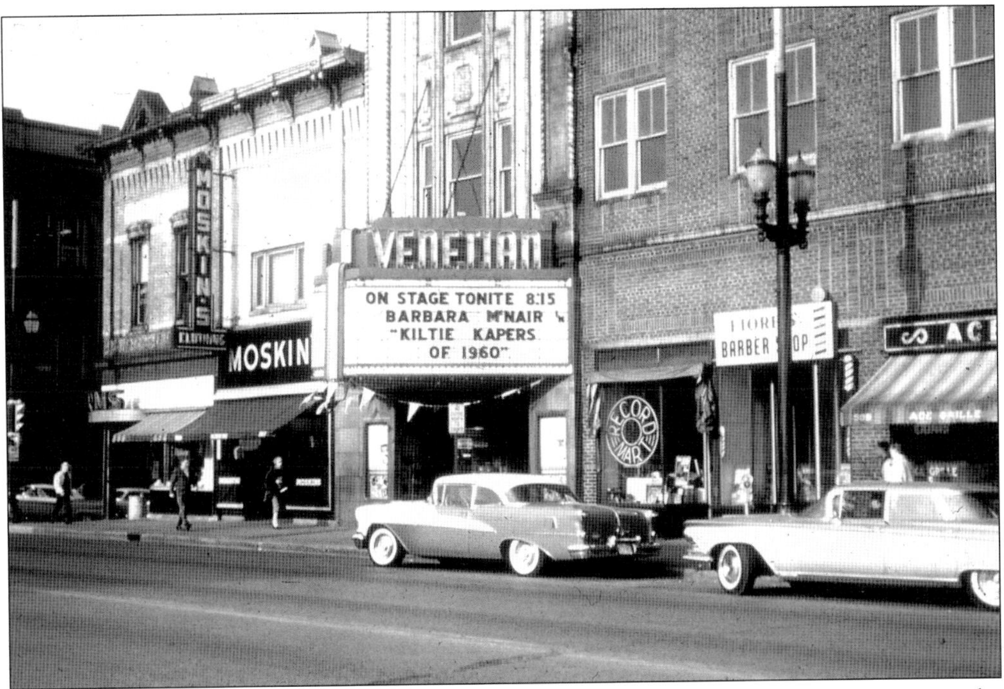

In the spring of 1950, the Kilties Parents Club undertook one of the greatest projects in the history of the corps. The first annual Kiltie Kapers, a 12-act variety show, was presented on April 20 at 8:00 p.m. at the Danish Brotherhood Hall in Racine. The Kiltie Kapers was very successful and, as a result, continued to be a major annual fund-raising event put on by the Kilties Parents Club for the next 20 years. The Kiltie Kapers would be held at various locations throughout the years. In 1960, it was held at the Venetian Theater.

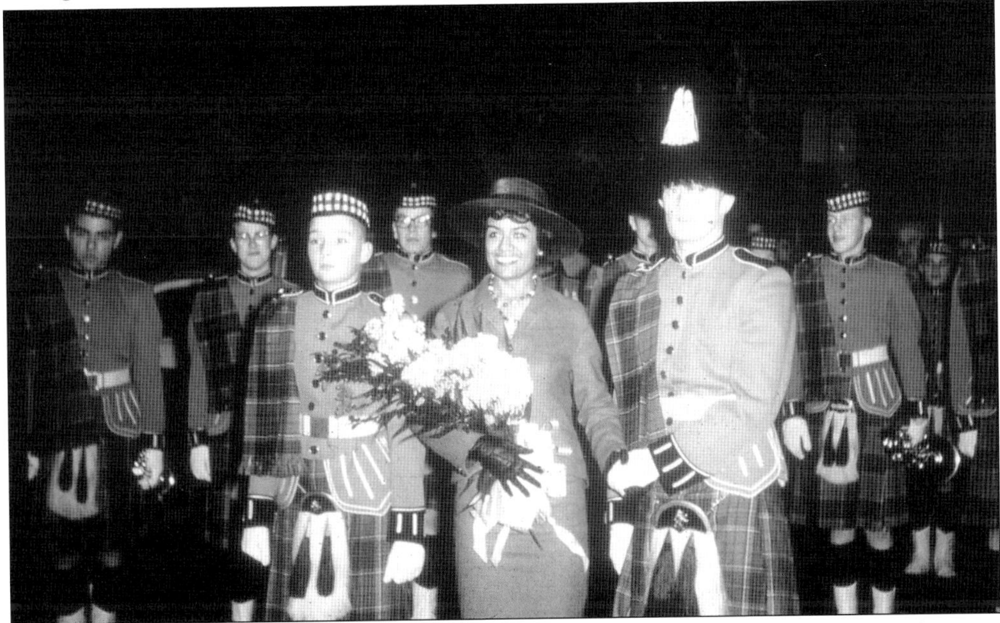

The Kiltie Kapers of 1960 starred the lovely singer Barbara McNair, a national recording star from Racine. Here the Kilties are seen greeting her at the train station in Racine.

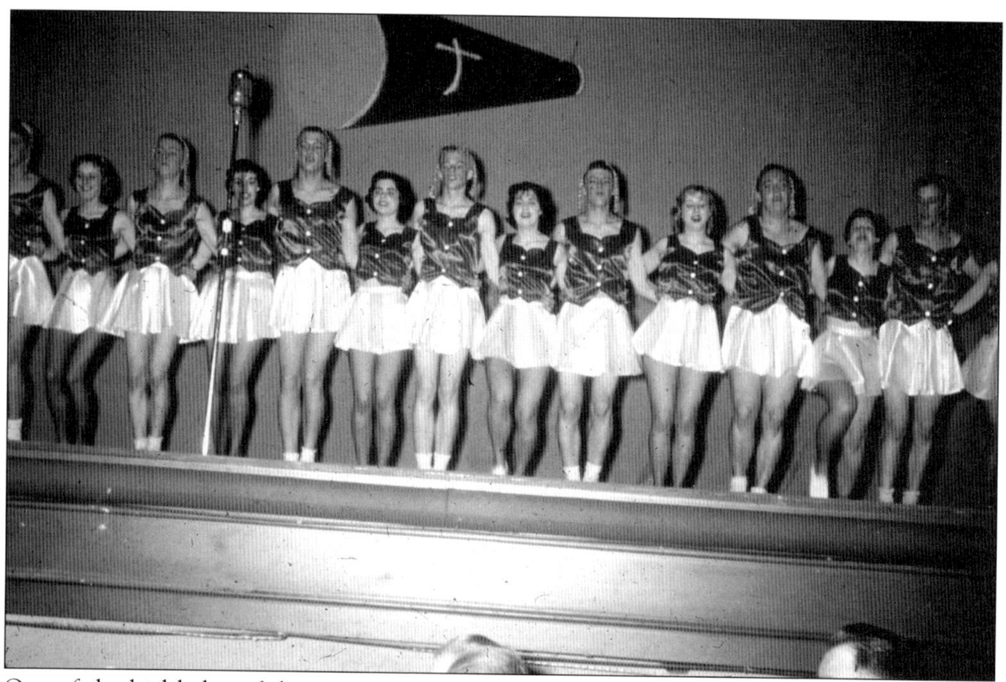

One of the highlights of the 1960 Kiltie Kapers happened when some members of the Kilties donned blond wigs, dressed up as female dancers, and performed a dance routine with similarly dressed young ladies as seen above. Every other person in this dance line is a male member of the Kilties.

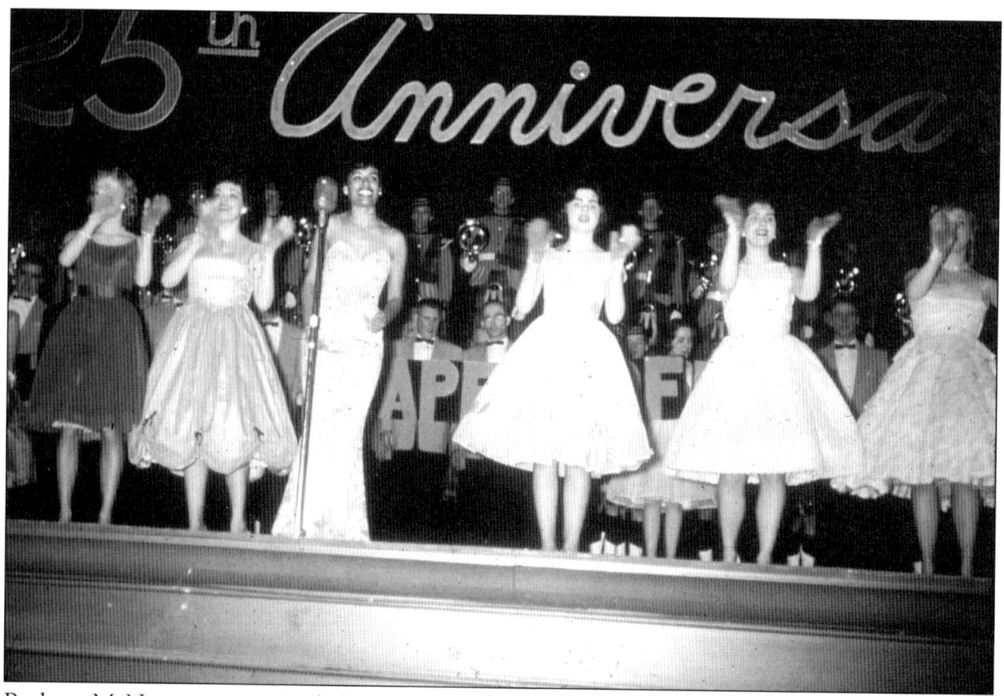

Barbara McNair, center stage behind the microphone, is having a great time entertaining the audience at the 1960 Kiltie Kapers.

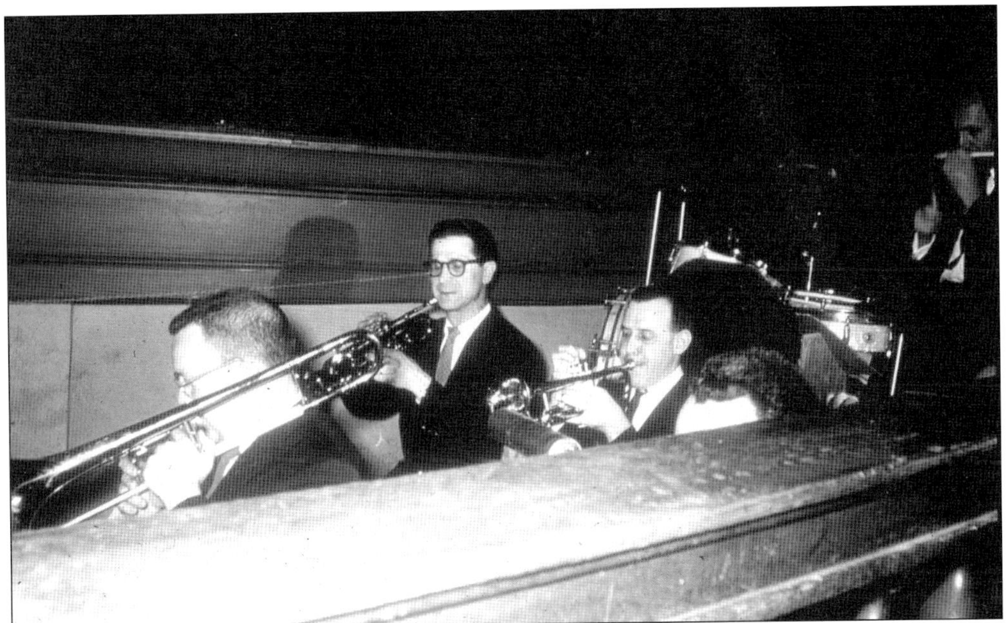

Emil Pavlik, trumpet player wearing black glasses, arranged the music for the Kiltie Kapers throughout the years. He is seen here playing trumpet with the Kiltie Kapers pit band during the performance of the 1960 Kiltie Kapers.

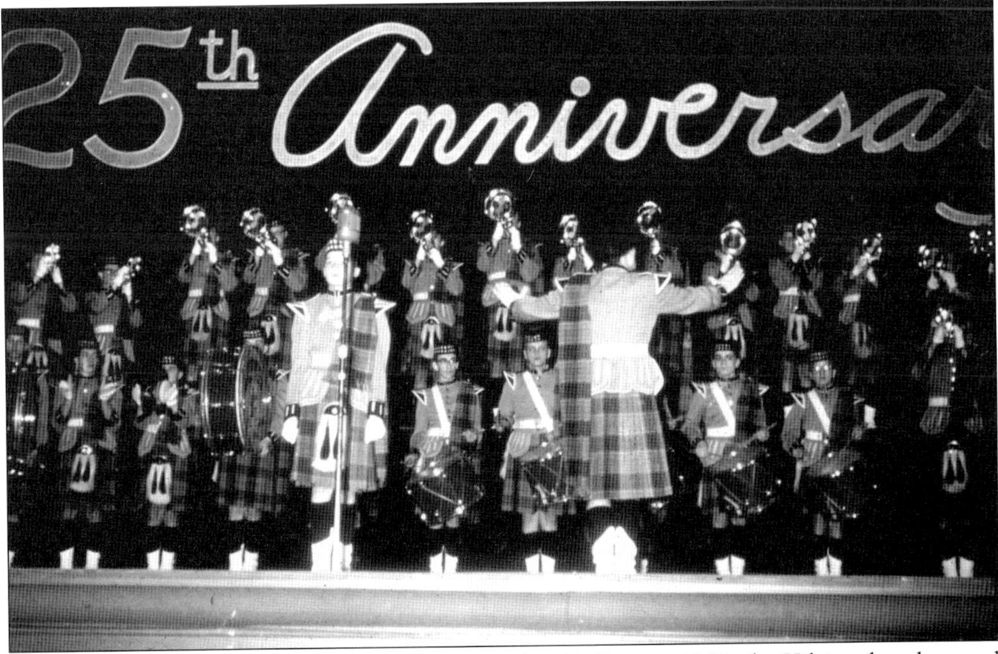

The Kilties are performing at the Kiltie Kapers of 1960. During 1960, the Kilties placed second at both the Wisconsin VFW Drum and Bugle Corps State Championship in Madison and at the Wisconsin American Legion Drum and Bugle Corps State Championship in Green Bay. The Kilties traveled to Detroit, Michigan, for the 1960 VFW Drum and Bugle Corps National Championship, where they placed 10th in preliminaries and 9th in finals. For 1960 and 1961, the whole corps wore Anderson plaid uniforms with the matching blue jackets exclusively.

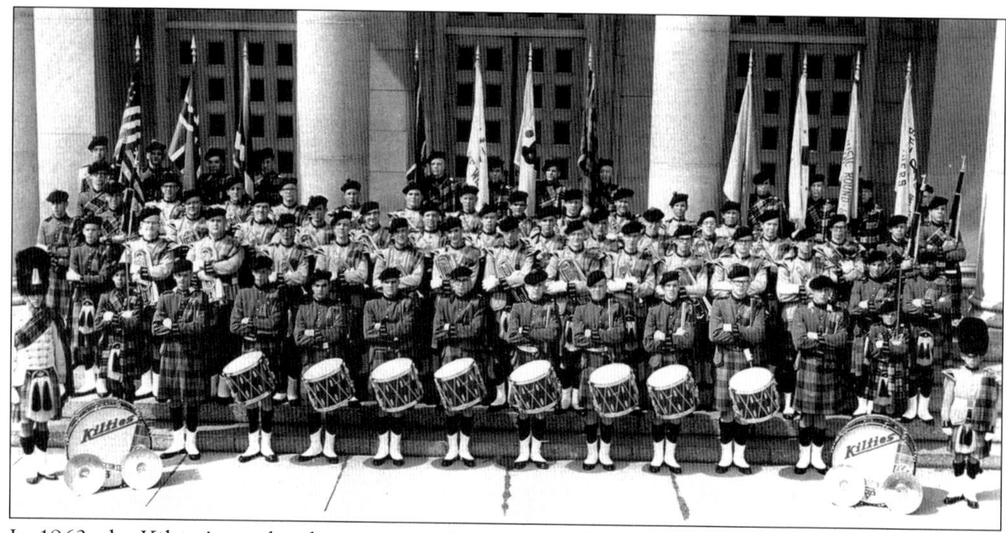

In 1963, the Kilties' membership continued to grow, making more uniforms necessary again. So the drum line switched to the old red jackets but still kept its Anderson plaid kilts and tartans. These uniform combinations, which remained the same through the 1973 season, created a very colorful appearance for the Kilties. The Kilties did not attend any national championships in 1963. They did, however, win the 1963 Wisconsin American Legion Drum and Bugle Corps State Championship. (Courtesy of RKAA.)

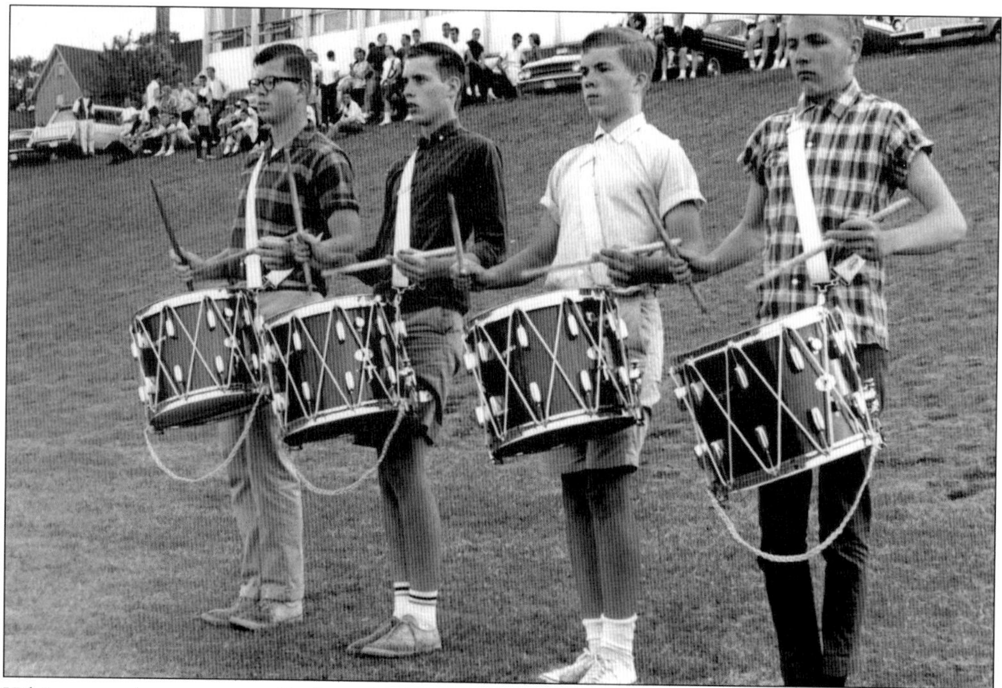

Kiltie snare drummers use Pershing Park behind the YMCA as a practice field sometime around July 1, 1963. The Kiltie snare drummers are, from left to right, Ronald Sorensen, John Pankow, Thomas Sorensen, and Charles Johnson. Tragically two of these Kilties were later killed in the line of duty. Johnson was killed in action in Vietnam. Pankow joined the Racine Fire Department and was killed while fighting a fire in 1980. (Courtesy of RKAA.)

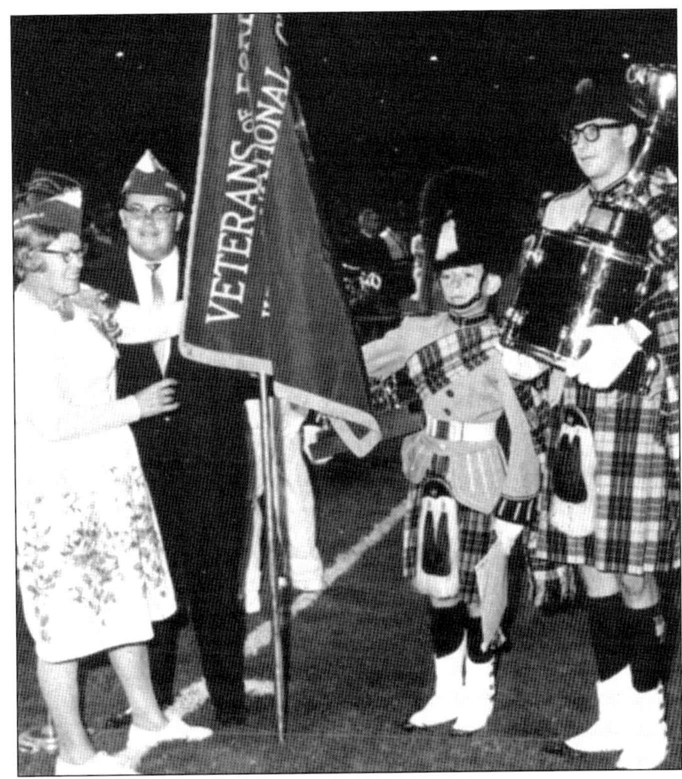

In competition with 44 other drum corps in preliminaries for the 1964 VFW Drum and Bugle Corps National Championship in Cleveland, Ohio, the Kilties solidly placed first, 1.4 points ahead of the second-place Chicago Royal Airs. Then at finals, in what *Drum Corps World* magazine stated was "a shocking display of personal determination," the Kilties convincingly won the championship. The second-place Royal Airs were one and a half points behind the Kilties in finals. In this photograph, Kilties drum major Scott Poulsen receives the national championship flag during finals at the 1964 VFW Drum and Bugle Corps National Championship. (Courtesy of RKAA.)

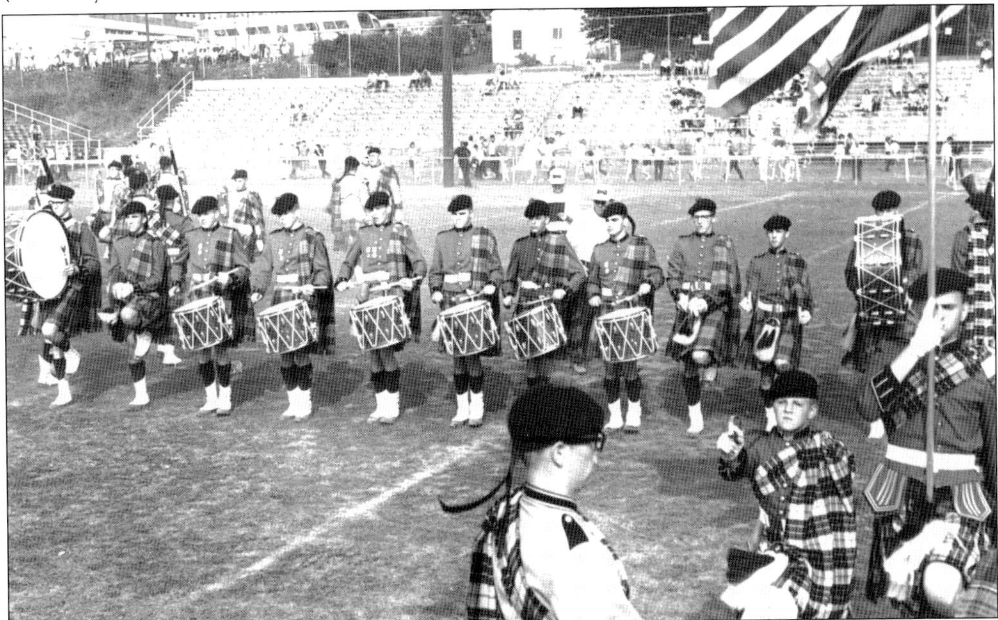

After winning VFW nationals in 1964, the Kilties continued out East, where they next competed in a contest at the 1964–1965 New York World's Fair on Saturday, August 29, 1964. In a very close scoring contest, the Kilties finished in fourth place. They lost out on winning first place because of a one-point flag penalty. This is, however, a photograph of the Kilties during preliminaries at the 1964 World Open. (Photograph by Moe Knox, courtesy of RKAA.)

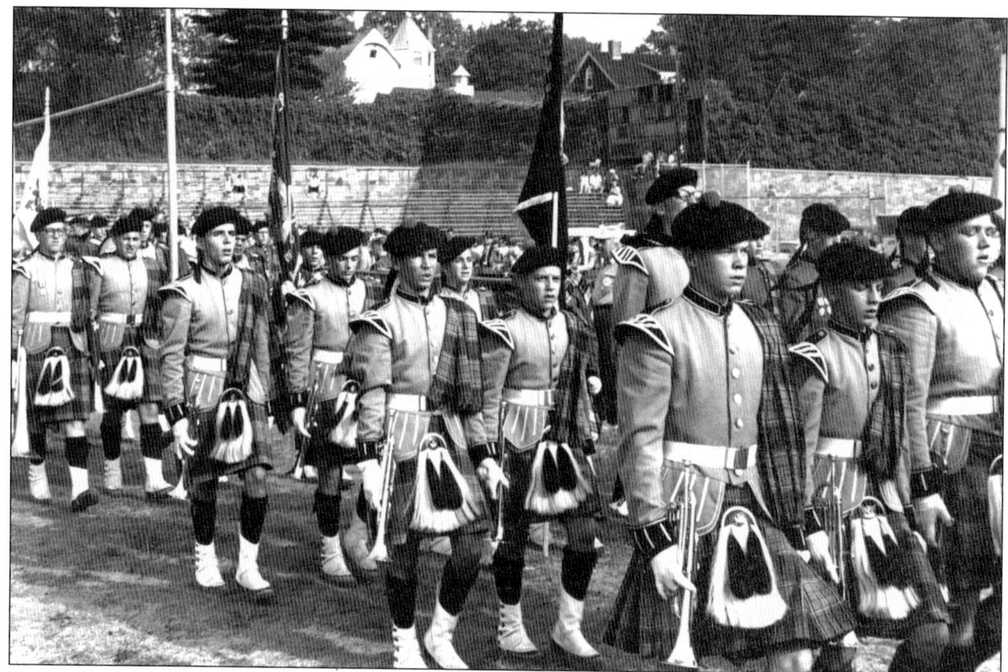

From the 1964–1965 New York World's Fair the Kilties then went to Bridgeport, Connecticut, to compete at the 1964 World Open. Sixty-three drum corps competed at preliminaries at the World Open with only the top 10 making finals. The Kilties placed seventh at finals. The Kilties are seen here on the field of competition during preliminaries at the 1964 World Open. (Photograph by Moe Knox, courtesy of RKAA.)

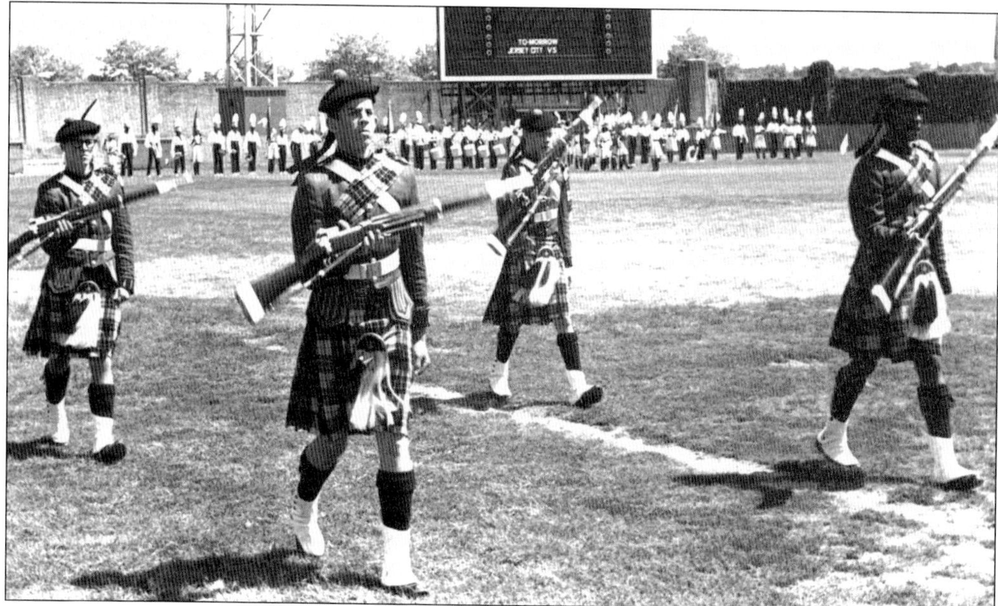

The Kilties rifles perform during preliminaries at the 1966 VFW Drum and Bugle Corps National Championship at Roosevelt Stadium in Jersey City, New Jersey. Just a few days earlier in the same stadium, the Kilties placed fifth at the National Dream contest. (Photograph by Moe Knox, courtesy of RKAA.)

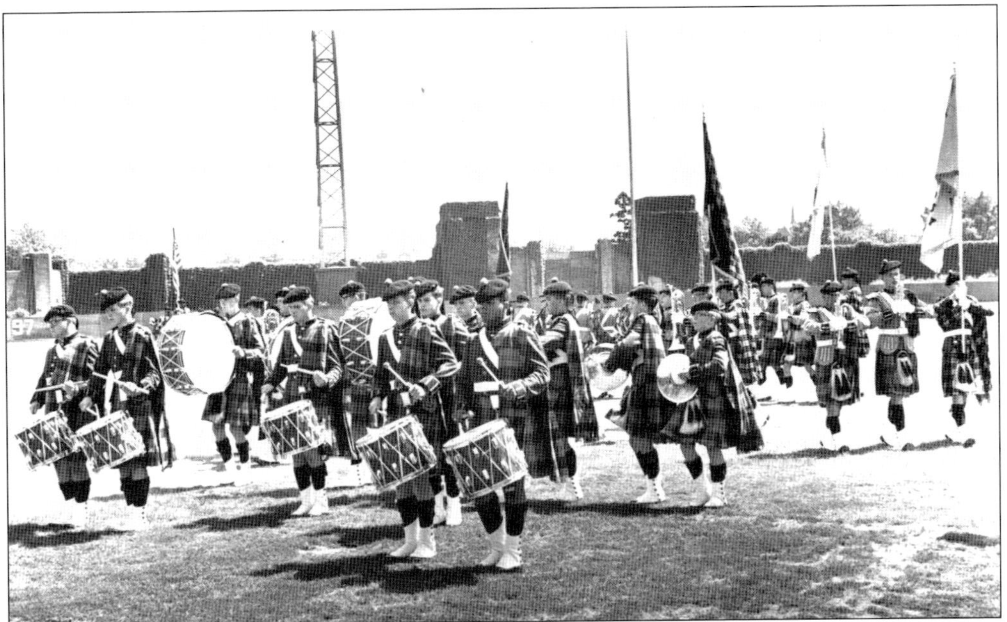

The 1966 VFW Drum and Bugle Corps National Championship in Jersey City featured two days of preliminary competition with 49 corps competing. The Kilties, seen here during their preliminary performance, took eighth place at preliminaries, which earned the group a spot in the 12-corps finals. (Photograph by Moe Knox, courtesy of RKAA.)

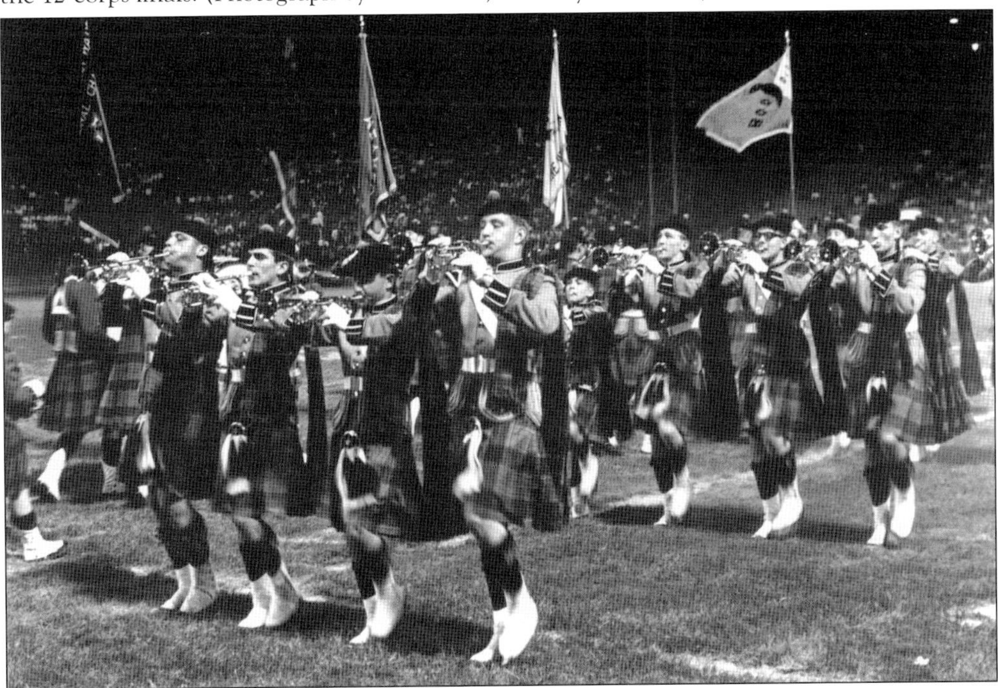

Playing themselves off the field at the conclusion of the grand finale at finals of the 1966 VFW Drum and Bugle Corps National Championship at Roosevelt Stadium in Jersey City are the members of the Racine Kilties. They finished in eighth place at finals too. (Photograph by Moe Knox, courtesy of RKAA.)

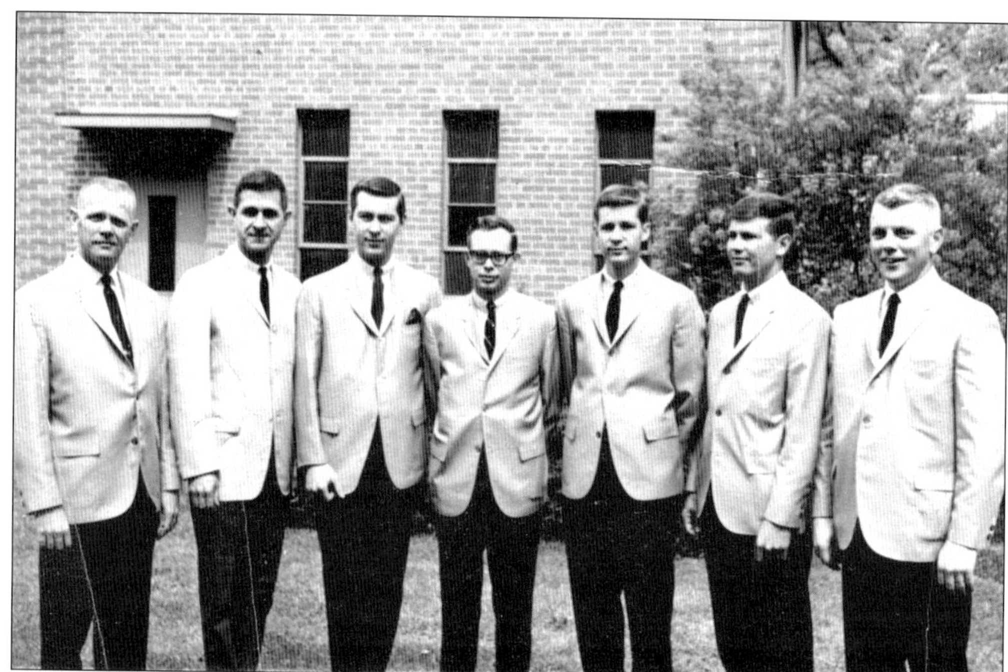

Pictured here are 7 of the 11 Kilties staff members during 1967. From left to right are Raymond Smith, director of marching; Emil Pavlik, music director; Gary King, associate music director; Daniel Ruud, assistant business manager; Lance King, assistant corps director; Thomas Wridt, corps director, and Harry Erickson, business manager. (Courtesy of RKAA.)

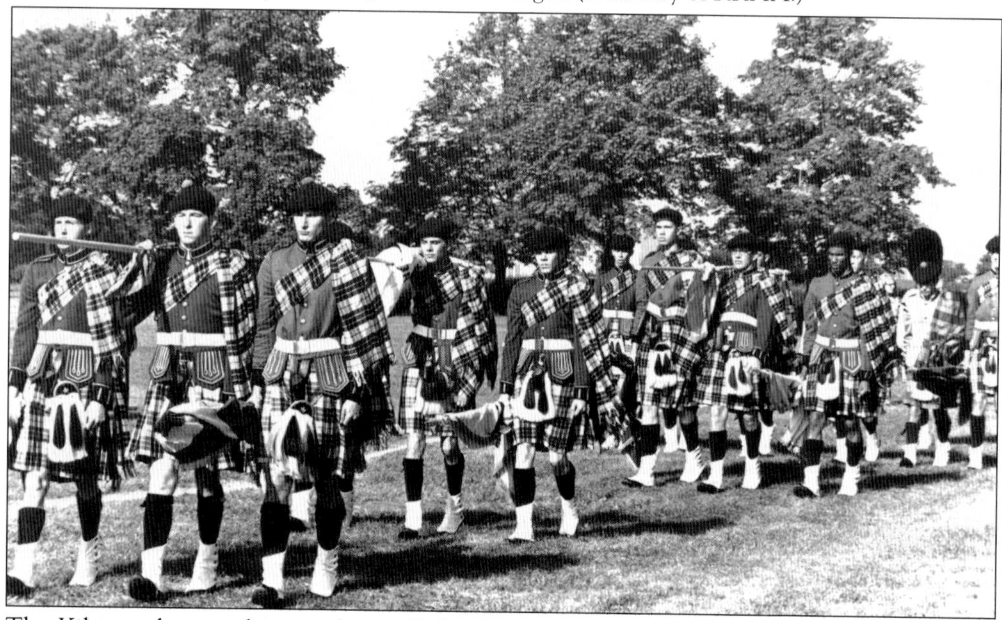

The Kilties color guard is marching off the field during preliminary competition at the 1968 VFW Drum and Bugle Corps National Championship. Forty-four corps competed in the preliminaries, which were held on Belle Island in Detroit. At preliminaries, the Kilties finished in a tie for fourth place with the Chicago Royal Airs. The Kilties won the coin flip and went on after the Royal Airs at finals. (Photograph by Moe Knox, courtesy of RKAA.)

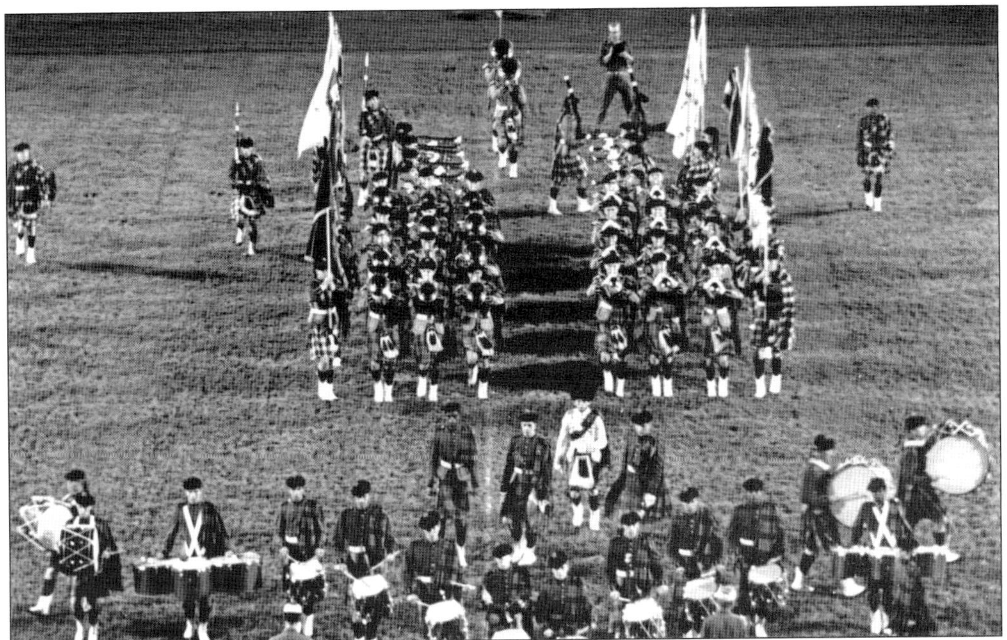
Members of the Kilties are setting up their famous train drill maneuver during finals at the 1968 VFW Drum and Bugle Corps National Championship at the University of Detroit stadium. The Kilties formed a train that moved toward the crowd while they played "Chattanooga Choo-Choo." (Photograph by Moe Knox, courtesy of RKAA.)

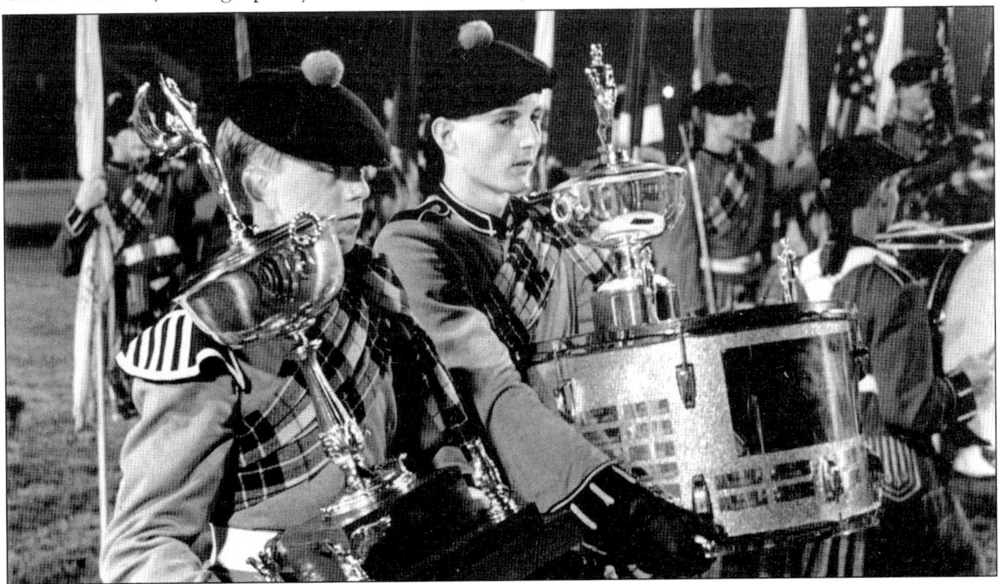
At the finals of the 1968 VFW Drum and Bugle Corps National Championship, the Kilties put on an electrifying performance that kept the crowd of 20,000 on its feet cheering the entire time the Kilties were on the field. The crowd roared with approval when the Kilties were announced as the new VFW national champions. While the Kilties played their encore concert after the finale, Gary Brack, left, holds the 1968 VFW Drum and Bugle Corps National Championship trophy, and Darrell Beth holds the trophy for the top drum score. (Photograph by Moe Knox, courtesy of RKAA.)

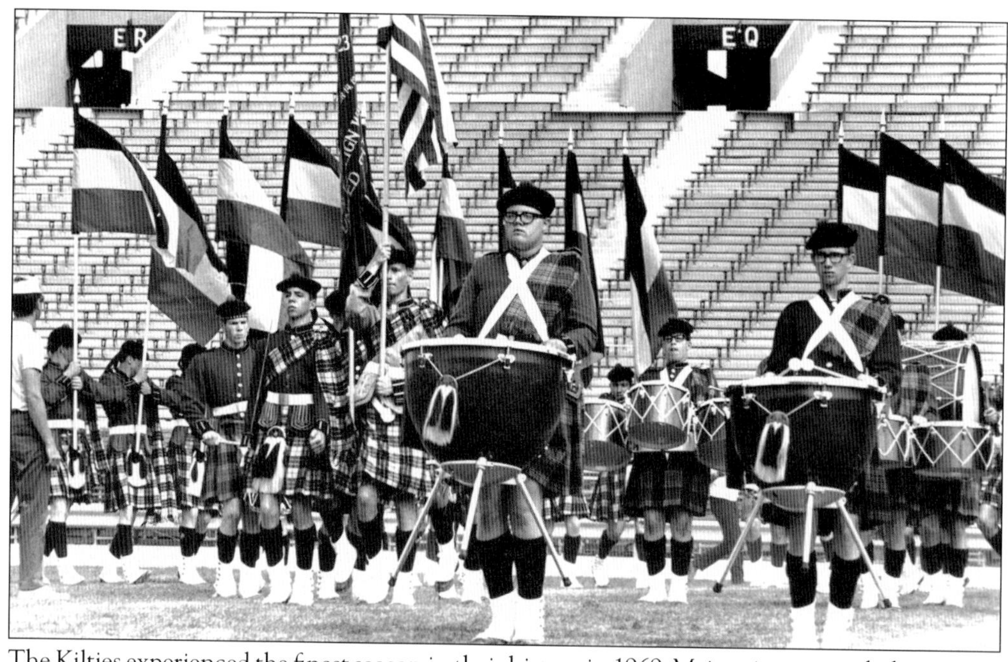

The Kilties experienced the finest season in their history in 1969. Major victories include winning the Wisconsin VFW Drum and Bugle Corps State Championship for the second year in a row, the 1969 Shriners International Championship in Toronto, the 1969 U.S. Open Championship in Marion, Ohio, and the Illinois Association Championship. Here members of the Kilties are performing during preliminaries at the 1969 VFW Drum and Bugle Corps National Championship in Philadelphia, Pennsylvania. (Photograph by Moe Knox, courtesy of RKAA.)

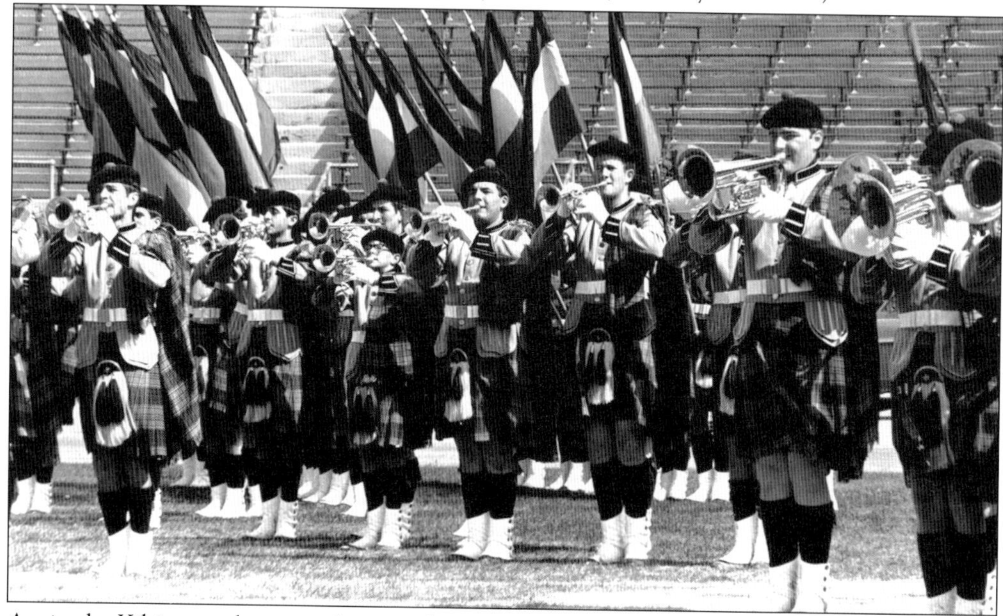

Again the Kilties are shown performing during preliminaries at the 1969 VFW Drum and Bugle Corps National Championship. This time the view is looking at the horn line stopped and playing the end of the Kilties flag presentation "Brotherhood of Man." (Photograph by Moe Knox, courtesy of RKAA.)

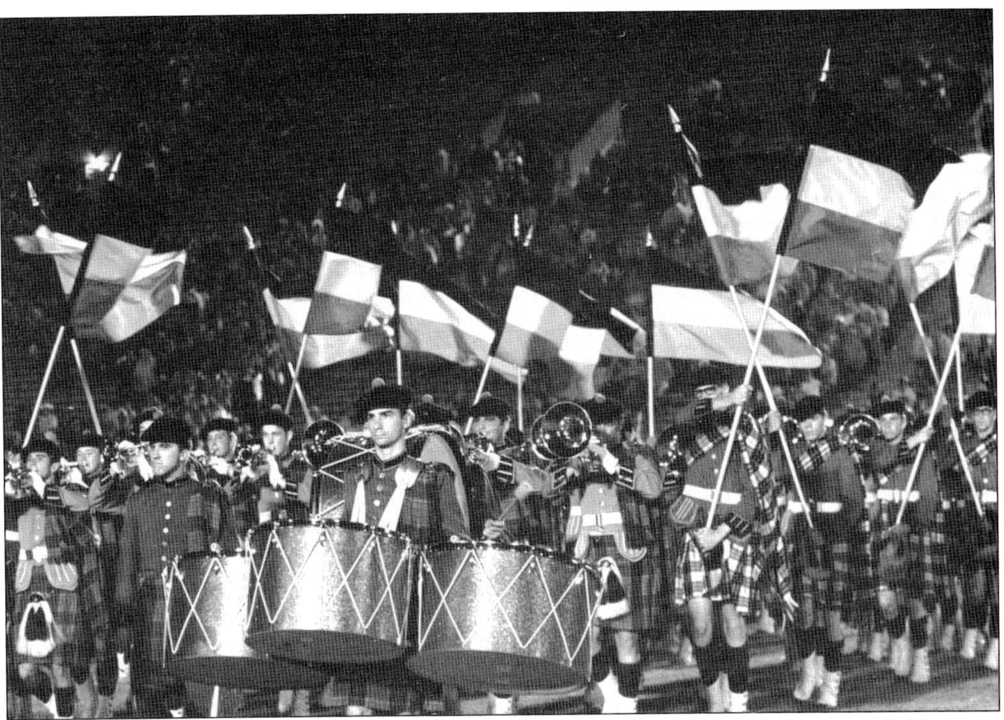

The Kilties are seen this time from ground level performing the group's famous train drill during "Chattanooga Choo-Choo" at the finals of the 1969 VFW Drum and Bugle Corps National Championship. (Photograph by Moe Knox, courtesy of RKAA.)

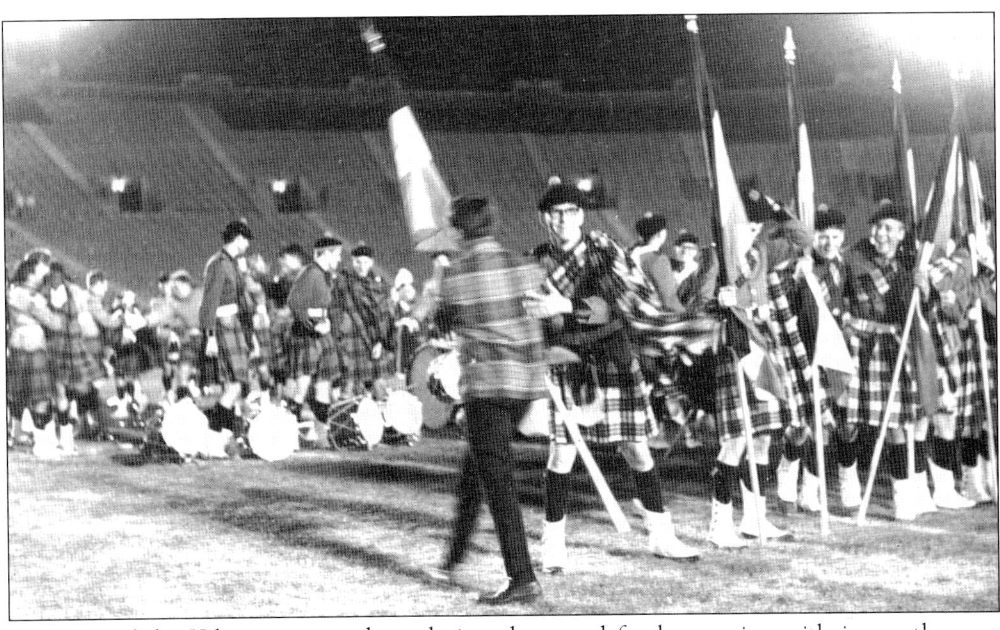

Members of the Kilties are seen here during the grand finale erupting with joy as they are announced as the 1969 VFW national champions. What an accomplishment! Sixty-three corps competed, which made it the best-attended VFW nationals ever. (Courtesy of RKAA.)

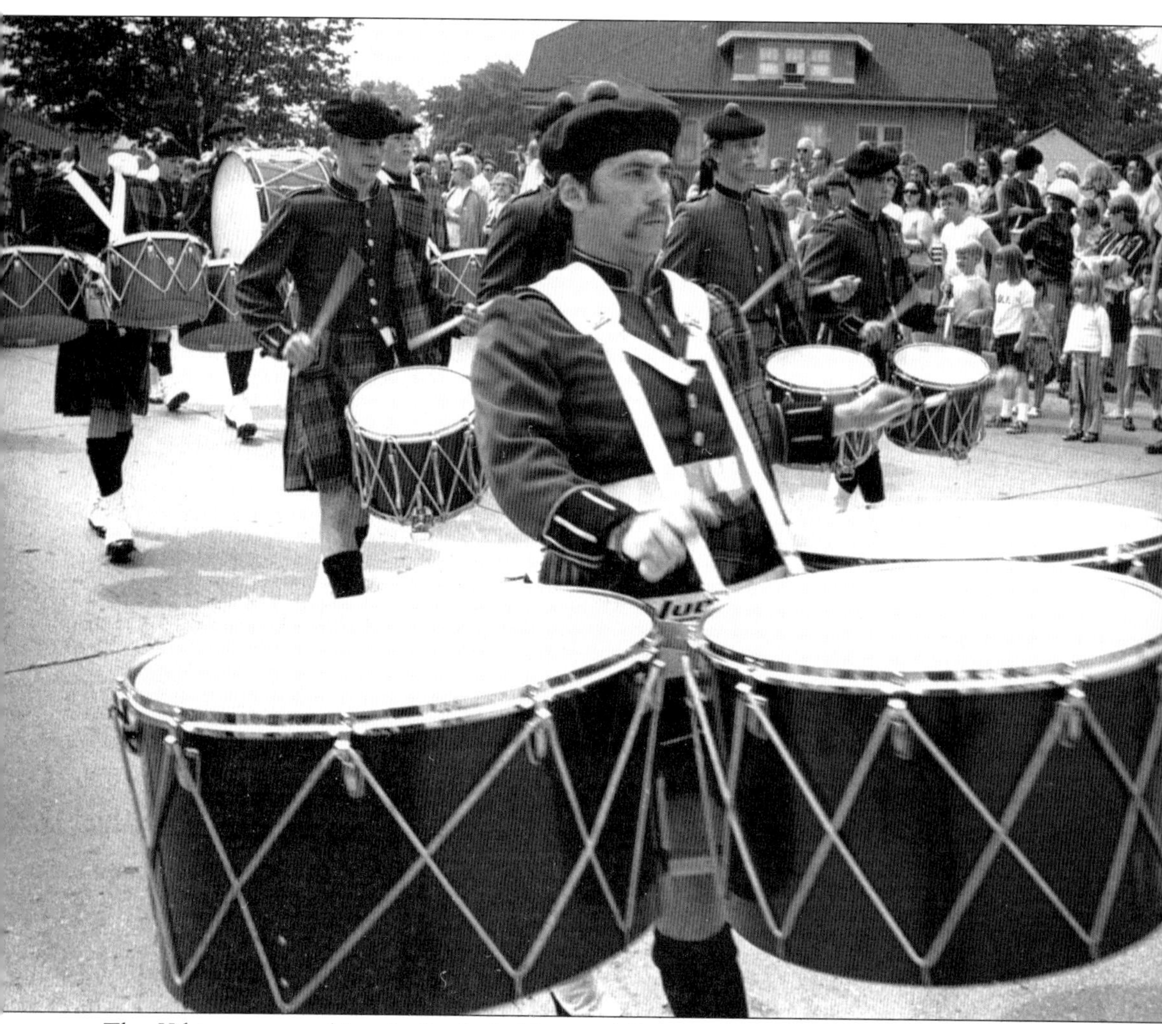

The Kilties are marching in Racine's Memorial Day parade of 1970. The Kilties produced another excellent drum corps in 1970. Right away in June the corps successfully defended two of its titles when it won the Shriners International Championship in Toronto again and its third consecutive Wisconsin VFW Drum and Bugle Corps State Championship in Green Bay. In August, the Kilties successfully defended their Illinois Association title for the second consecutive year in Bradley, Illinois. Unfortunately a broken drumstick kept the Kilties from repeating as champions at the U.S. Open in Marion, Ohio. The Kilties received a half-point penalty for the broken drumstick, which kept the group from tying the Madison Scouts for the 1970 U.S. Open Championship. At the 1970 VFW Drum and Bugle Corps National Championship in Miami, Florida, the Kilties also were not able to defend their title. There the group placed fifth in preliminaries and sixth in finals. (Courtesy of RKAA.)

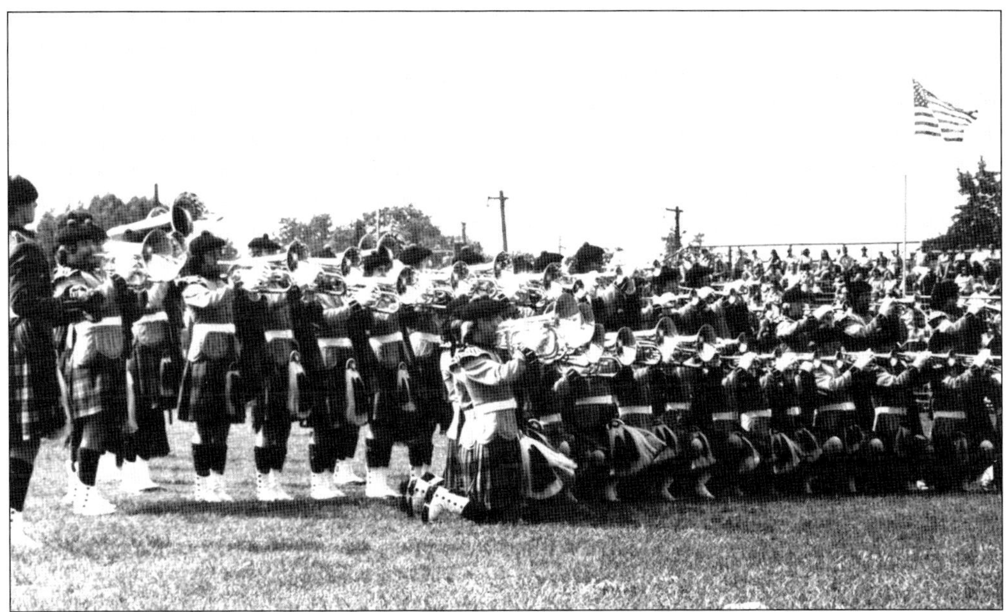

This is the 1972 or 1973 Kilties Drum and Bugle Corps. Both years were very successful for the group. During the summer of 1972, the Kilties won 11 contests, including South Milwaukee's Spectacle of Music, the World Open Championship in Boston, and the Danny Thomas Invitational, also in Boston. During 1973, the Kilties won five contests, including South Milwaukee's Spectacle of Music for the second consecutive year and the Illinois Association Championship for the fourth time in five years. The Kilties finished in eighth place in finals at the Drum Corps International (DCI) Championship in 1972 and took fifth place in finals in 1973. Both were held in Whitewater. (Courtesy of RHM.)

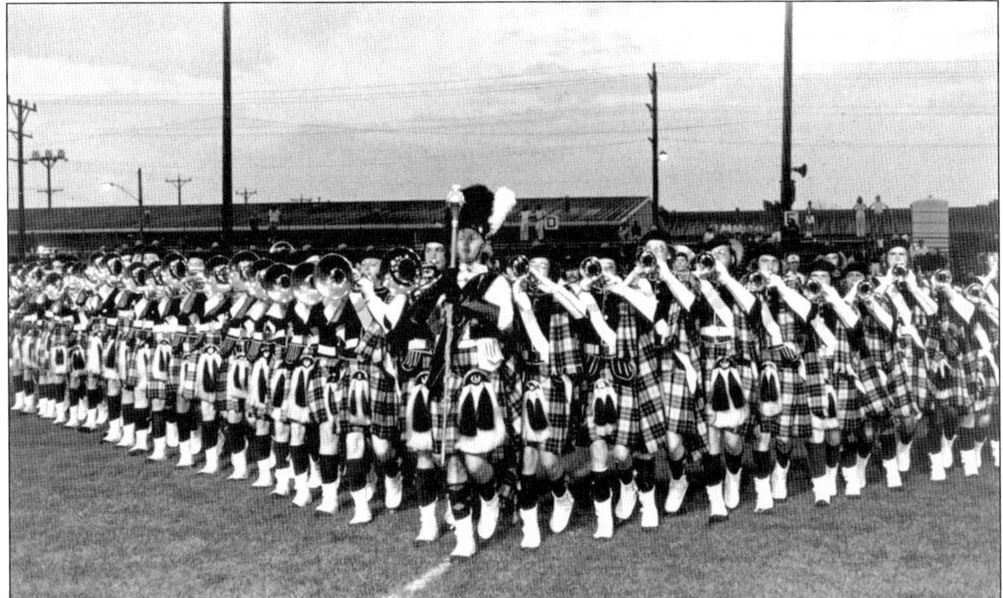

Led by Kilties drum major Kenneth Morrell, the Kilties perform one of the group's classic drill maneuvers called "the wedge" at Racine's Horlick Field in 1974. At the 1974 DCI Championship in Ithaca, New York, the Kilties placed sixth in finals. (Courtesy of RHM.)

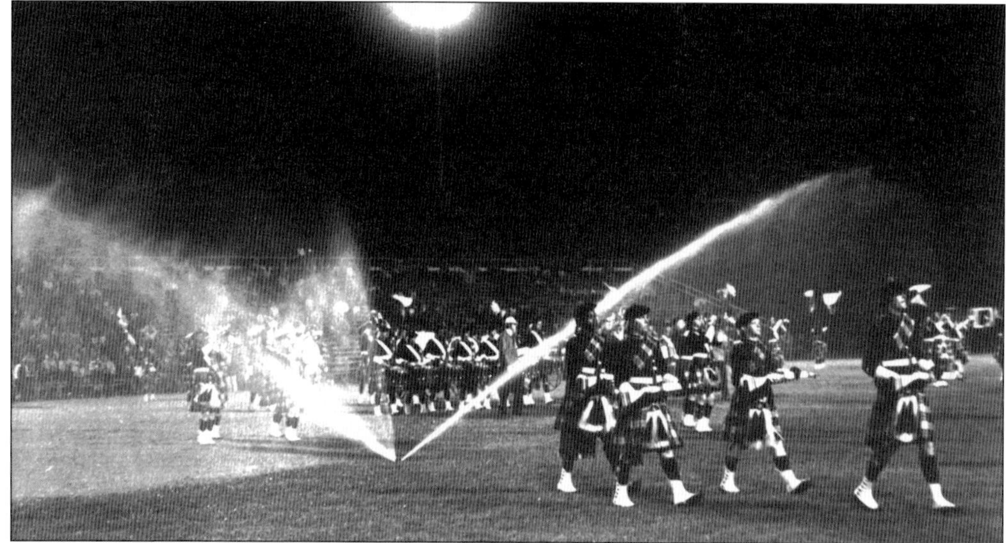

The Kilties were a very competitive and highly entertaining drum corps in 1974. The whole corps was now in new yellow and black McLeod plaid kilts and tartans with black jackets. During 1974, the Kilties won the Wisconsin American Legion Drum and Bugle Corps State Championship and finished second at the World Open in Lowell, Massachusetts. Midway through the Kilties' performance at finals in the 1974 World Open, a malfunction occurred, sending jets of water all over the field and drenching the Kilties as seen above. (Photograph by Moe Knox, courtesy of RKAA.)

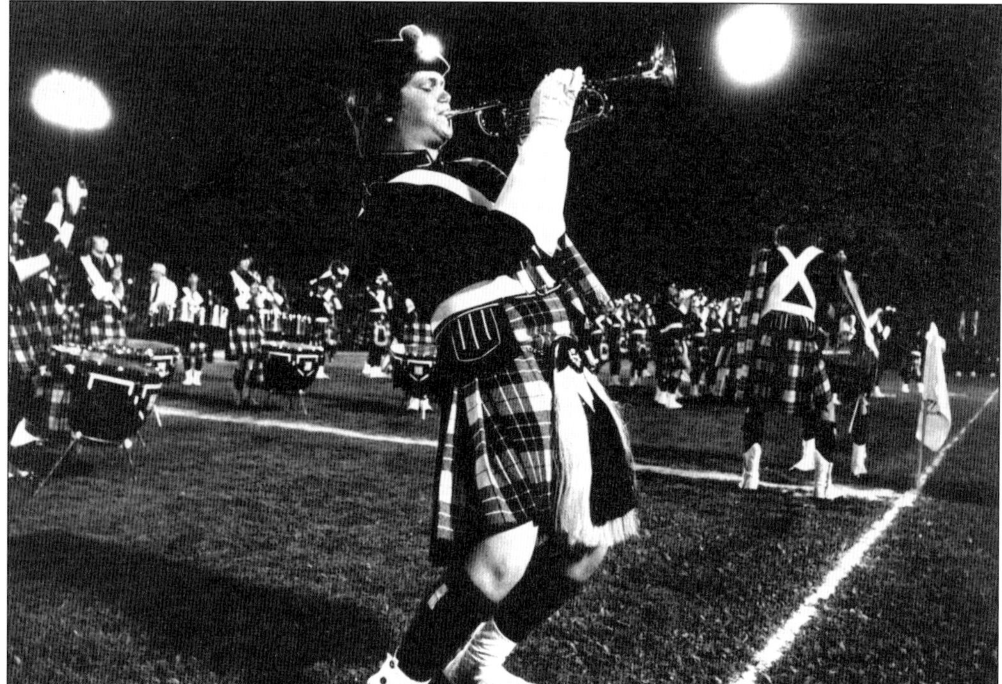

Kilties soloist Thomas Meredith is wailing away on his soprano bugle during the mid-1970s. After 1974, the Kilties would be a DCI finalist three more times: 7th place in 1975 in Philadelphia, 10th place in 1977 in Denver, and 12th place in 1978, also in Denver. (Courtesy of RHM.)

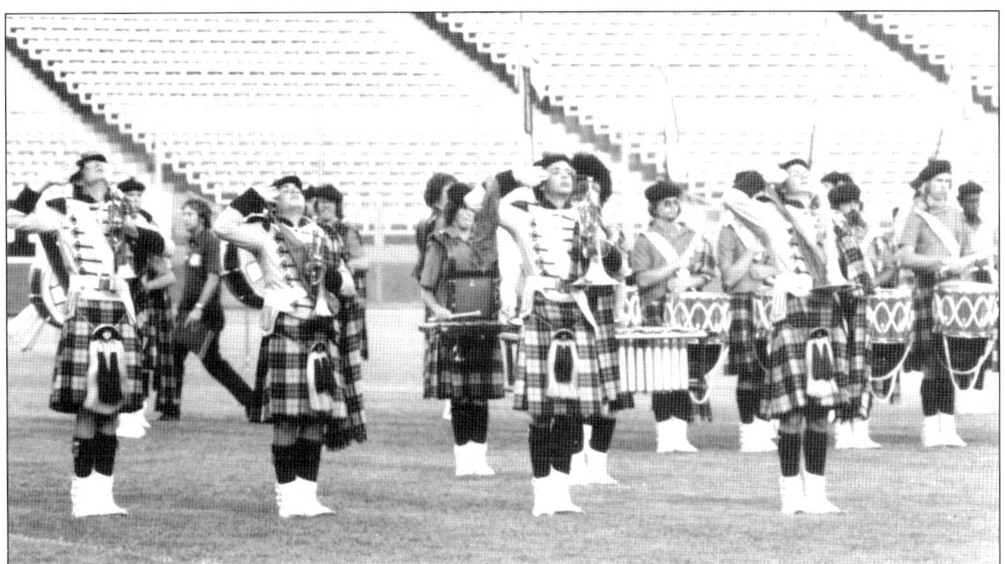

The 1978 Kilties retained the familiar yellow and black McLeod plaid kilts and tartans but changed from black to yellow jackets. In the spring of 1978, the Kilties opened up membership to allow females to join. The last contest the Kilties won was at Indianapolis in 1979. The Kilties took the year off in 1980. The group reorganized and fielded corps again in 1981 and 1982. After that, financial difficulties silenced the Kilties for good. (Courtesy of RHM.)

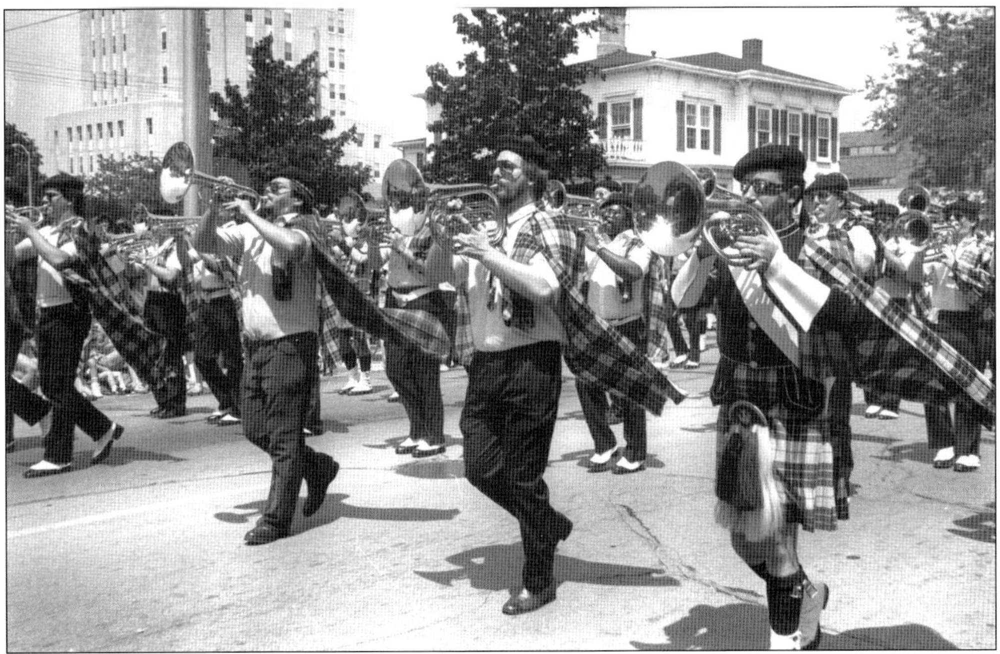

The Kilties alumni drum and bugle corps is pictured here marching in Racine's 1986 Fourth of July parade. It celebrated the 50th anniversary of the Kilties' first public appearance in Racine's 1936 Fourth of July parade. The corps also made a special appearance the night before at the Boys of 76's July 3rd Spectacular. In 1992, Joseph Fazzari organized another Kilties alumni corps. This time the purpose was to play a standstill concert at DCI finals in Madison as part of DCI's 20th anniversary celebration. (Courtesy of RKAA.)

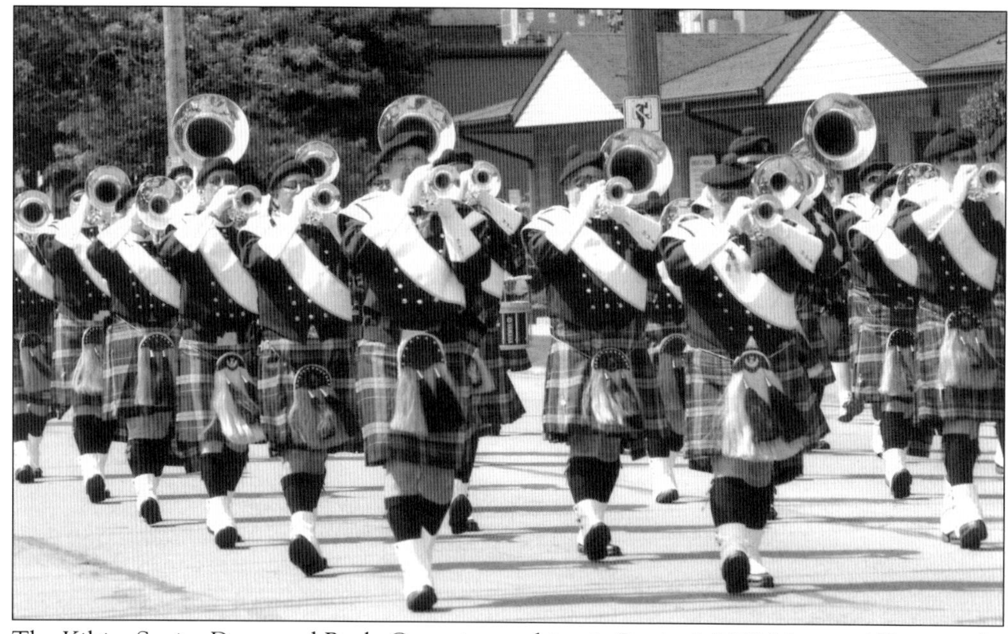

The Kilties Senior Drum and Bugle Corps is marching in Racine's 2007 Memorial Day parade. Organized by Kilties alumni in the fall of 1992 as a result of the enthusiasm generated by the successful appearance of the Kilties alumni corps at DCI finals in Madison in 1992, the Kilties Senior Drum and Bugle Corps of today continues to be a crowd-pleasing, successfully competing drum and bugle corps. In 1997, the Kilties became the official musical organization for the Clan Buchanan Society.

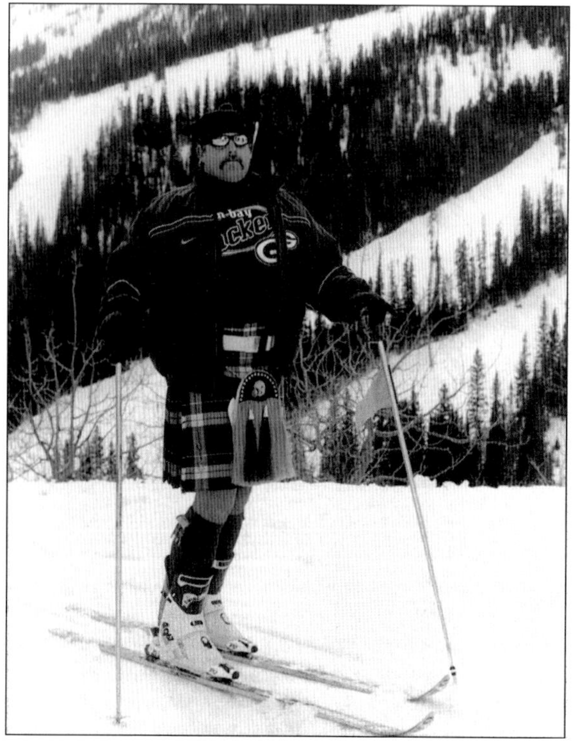

Raymond "Moon Eyes" Johnson is skiing in what he calls his Green Bay Packer Kiltie outfit. He has skied over the years in his Packer Kiltie attire in Colorado, Utah, California, and Canada. He is seen here skiing at Aspen, Colorado. No one has been a member of the Kilties longer than he has. He has been a member of the various Kilties organizations for 30 years: the Kiltie Kadets from 1966 through 1969, the Kilties from 1970 through 1977, both the 1986 and 1992 Kilties alumni corps, and the senior Kilties from 1992 to the present. (Courtesy of RKAA.)

Five

Kiltie Kadets

JOHN SPARKMAN, ALA., CHAIRMAN

WILLIAM PROXMIRE, WIS. JOHN TOWER, TEX.
HARRISON A. WILLIAMS, JR., N.J. WALLACE F. BENNETT, UTAH
THOMAS J. MC INTYRE, N.H. EDWARD W. BROOKE, MASS.
ALAN CRANSTON, CALIF. BOB PACKWOOD, OREG.
ADLAI E. STEVENSON III, ILL. BILL BROCK, TENN.
J. BENNETT JOHNSTON, JR., LA. ROBERT TAFT, JR., OHIO
WILLIAM D. HATHAWAY, MAINE LOWELL P. WEICKER, JR., CONN.
JOSEPH R. BIDEN, JR., DEL.

DUDLEY L. O'NEAL, JR.
STAFF DIRECTOR AND GENERAL COUNSEL

United States Senate
COMMITTEE ON BANKING, HOUSING AND URBAN AFFAIRS
WASHINGTON, D.C. 20510

August 27, 1973

Racine Kiltie Kadets
Post Office Box 361
Racine, Wisconsin 53401

I am sure that the Kilties and the Kiltie Kadets have been of immeasurable value to Racine and to Wisconsin. They have always represented the city and state with honor and have demonstrated the vitality and versatility of the people -- young and not-so-young -- of Racine. The public relations value alone is great.

Keep up the good work. It is fine for the young people who participate, giving them the opportunity to excel. And it gives the people of Racine and of Wisconsin the opportunity for justifiable pride.

With warmest wishes for continued success, I am

Sincerely,

William Proxmire, U.S.S.

WP:ced

This is a letter dated August 27, 1973, from Sen. William Proxmire to the Racine Kiltie Kadets acknowledging their value as a youth organization. (Courtesy of RKAA.)

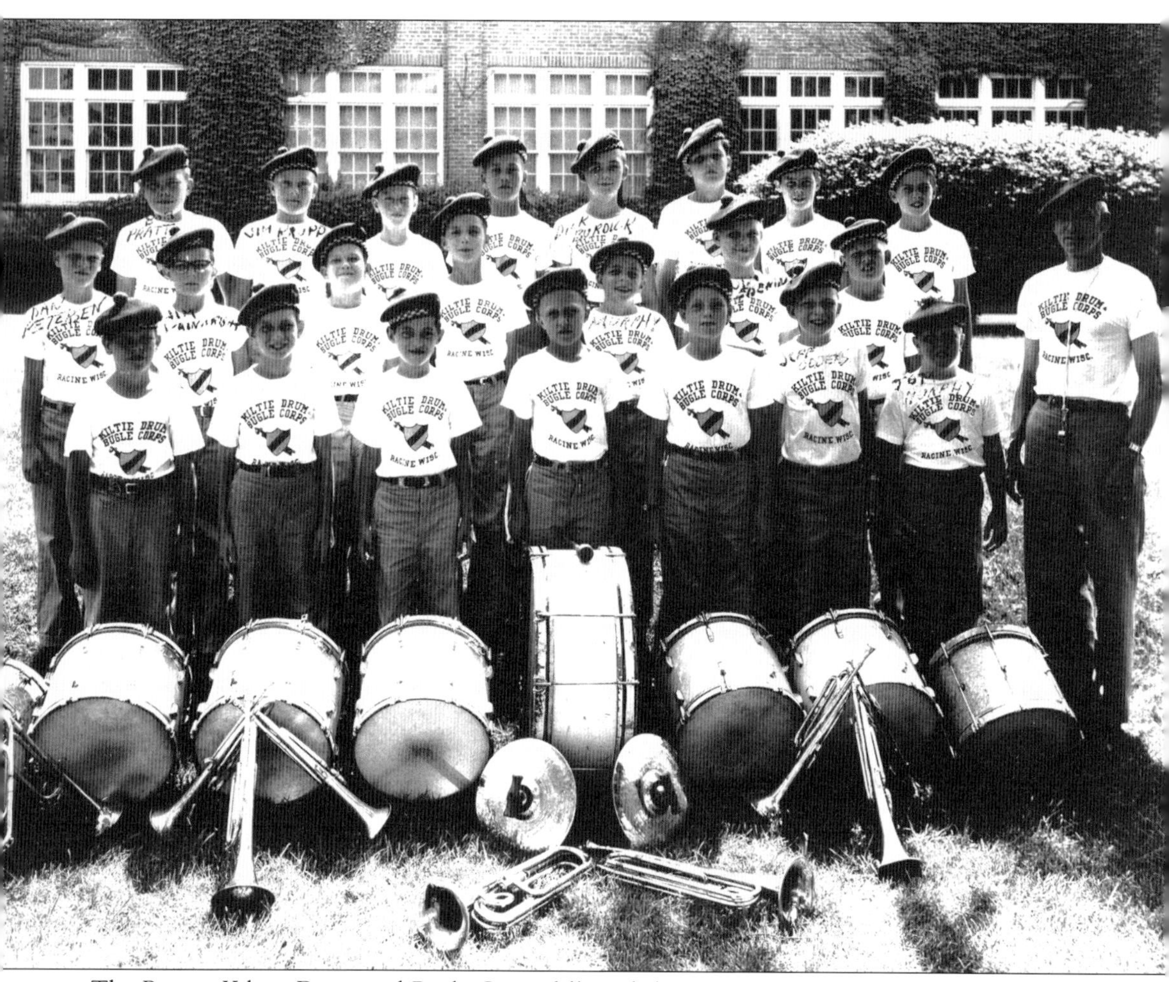

The Racine Kilties Drum and Bugle Corps followed the growing trend among Midwest junior corps in the 1950s by starting a rookie, or a training, drum and bugle corps. The members consisted of rookies and others who needed more training before they could become regulars in the Racine Kilties Drum and Bugle Corps. The photograph above shows the 1957 Racine Kilties Rookie Drum and Bugle Corps with drillmaster Russell Gladys standing on the far right. During 1957, the group rehearsed once a week and appeared in a few local parades. In the fall of 1958, the Kilties Rookie Drum and Bugle Corps was reorganized into the Racine Kiltie Kadets Drum and Bugle Corps. The Kiltie Kadets' purpose was to provide a training ground for boys aged 10–13 who were interested in becoming a Kiltie. The Kiltie Kadets made their first marching appearance in Racine's 1959 Memorial Day parade. The group grew rapidly, and by 1962, it was a very competitive Class C drum and bugle corps. The 1963 season saw the Kiltie Kadets place first 12 times, including winning the Wisconsin VFW Drum and Bugle Corps State Championship in Class B. (Courtesy of RKAA.)

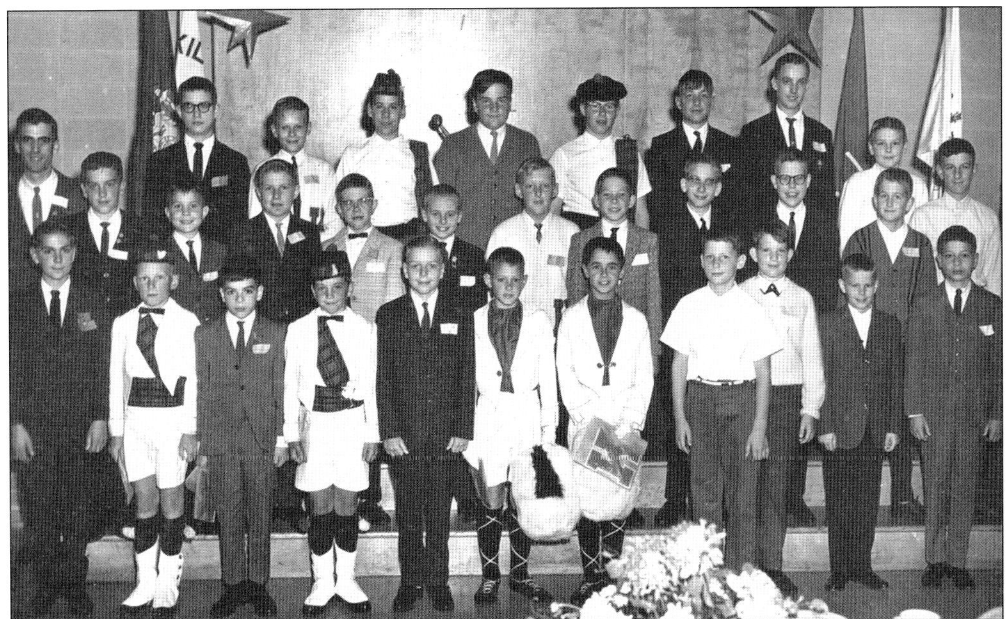

At the end of the competition season, usually in September, the Kiltie Kadets would have a banquet. The banquet seen here is the 1965 banquet. At these banquets, awards were given out, including the presentation of a red letter *K* to each deserving rookie in thanks for their first year of service to the corps. Members of the Kiltie Kadets would sew their letters onto a white cardigan sweater. Each year thereafter members of the Kiltie Kadets earned a gold pin for attachment to their letter. A red letter *K* can be seen in this photograph being held in the front row by James Chambasian. (Courtesy of RKAA.)

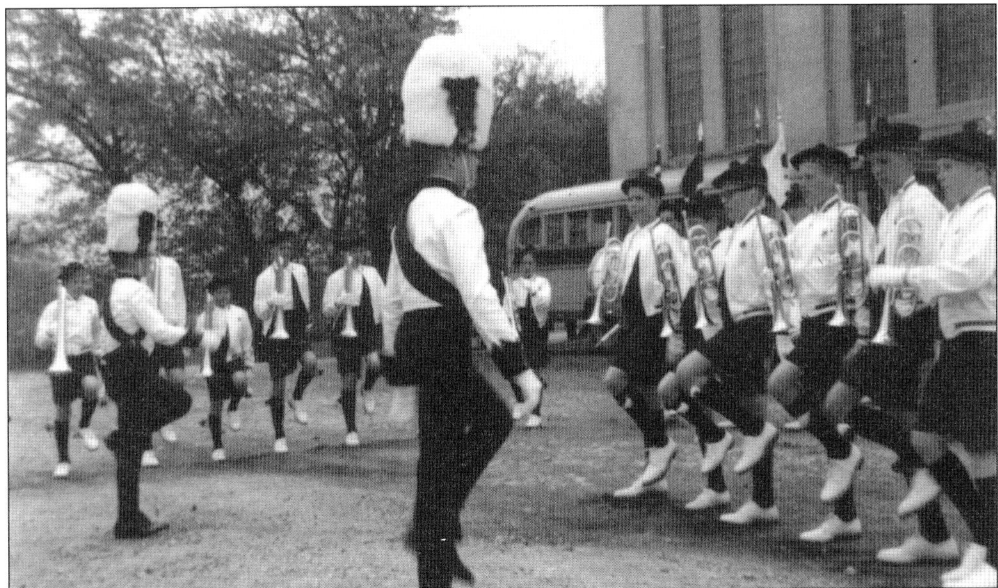

The Kiltie Kadets are seen here on a cool day in 1965 wearing jackets while warming up before a parade in Stoughton. Probably the best showing for the Kiltie Kadets during 1965 was their third-place finish in Class B competition at the Wisconsin VFW Drum and Bugle Corps State Championship on Saturday, June 26, in Appleton.

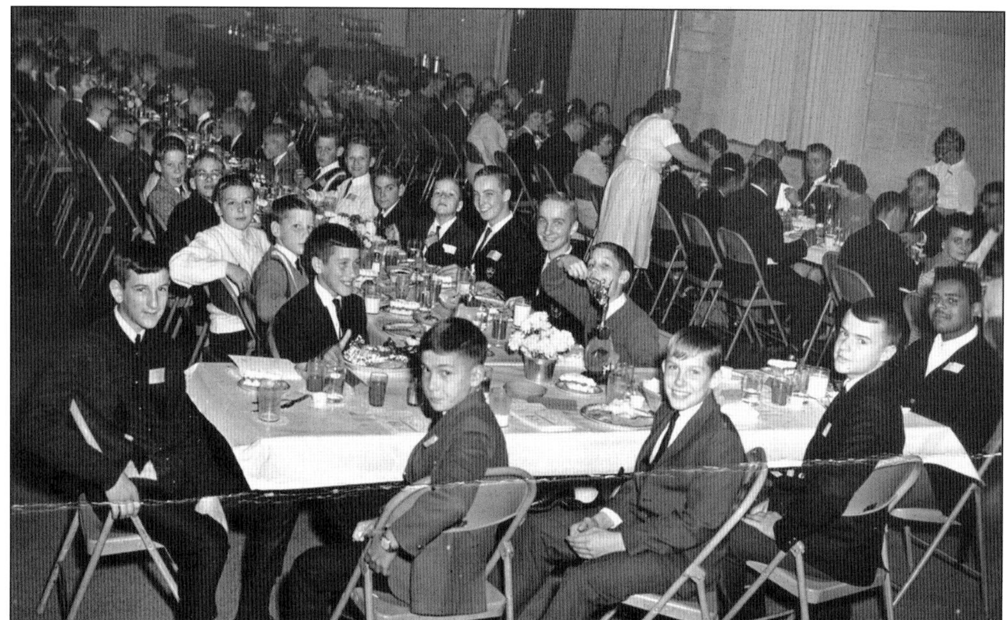

This is another photograph of the Kiltie Kadets' 1965 banquet. It was held at the Racine Labor Center. The five members of the Kiltie Kadets who are seated at the head table are the "age outs." Being too old for membership in the Kiltie Kadets, many age outs would go up to, or join, the Kilties. (Courtesy of RKAA.)

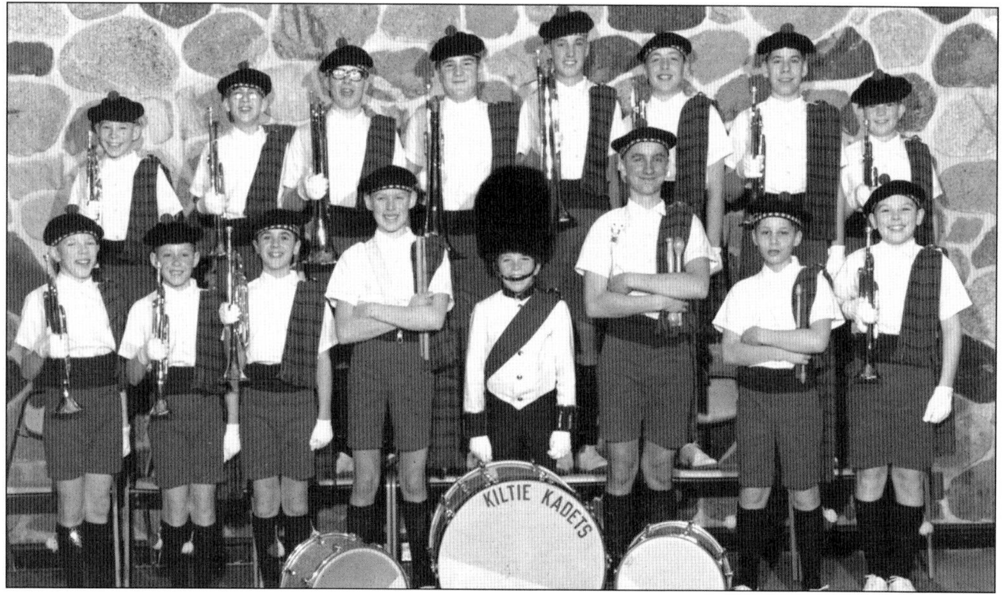

Small corps competition was organized around 1959 by Wisconsin's Badgerland Association in an attempt to make the drum and bugle corps activity year-round. Fifteen members of a drum and bugle corps would play a five-minute standstill concert in judged competition. The small corps activity quickly spread to neighboring states where some of their drum corps also organized small corps. The 1966 Racine Kiltie Kadets Drum and Bugle Corps' competitive winter small corps is shown in this photograph. This photograph was taken on April 4, 1966, at the Spring Spectacle in Madison, which the Kiltie Kadets handily won. (Courtesy of RKAA.)

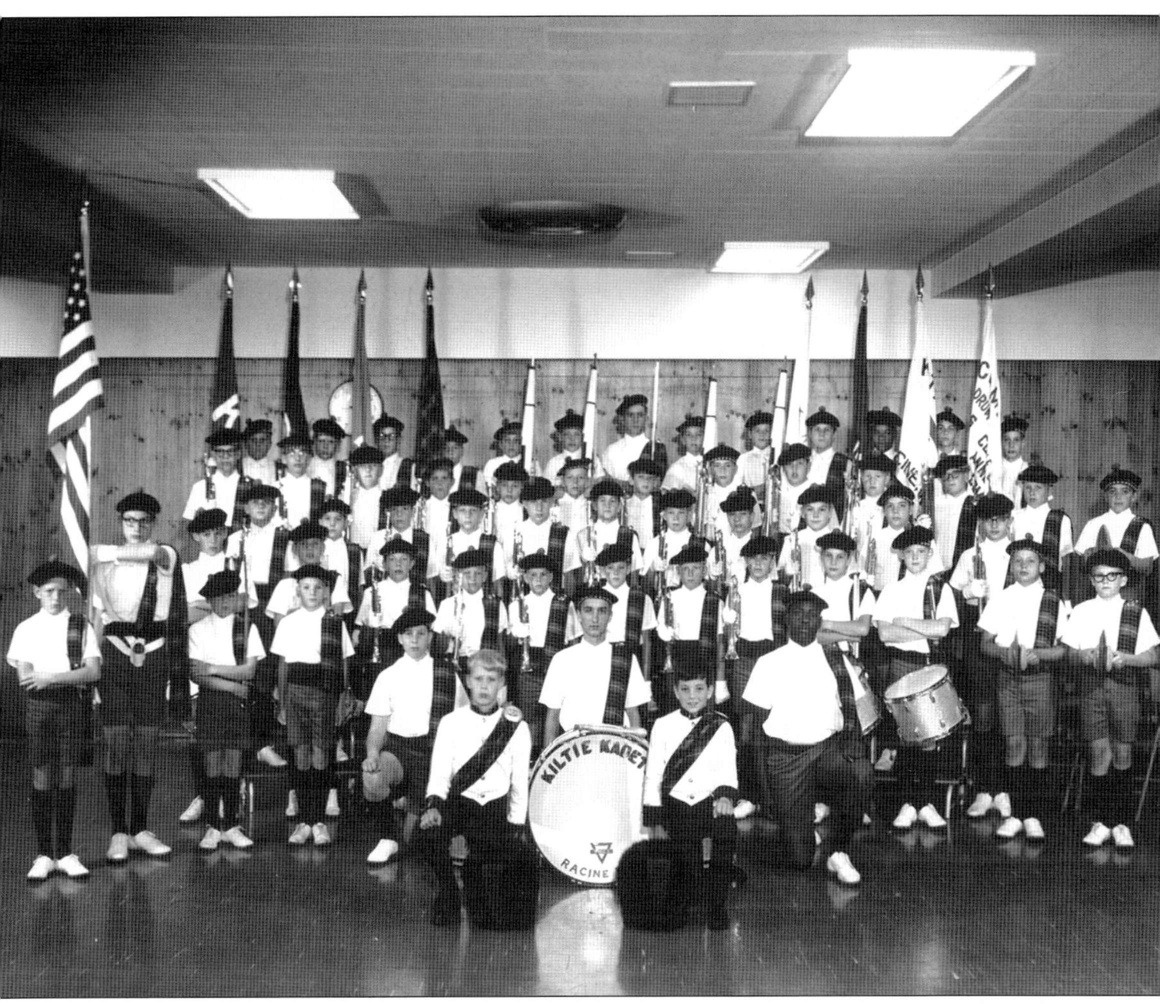

This photograph of the Kiltie Kadets was taken in 1966 inside the Racine YMCA. The Kiltie Kadets fielded an excellent corps in 1966, placing in the top three in nearly every contest throughout the summer. In fact, the Kiltie Kadets narrowly missed winning the Class B title at the Wisconsin VFW Drum and Bugle Corps State Championship in Janesville on June 25 when they finished a close second to a much older and more experienced Class B corps, the Kenosha Queensmen. Unfortunately no separate competition for Class C corps was offered. This forced the Kiltie Kadets, along with all the other Class C corps in Wisconsin, to compete in Class B against older and more experienced corps. (Courtesy of RKAA.)

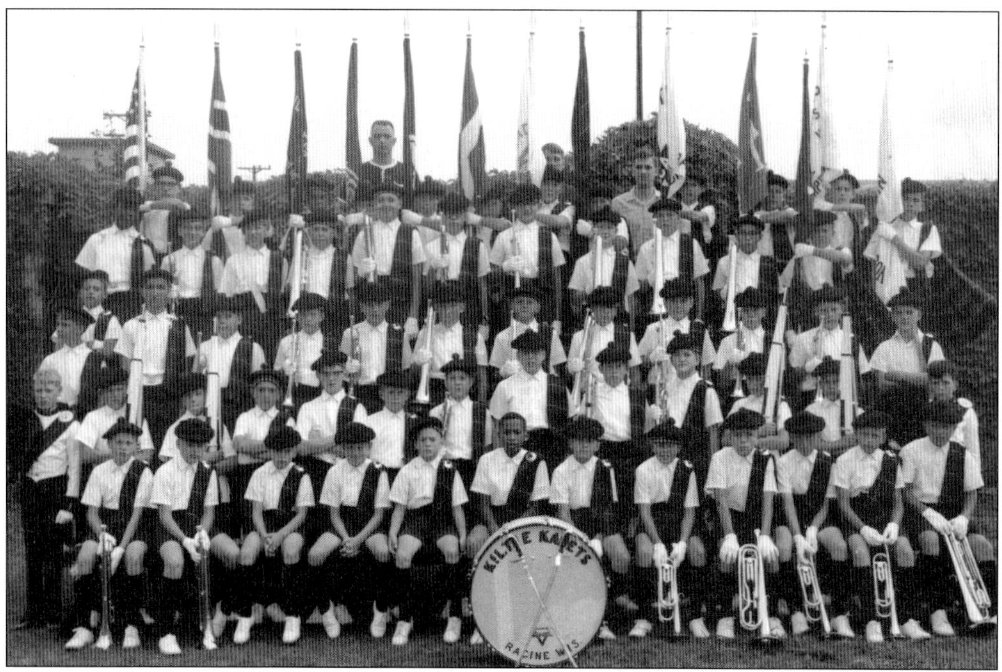

This 1966 photograph of the Kiltie Kadets was taken at Racine's Horlick Field. The Kiltie Kadets began the summer of 1966 on a positive note by taking first place in Class C competition at the Badgerland Association's annual Summer Preview in Wauwatosa on Saturday, June 4. Successes continued throughout the summer for the Kiltie Kadets as the group fielded one of its best corps to date. (Courtesy of RKAA.)

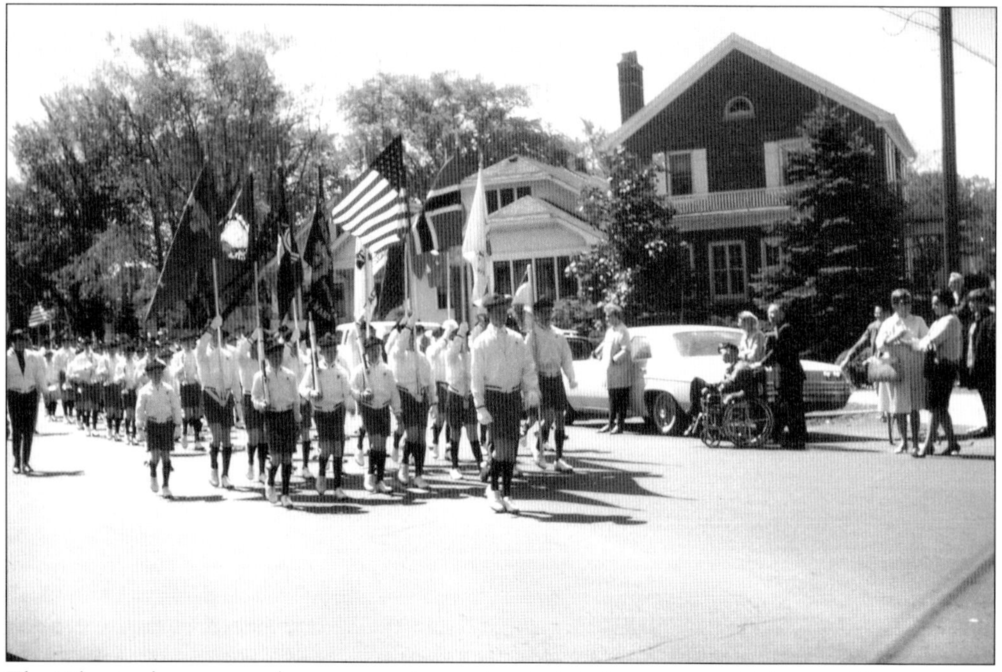

The Kiltie Kadets are seen here on parade wearing their jackets on a cool Memorial Day morning in 1966 in Racine. (Courtesy of RKAA.)

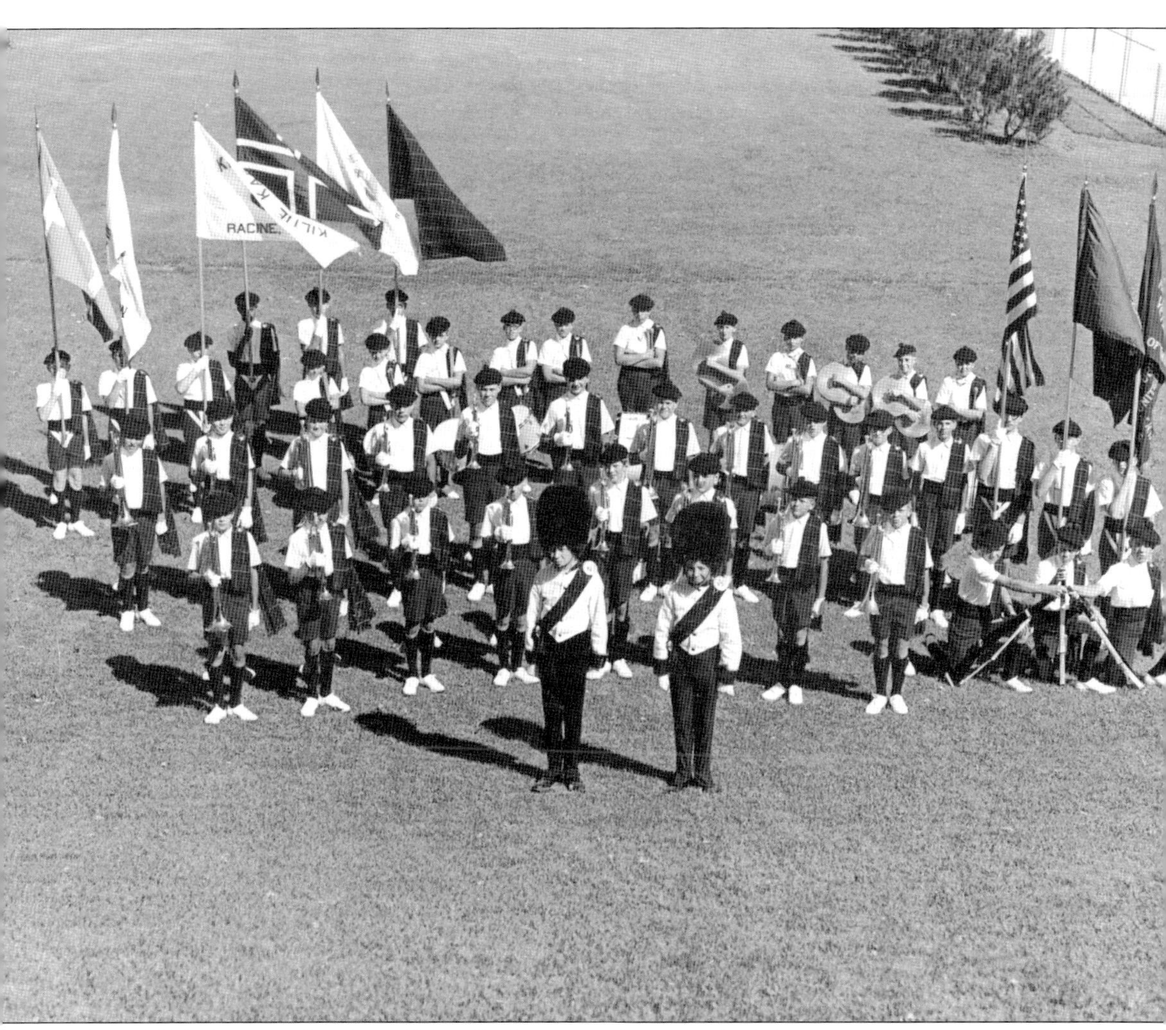

This 1967 photograph of the Kiltie Kadets was taken on the hill near the tennis courts in Racine's Pershing Park. Even though the group had a much younger corps than in past years, the Kiltie Kadets were still able to consistently take third or fourth place in Class C contests throughout 1967. (Courtesy of RKAA.)

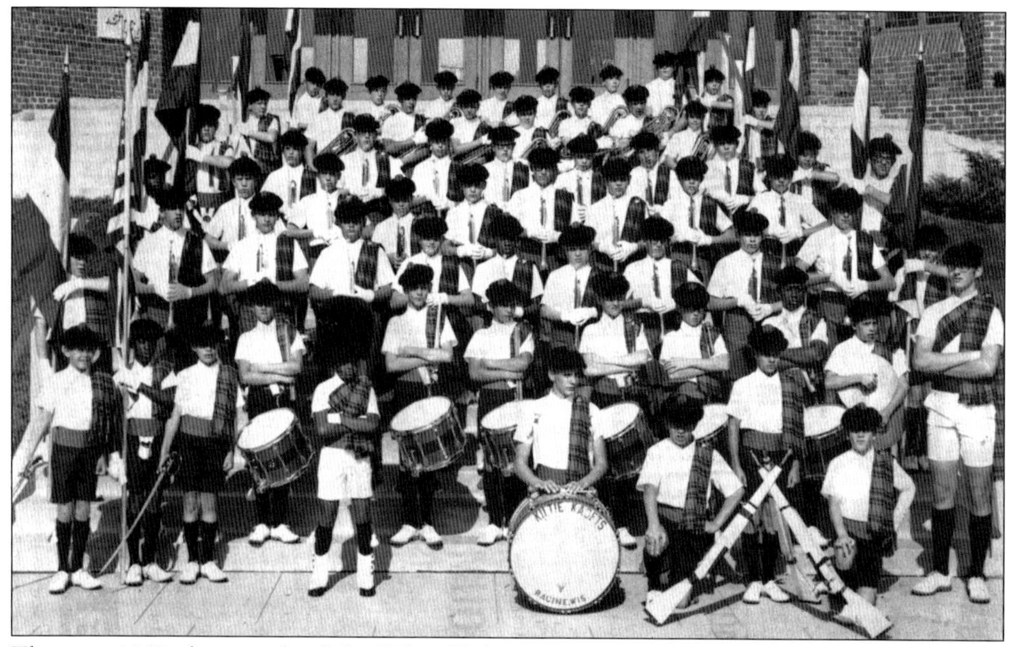

This is a 1969 photograph of the Kiltie Kadets. In 1969, the Kiltie Kadets became the first Class C drum and bugle corps in the country to equip with the new G-F bugle, which permits any musical score to be played. The purchase of these new G-F bugles was consistent with the Kiltie Kadets' goal of offering the highest quality musical instruction program available anywhere. The Kiltie Kadets won numerous small corps contests in 1969. Victories during the summer in Class C competition included at Cedarburg, New Berlin, the Music Round-Up at Kenosha, and the Wisconsin State Fair in West Allis. (Courtesy of RKAA.)

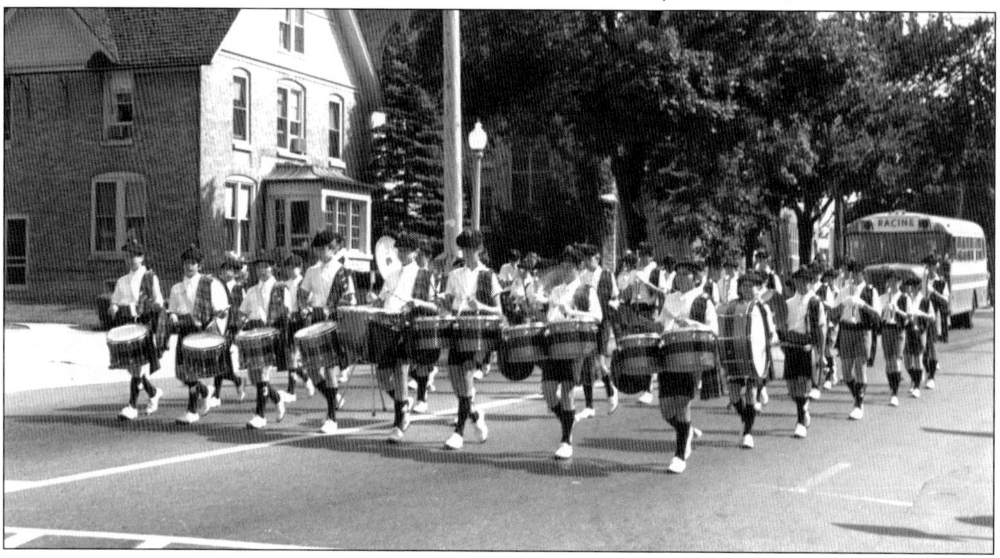

This is an early-1970s photograph, probably from 1973, of the Kiltie Kadets on parade in Burlington. During 1973, the Kiltie Kadets did a pregame performance at the Green Bay Packers inter-squad game in front of 56,000 people. Just two years earlier, the Kiltie Kadets won their first national championship when they won the Class C championship at the 1971 North American Championships in Milwaukee. (Courtesy of RKAA.)

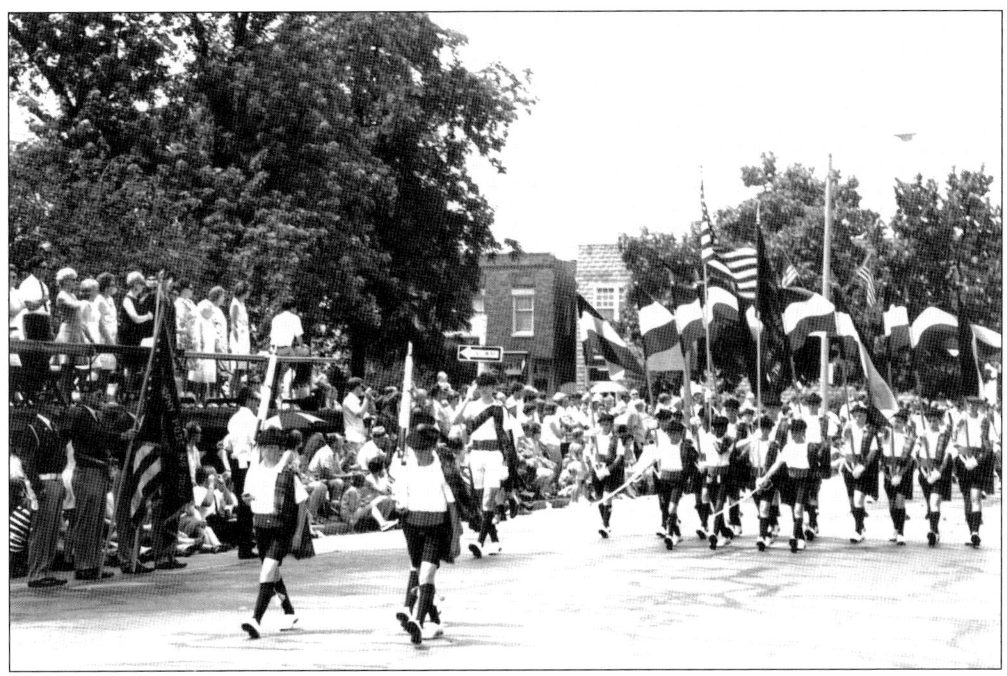

The Kiltie Kadets are seen here passing the reviewing stand during the afternoon parade held in conjunction with the 10th annual Pageant of Drums in Burlington on July 29, 1973. Sponsored jointly by the Racine Kilties and Burlington's Anderson-Murphy VFW Post 2823 since 1964, the 1973 Pageant of Drums was the last one ever held. (Courtesy of RKAA.)

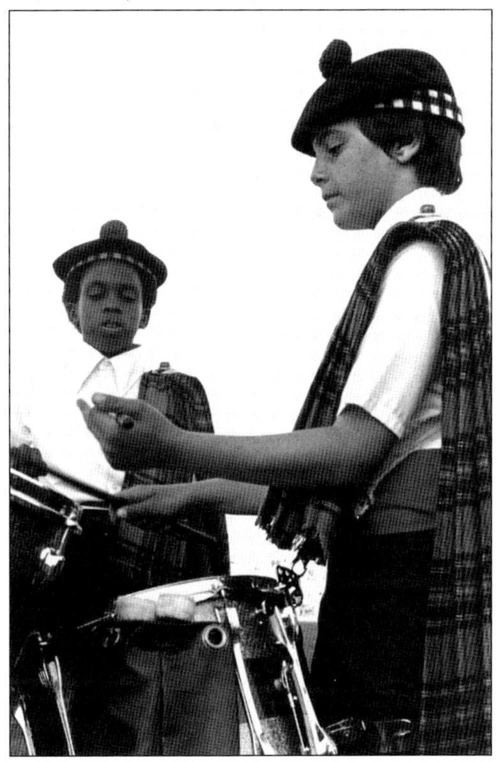

A Kiltie Kadets drummer is performing at Racine's Drum Corps Days in 1974 at Pershing Park. The Kiltie Kadets' buses and equipment truck were broken into sometime during Christmas vacation in December 1973 and equipment and instruments were vandalized and destroyed. This happened again in June 1974, with equipment and instruments again being vandalized and destroyed. The Kiltie Kadets and the parents' club did anything and everything to raise the funds necessary to repair or replace everything that they needed to as a result of the first incident in December 1973. Then they had to do it all over again in June 1974. (Photograph by Ruth Mainland, courtesy of RKAA.)

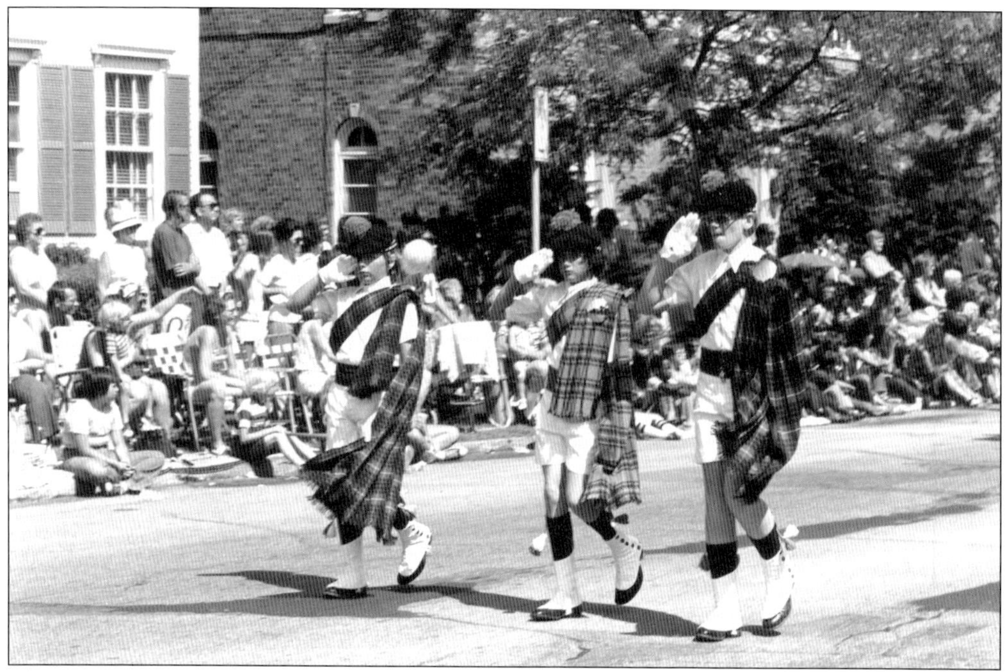

The Kiltie Kadets' three drum majors are proudly saluting during Racine's 1975 Fourth of July parade. By this time, the Kiltie Kadets were traveling 5,000 to 8,000 miles per year. (Photograph by Ruth Mainland, courtesy of RKAA.)

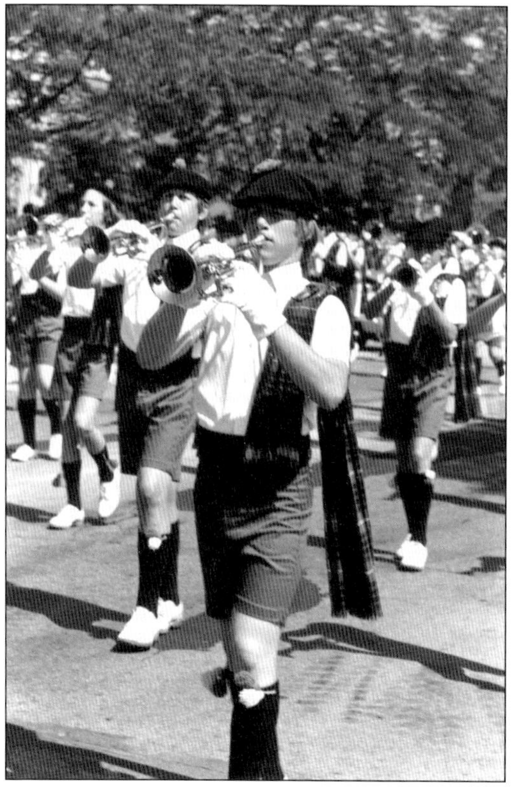

The Kiltie Kadets had been so successful throughout the early 1970s that by 1975 they found themselves being excluded from Class C competitions in an attempt to force them to compete in Class B and Open Class against corps with older and more experienced members. The Kiltie Kadets accumulated over 100 trophies and titles from 1969 through 1975. In this photograph are soprano buglers of the Kiltie Kadets playing during Racine's Fourth of July parade in 1975. (Photograph by Ruth Mainland, courtesy of RKAA.)

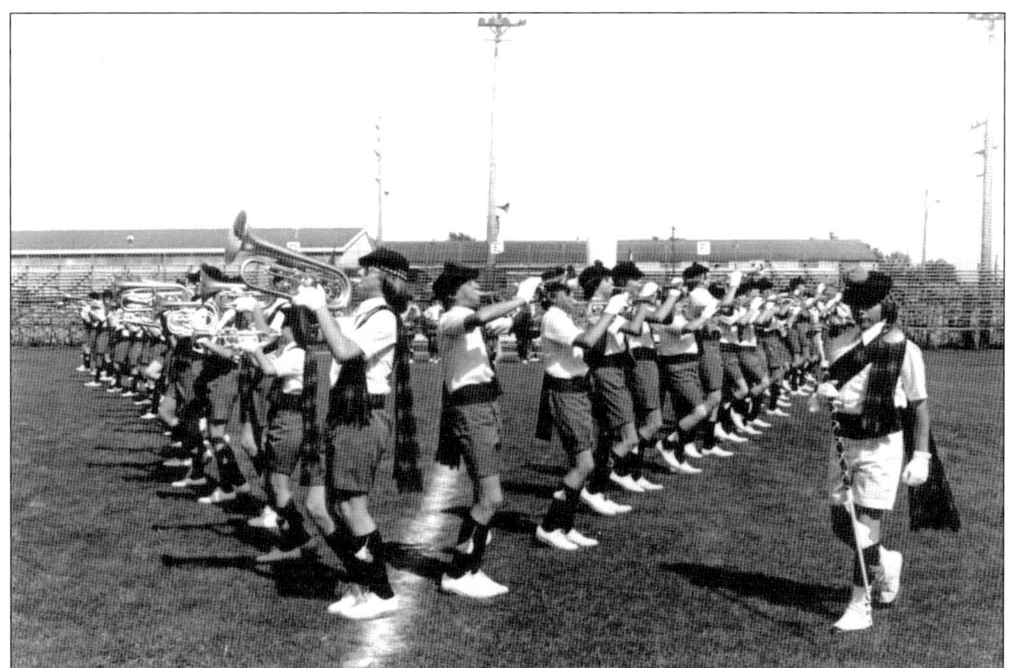

The Kiltie Kadets are on the field of competition at Racine's Horlick Field during the summer of 1976. This would be the last year the group wore its famous white shirts, blue cummerbunds, and red shorts with a red plaid tartan. During 1976, the Kiltie Kadets took first place in Class C at the Wisconsin VFW Drum and Bugle Corps State Championship in Wausau and were the 1976 Cadet Corps International (CCI) round-robin champions. (Courtesy of RKAA.)

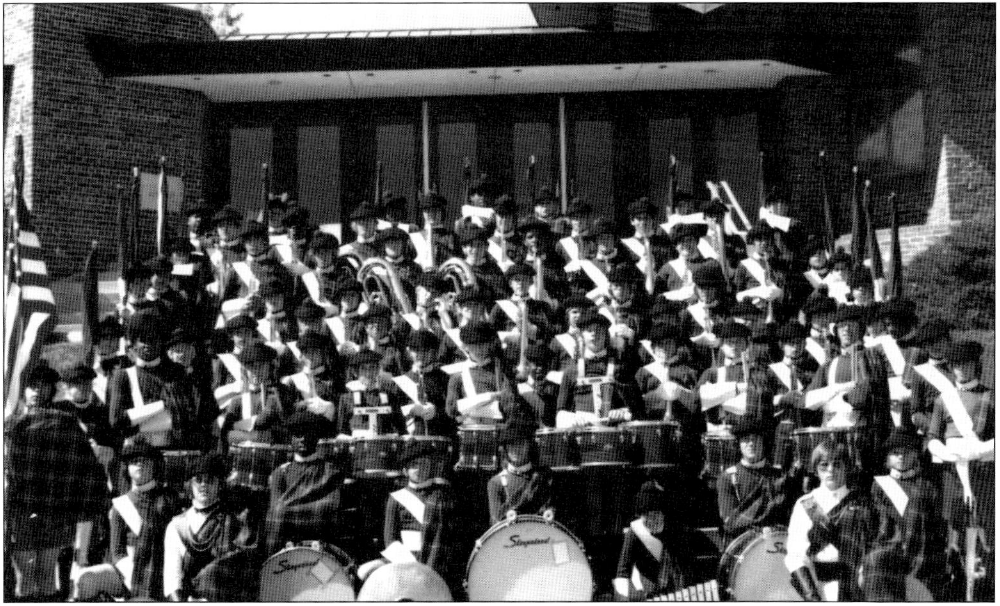

The 1977 Kiltie Kadets are seen here in their new uniforms. This was the first year the CCI Championship was held. The Kiltie Kadets took third place at the CCI Championship in both 1977 and 1978. This was followed up by a second place at the CCI Championship in 1979. (Courtesy of RKAA.)

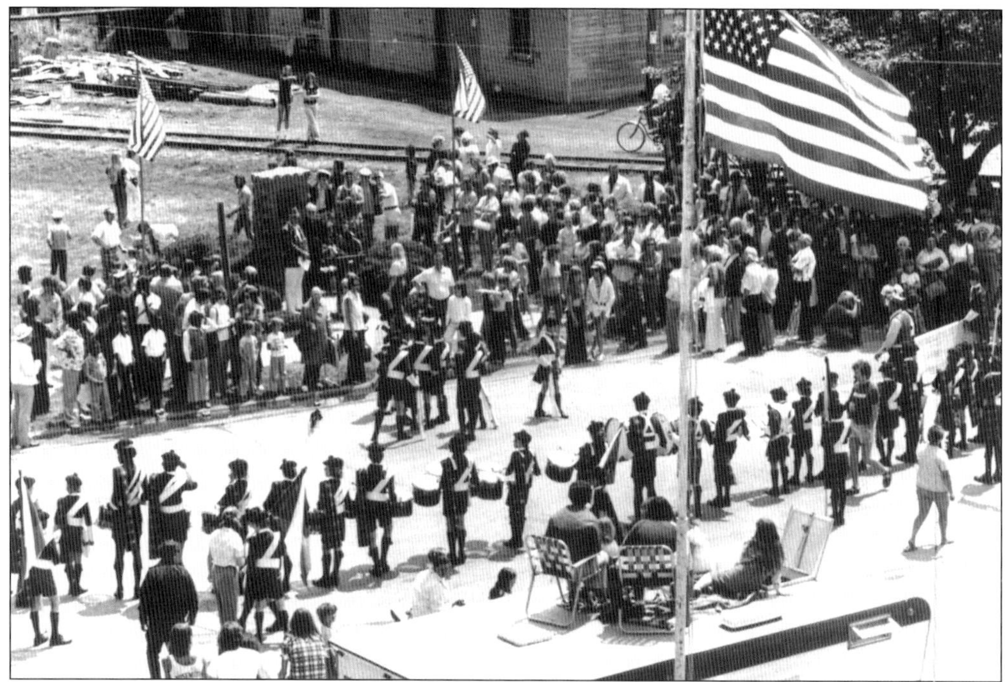

The Kiltie Kadets are seen in concert at the 1977 Veterans Day ceremony in Sturtevant. The location of this photograph is at the historical marker just north of the railroad tracks, on the east side of Highway H. (Courtesy of RKAA.)

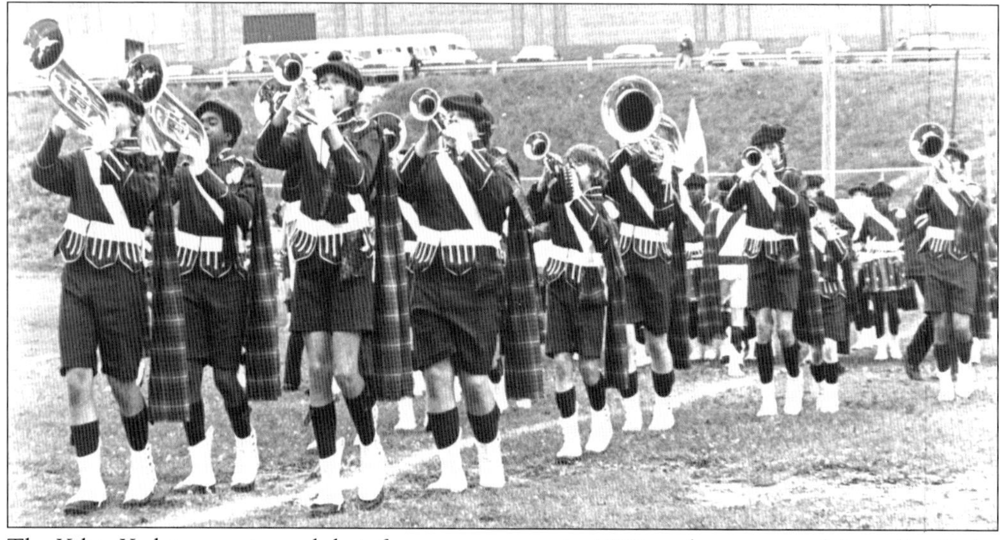

The Kiltie Kadets experienced their finest season ever in 1980, as they went undefeated in Cadet Class competition. Then at the 1980 DCI Championship in Birmingham, Alabama, the Kiltie Kadets came in 12th place in the Class A/All-Girl preliminaries. The 1980 season culminated with the Kiltie Kadets winning the CCI Championship on August 24 in Racine. The drum corps activity would unfortunately be able to enjoy the Kiltie Kadets for only one more season. The group folded after the 1981 season, creating a huge void in the drum corps scene of Racine and nationwide as well. (Courtesy of RKAA.)

Six

AMBASSA"DEARS" AND NEW DAY

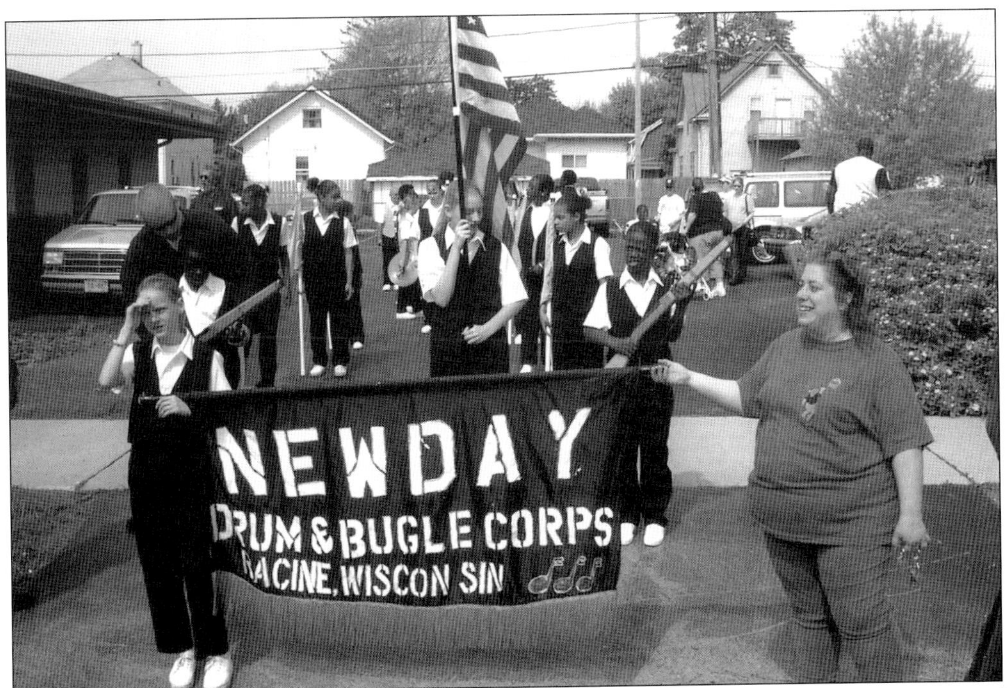

The Racine New Day Drum and Bugle Corps was formed in the fall of 1972 from the merger of the Racine Ambassa"Dears" Drum and Bugle Corps and the Racine Citations Color Guard. This photograph shows the New Day in the staging area for Racine's 2002 Memorial Day parade.

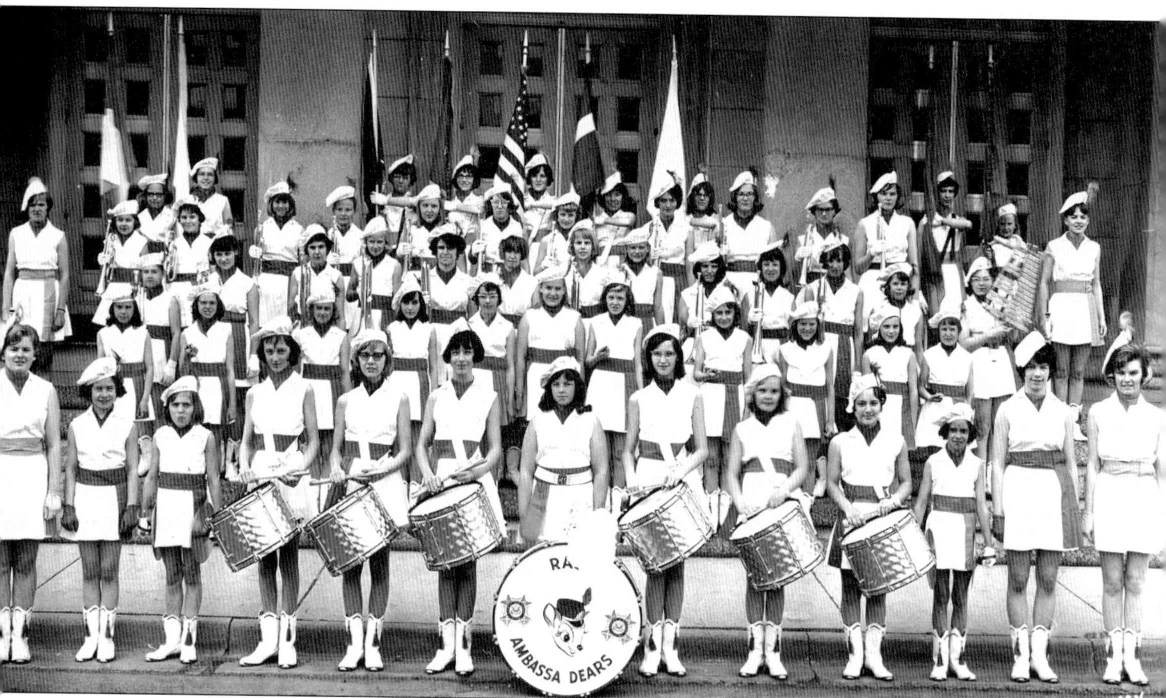

The Racine Ambassa"Dears" All-Girl Drum and Bugle Corps was organized on September 8, 1963, by Kaye Poulsen and Cheryl Johnson. At first the corps bought drums from the Racine Boy Scout Junior Drum and Bugle Corps and played fifes, which were bought for 39¢ a piece. The corps purchased its first bugles in 1964. The first uniforms adopted by the girls were of a design similar to those worn by Gussie Moran, a famous female tennis player. The corps members made their own uniforms. The girls are still found wearing this style uniform in this 1965 full corps photograph of the Ambassa"Dears," which was taken on the steps of Memorial Hall in Racine. (Courtesy of RHM.)

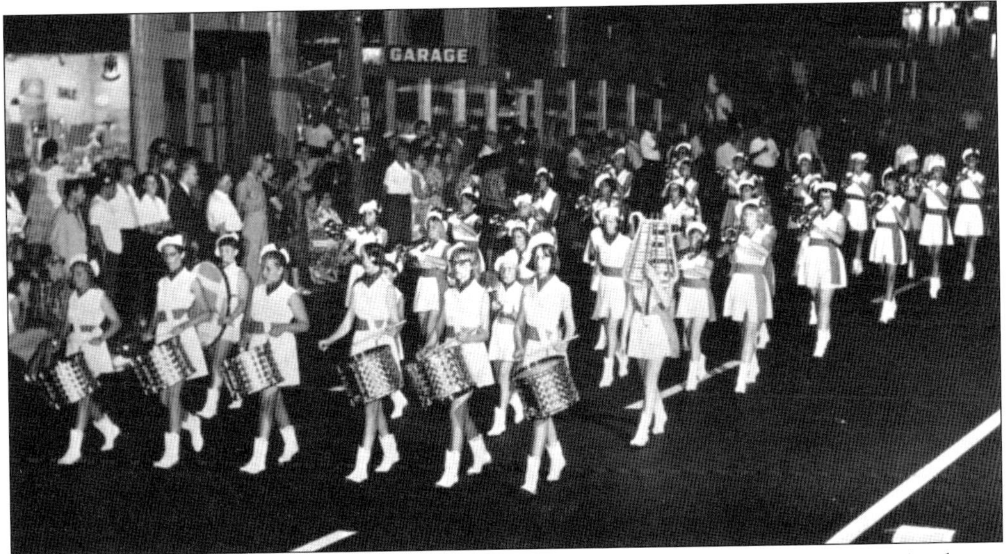

In 1965, the Ambassa"Dears" competed at the Wisconsin VFW state championships in Appleton, where they finished fourth in their class. Here the Ambassa"Dears" are seen on parade in the 1965 VFW national convention parade in Chicago.

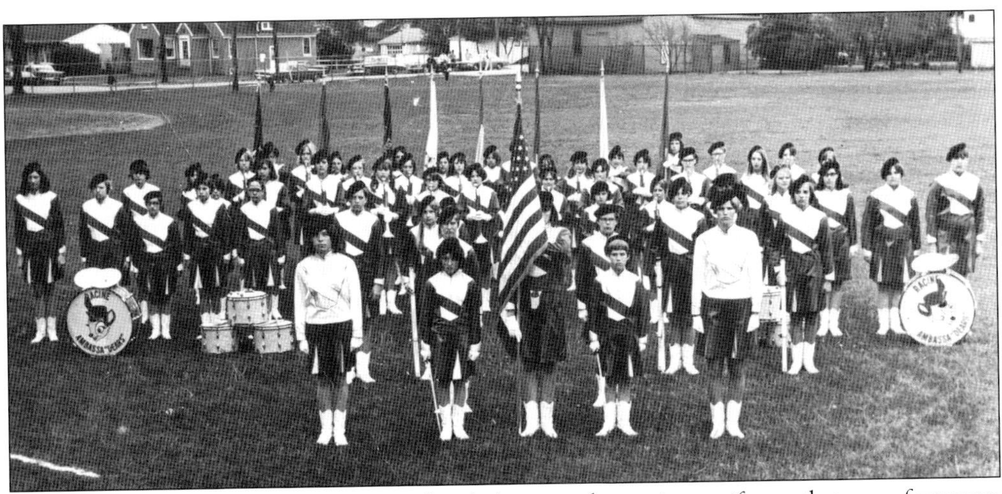

The Ambassa"Dears" appear in this undated photograph wearing uniforms that were first worn by them in 1967. The Ambassa"Dears" traveled extensively and competed successfully in their class until after the 1972 season, when the corps was reorganized as the New Day Drum and Bugle Corps. (Courtesy of RHM.)

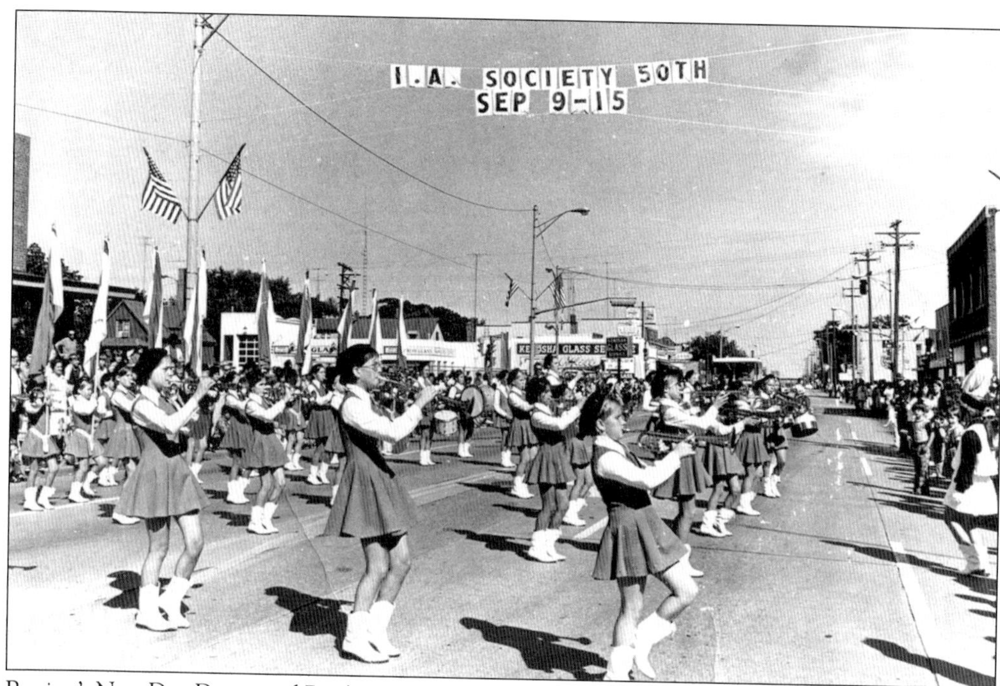

Racine's New Day Drum and Bugle Corps is seen here on parade in 1974 in Kenosha for the 50th anniversary of Kenosha's Italian American Society. (Courtesy of RKAA.)

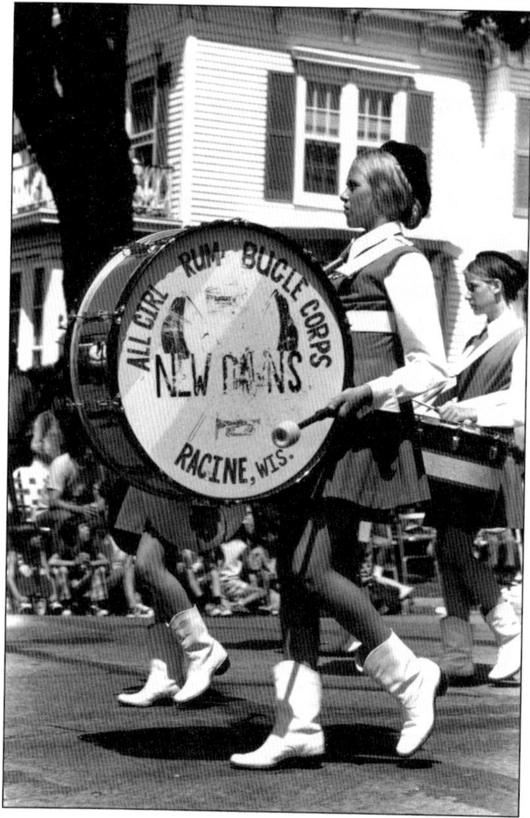

On parade in Racine's Fourth of July parade of 1975 is the Racine New Dawns All Girl Drum and Bugle Corps. The New Dawns were a Class C corps formed in 1973 as a training corps for the New Day. The corps had its first competition in 1974. It fielded a corps through the 1977 season. In fact, the New Dawns corps was larger than New Day and for three years running won its division at the Badgerland Association Championship. (Photograph by Ruth Mainland, courtesy of RKAA.)

Both of these New Day drummers were photographed during their exhibition in 1974 at Pershing Park for Racine's Drum Corps Day. The all-girl New Day came close to folding when the all-male Racine Kilties took in girls in 1978. This caused the New Day, composed of older girls, and the New Dawns, a training corps for younger girls, to merge. Even with the merger, the New Day was unable to have enough members to field a competitive corps. Although folding the corps was discussed, the 17 remaining girls decided not to give up. Their "don't give up–don't quit" spirit made it possible for the New Day to survive. In 1982, the group reentered competition. One of New Day's winter guard highlights occurred in 1993, when it made finals at the Winter Guard International (WGI) Midwest regional competition. The New Day and its winter guard competed throughout the United States and Canada through the 1996 season, when more problems beset the corps. The New Day disappeared for good after the summer of 2002. (Photographs by Ruth Mainland, courtesy of RKAA.)

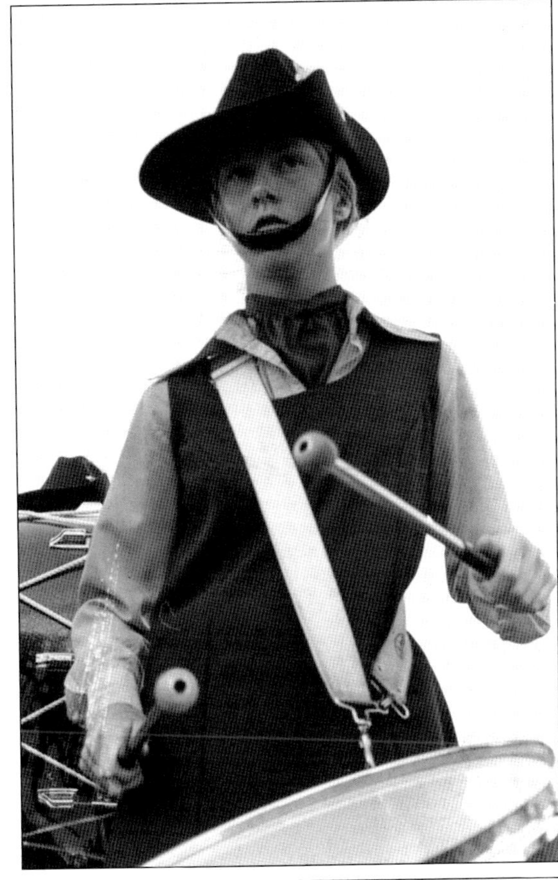

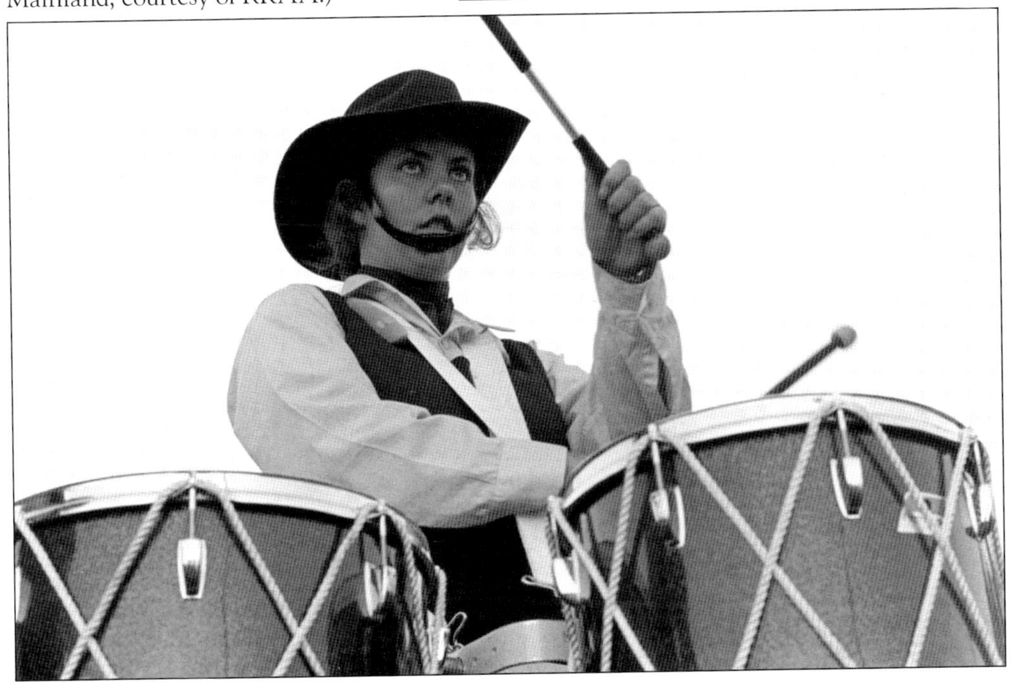

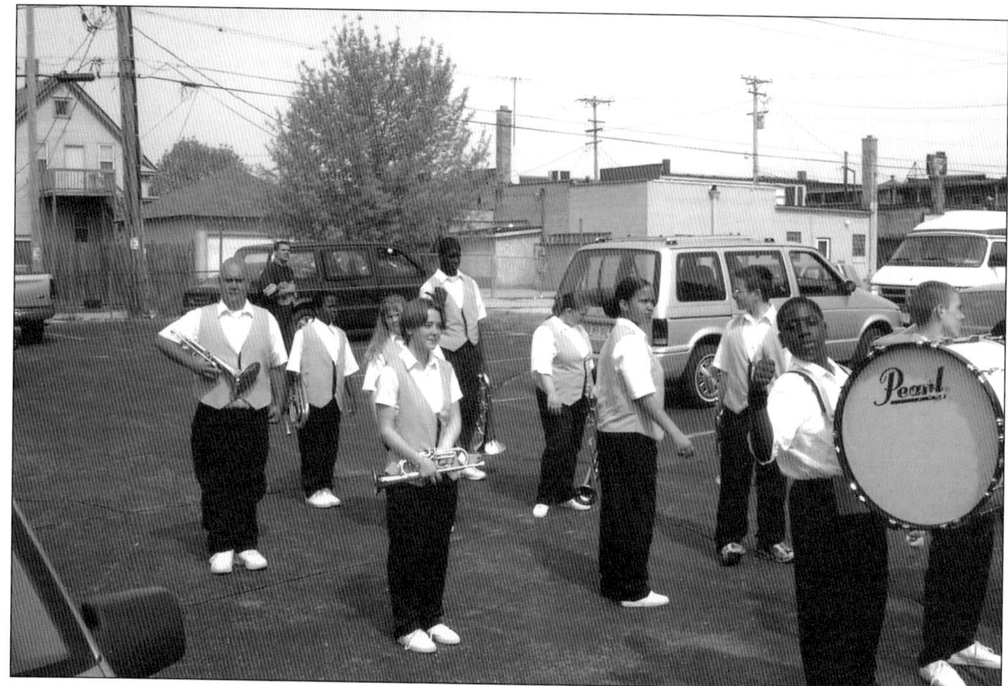

The New Day buglers above and drummers below were photographed on May 27, 2002, while they waited in the staging area for their turn to march in Racine's Memorial Day parade. The New Day was now open to boys. The group was delightful, enthusiastic, and highly spirited. Unfortunately New Day disappeared for good after this summer.

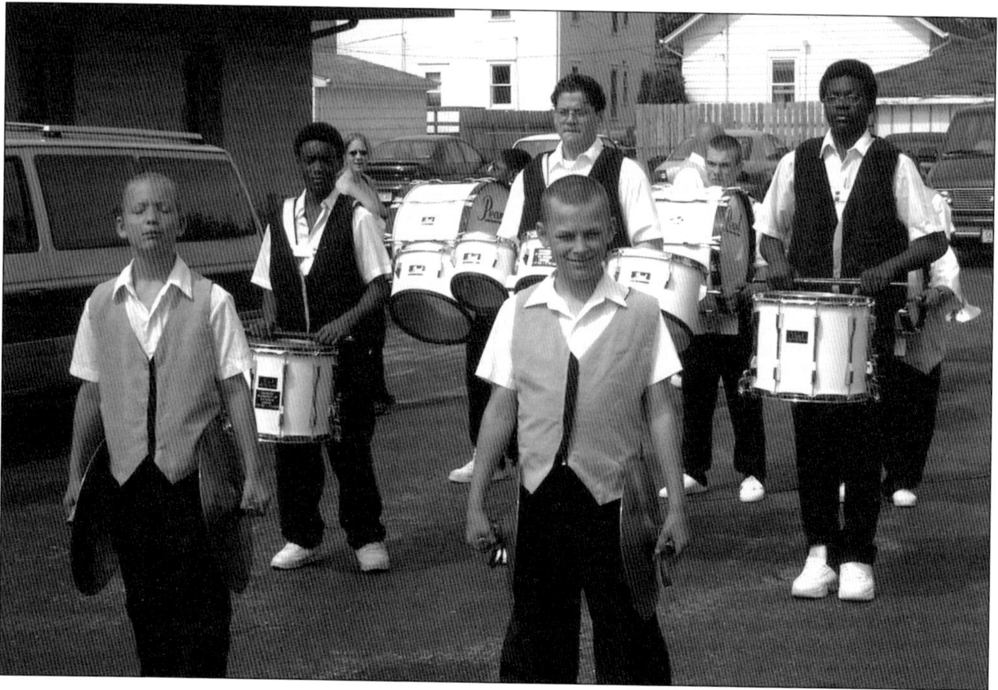

Seven

Other Racine Units

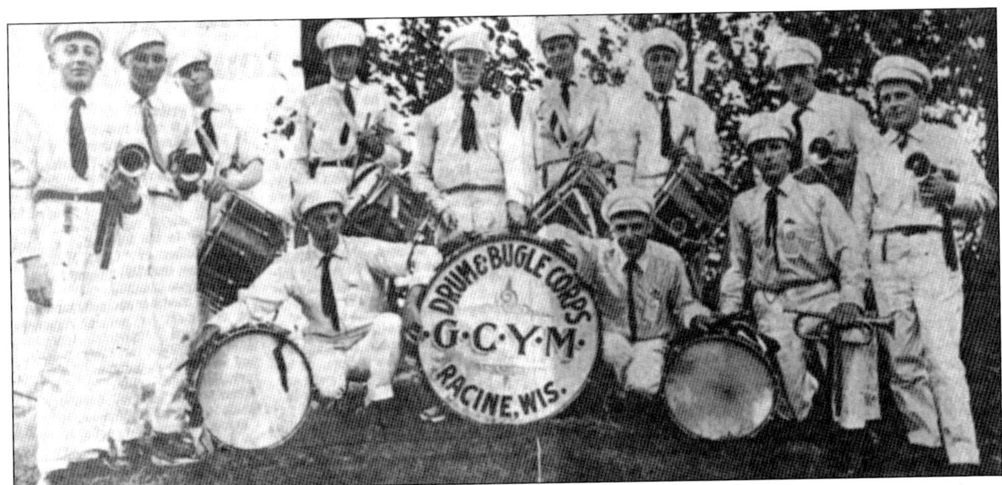

The Racine German Catholic Young Men's Association sponsored a drum and bugle corps from 1903 to 1919. Frederick Schulte was the drum corps' first drum instructor, and Herman Freres was the drum corps' first bugle instructor. The Racine German Catholic Young Men's Association dates back to 1866, when it was founded as the German Catholic Singing Society. The year this photograph was taken is unknown.

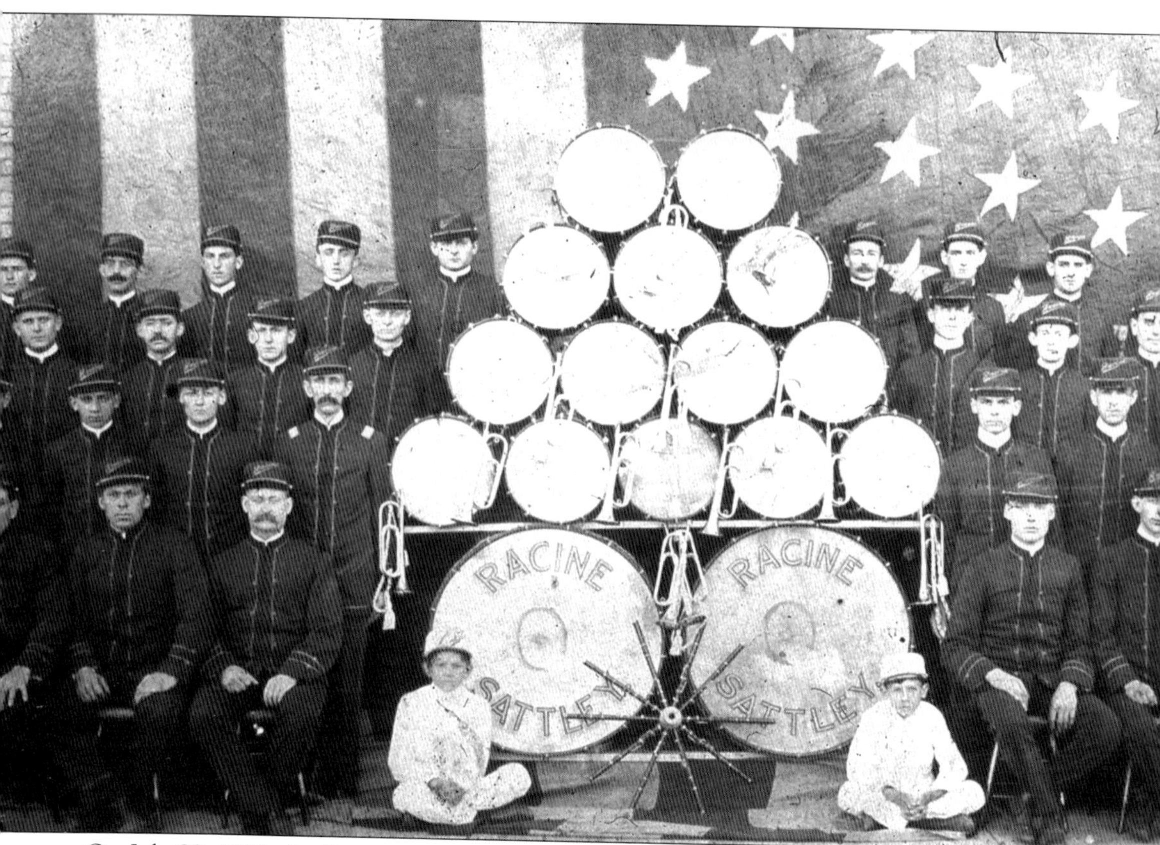

On July 28, 1903, the Racine Wagon and Carriage Company and the Sattley Manufacturing Company of Springfield, Illinois, a large manufacturer of plows and implements, consolidated into the Racine-Sattley Company. The new company became the only concern in the world up to that time that manufactured plows, implements, farm wagons, and spring vehicles of that kind. Endeavors had been made in the past to consolidate plow companies with vehicle concerns, but this was the first successful consolidation of its kind. However, by September 1915, the Racine-Sattley Company was in bankruptcy proceedings. The Racine-Sattley fife, drum, and bugle corps was organized in 1903. It was sponsored by the company and proclaimed itself to be the largest and best equipped of its kind in the country. At the time of the consolidation in July 1903, the Racine Wagon and Carriage Company had 900 employees in Racine. The Racine-Sattley fife, drum, and bugle corps existed until July 15, 1905, when 22 of its members joined Racine Council No. 77 of the National Fraternal League as a group. They immediately became the Racine National Fraternal League fife, drum, and bugle corps. (Courtesy of RHM.)

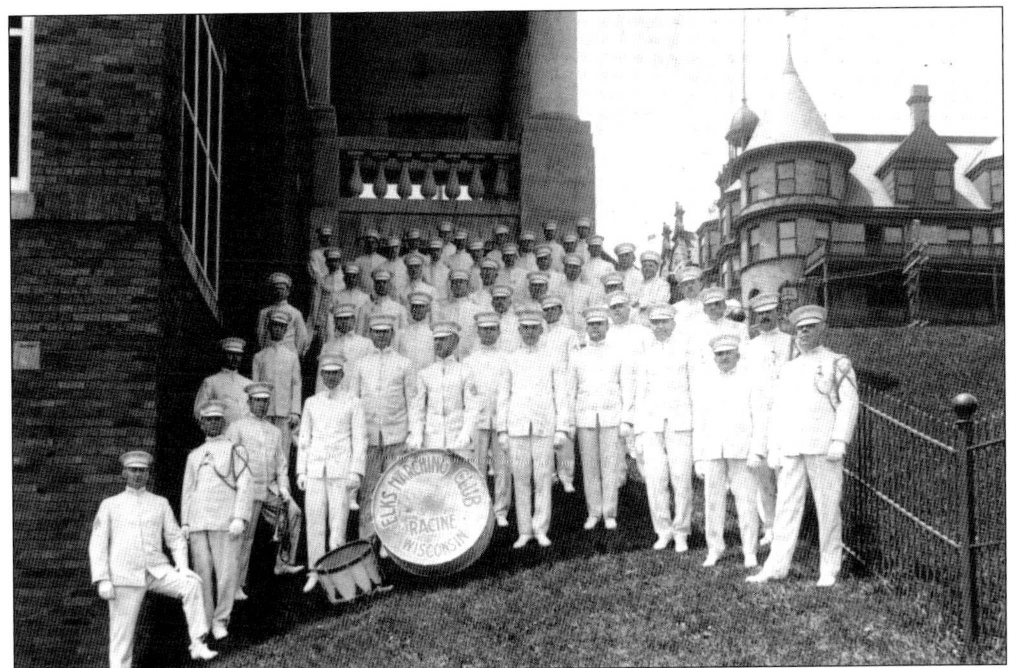

Members of the Racine Elks Marching Club are posed on the front lawn of the Elks Club in downtown Racine. The original Hotel Racine is in the background. The club was organized by Racine Elks Lodge 252, Benevolent and Protective Order of Elks, in September 1913. Initially the Racine Elks Marching Club had over 100 members. By the summer of 1920, the organization could only claim about 15 members. By the end of 1920, it had dissolved. (Courtesy of RHM.)

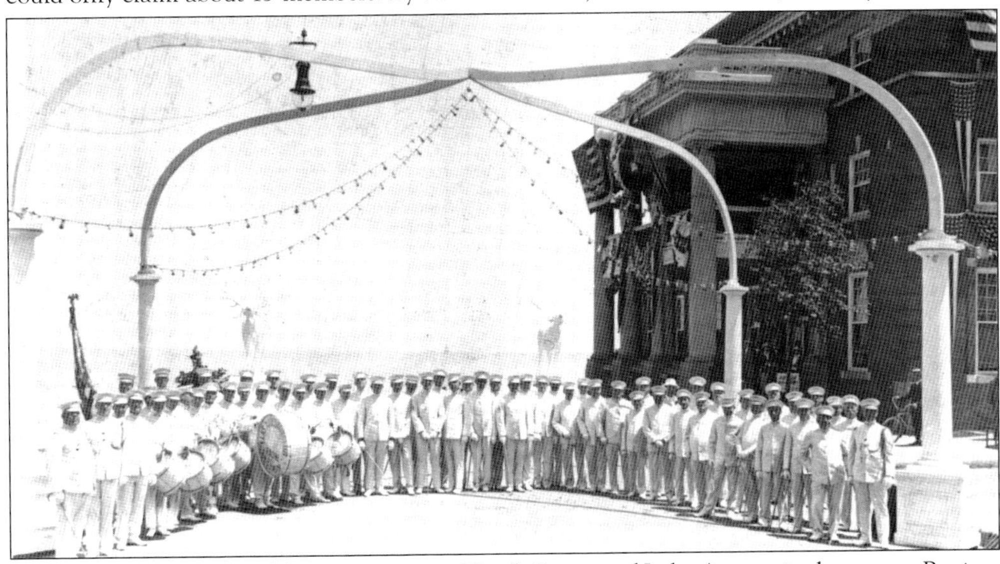

Standing in the middle of the intersection of Sixth Street and Lake Avenue in downtown Racine, the Racine Elks Marching Club poses for this photograph under a decorative arch. The front of the Racine Elks Club is in the background. The Racine Elks Marching Club immediately rose to become the classiest organization of its kind in Wisconsin. It was named the best-appearing marching club in the annual convention parade of the Wisconsin state association of Elks in Wausau in 1914 and in Oshkosh in 1915. (Courtesy of RHM.)

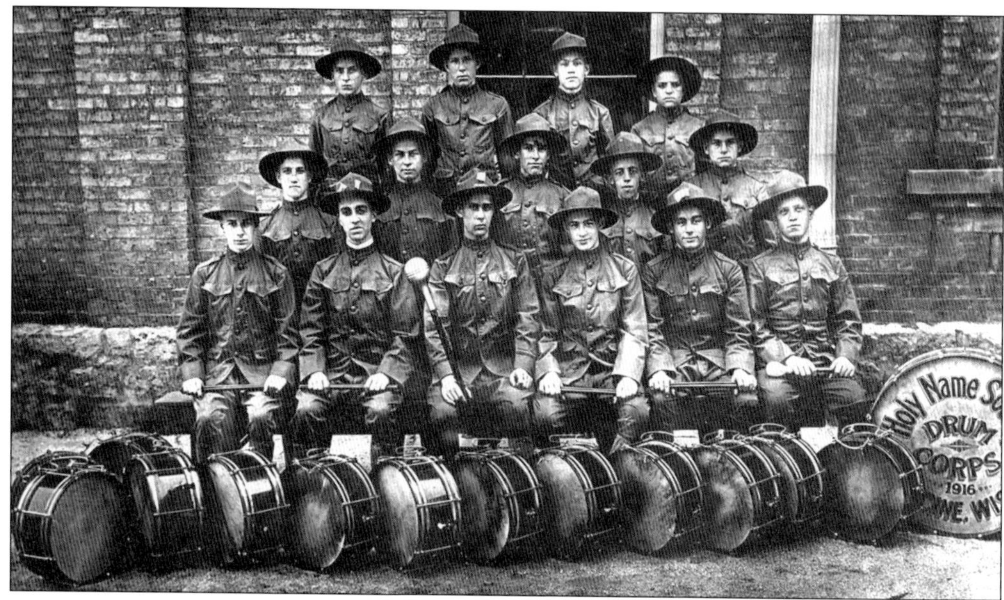

The Racine Holy Name Society Drum Corps was organized in April 1916. Its initial membership consisted of 10 drummers. There were no other musicians at the onset. After a few weeks of practicing indoors almost every night, one nice April night at 9:00 in the evening the Racine Holy Name Society Drum Corps took the Lakeside neighborhood by surprise when it decided to move outside and march up and down the streets. Some of the workers at the J. I. Case South Works actually thought war was declared. (Courtesy of RHM.)

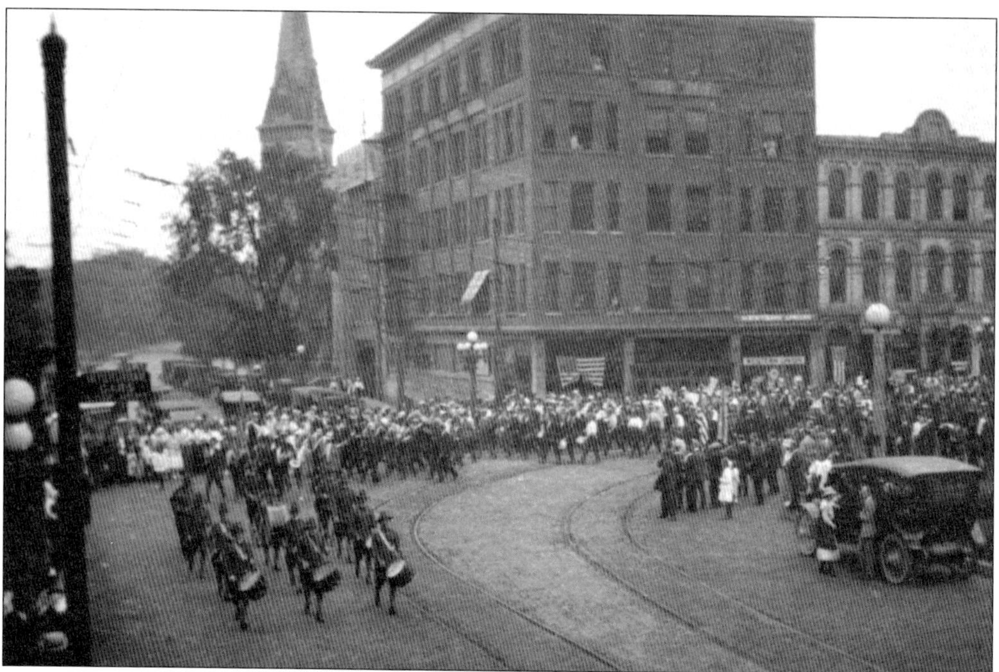

The Racine Batteries C and F Drum and Bugle Corps is seen here on parade in 1917 making the turn from Sixth Street onto Main Street. It is now heading north on Main Street in downtown Racine. The group looks strikingly similar to the Racine Holy Name Society Drum Corps.

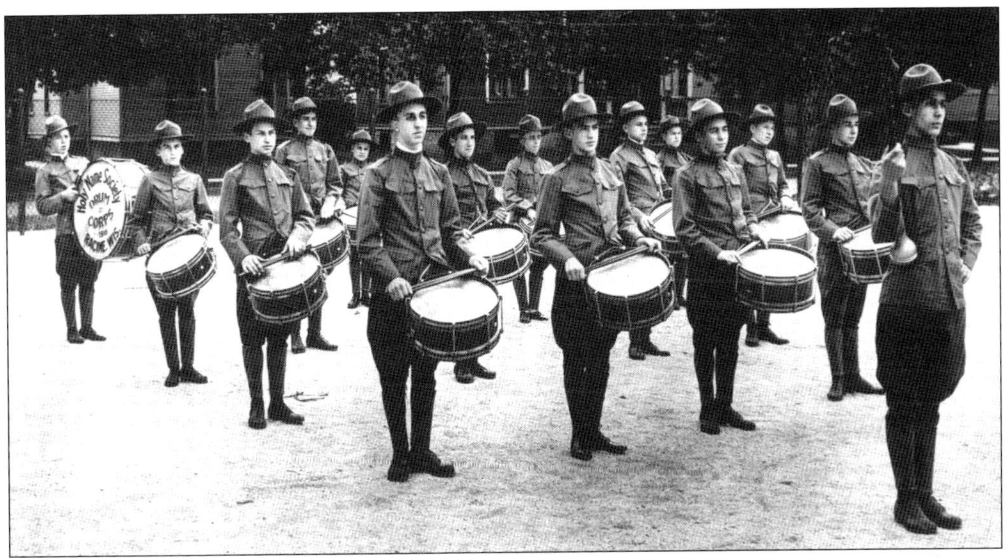

The Racine Holy Name Society Drum Corps is shown here in parade formation around 1916. The group was also known as the South Side Drum and Bugle Corps of Holy Name Church. (Courtesy of RHM.)

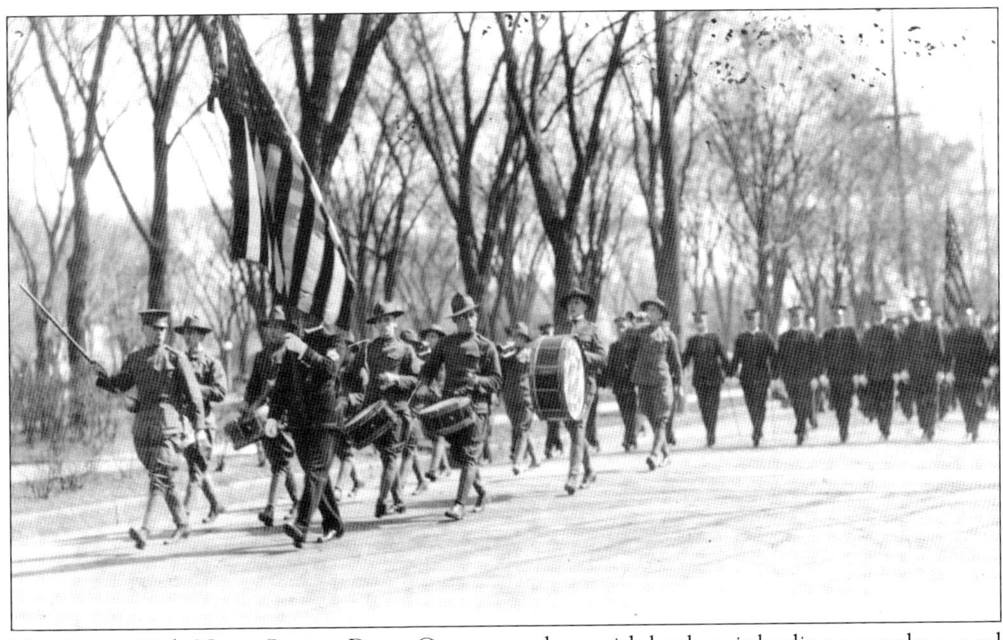

The Racine Holy Name Society Drum Corps, seen here with buglers, is leading a parade around 1918. It was very active in local community and Catholic events during its short three-year existence. The group was also a regular at the annual convention of the Racine County Federation of Catholic Societies and at the annual state conventions of both the German Catholic Society and the Knights of Columbus. (Courtesy of RHM.)

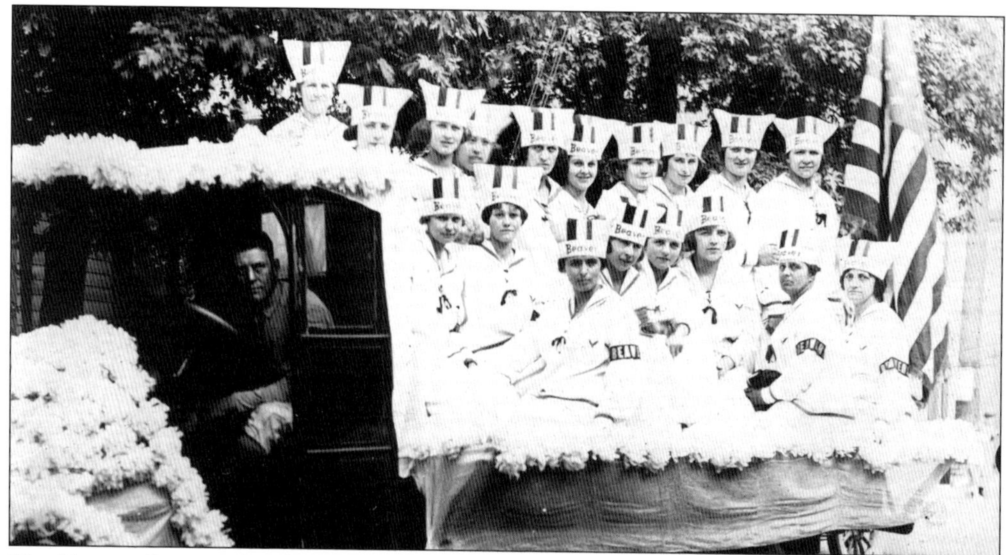

The Beavers Reserve Fund Fraternity girls' drill team of Racine Beaver Colony No. 1002 was organized sometime around 1917 and continued until the late 1920s. This photograph was taken during the Beavers' biennial convention, which was held in Racine on June 23 and 24, 1920. The drill team rode this decorated truck to the various events that were held throughout Racine in connection with this convention. (Courtesy of RHM.)

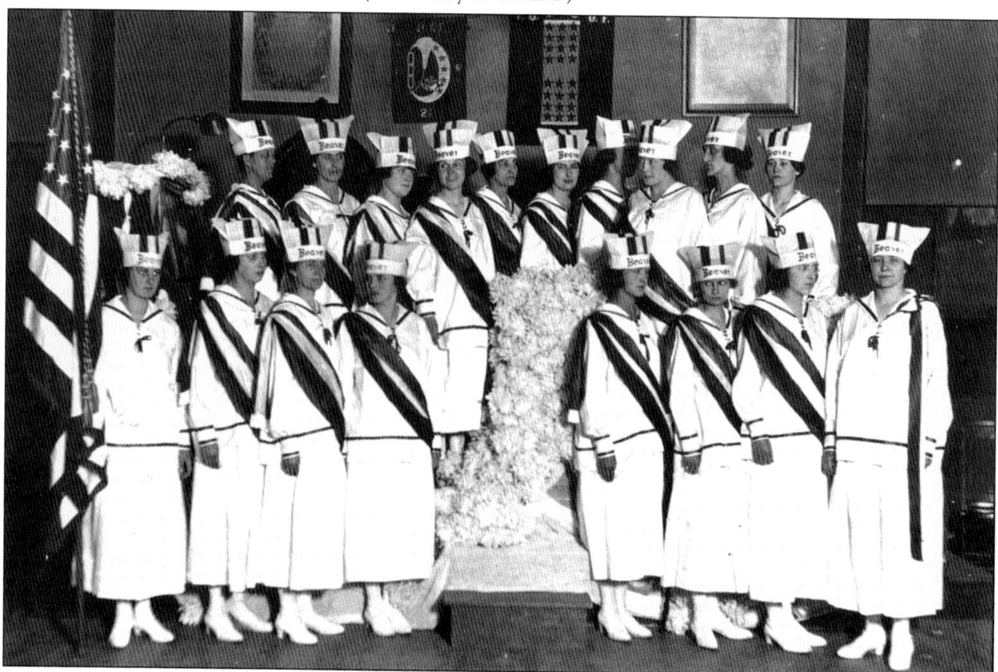

The Beavers Reserve Fund Fraternity was incorporated under the laws of the State of Wisconsin in January 1902 and was still doing business as an insurance fraternity when this photograph of Racine's Beavers Reserve Fund Fraternity girls' drill team was taken in 1924. The girls' drill team of the Racine Beavers Reserve Fund won a flag for taking second place in a drill team competition in 1917 among eight drill teams on Fraternity Day at the Wisconsin State Fair. (Courtesy of RHM.)

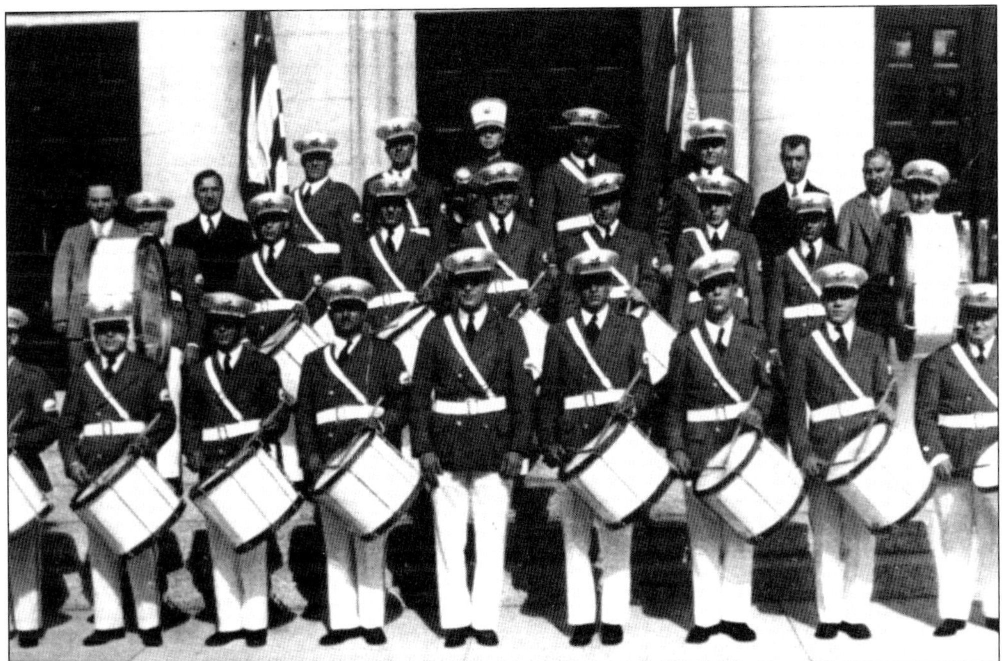

The Roma Lodge Drum and Bugle Corps poses in front of Memorial Hall for this photograph on October 12, 1930. The group's only competitive appearance was at the Chicagoland Music Festival in 1934. It was one of only four drum and bugle corps to compete in the senior division. Wearing its purple and white uniforms, the group put on a fine showing; however, it was outclassed by the other three senior corps, which were all top corps from Chicago, and had to settle for a distant fourth place. (Courtesy of Racine Roma Lodge.)

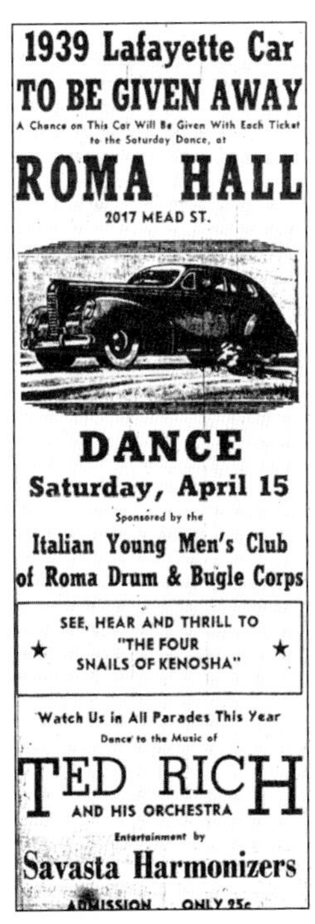

To raise money for new bugles, during the spring of 1939 the Racine Roma Lodge Drum and Bugle Corps sold tickets on a new Nash Lafayette automobile. The car was raffled off on April 15 at the Roma Lodge, which was then located at 2017 Mead Street in Racine. The Racine Roma Lodge Drum and Bugle Corps, organized in 1929, had a membership of 52 plus four drum majors in 1939. It folded about a year later.

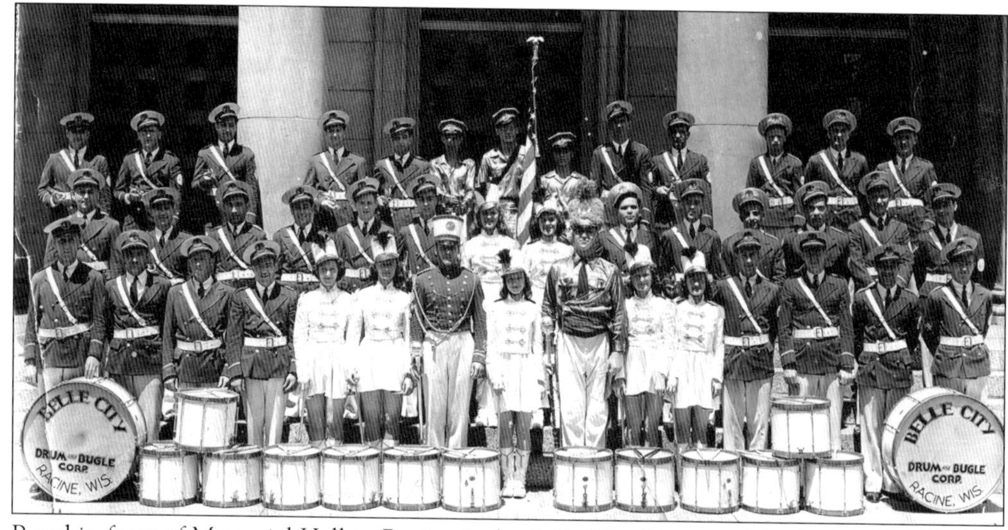

Posed in front of Memorial Hall in Racine is the Belle City Drum and Bugle Corps. The Belle City Drum and Bugle Corps was organized during the summer of 1940 after purchasing the uniforms and instruments from the Racine Roma Lodge Drum and Bugle Corps. However, the Belle City Drum and Bugle Corps only managed to last through 1942. During its brief existence, the group practiced at Island Park in Racine and participated in many of the area's civic events. (Courtesy of RHM.)

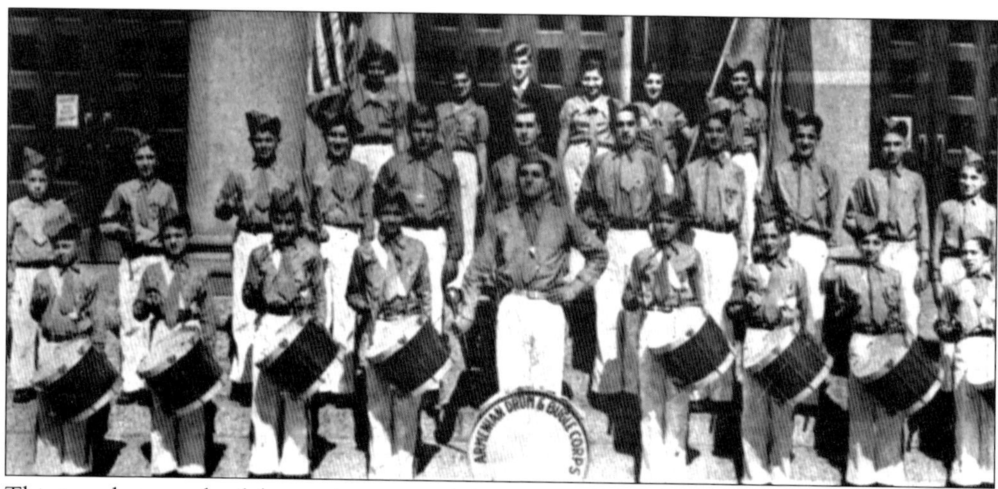

This is a photograph of the newly organized Armenian Drum and Bugle Corps of Racine taken in front of Memorial Hall in Racine in 1937. The corps was organized in 1937 by the Racine Armen Garb Chapter of Tszgagrone (Armenian Youth) and was the only drum corps of its kind that ever existed in the United States. The group went inactive just a few years later and reorganized in 1951. The drum corps disappeared for good sometime around 1955.

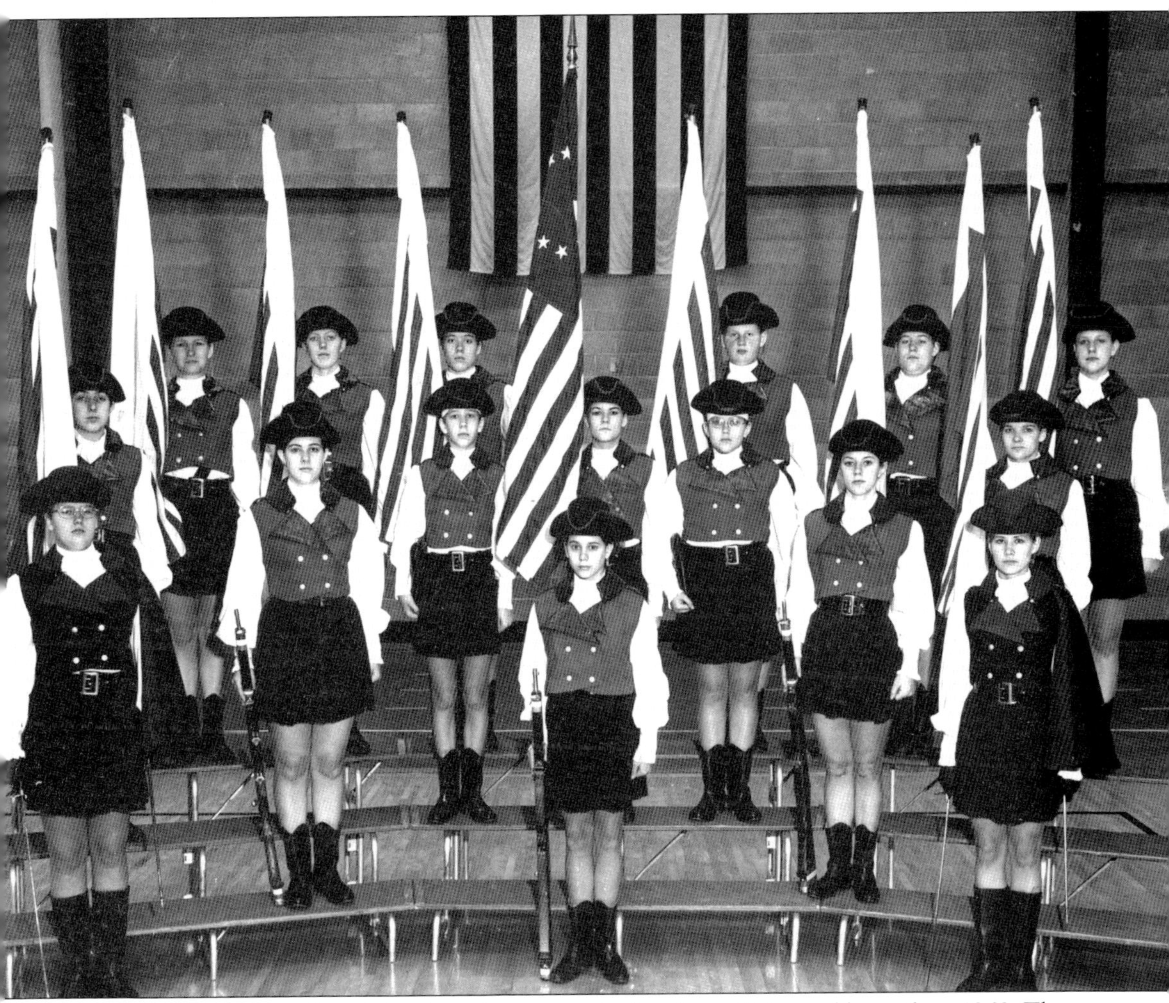

The Racine Liberty Belles Color Guard was organized by Jerry Kisler and his wife in 1968. The Liberty Belles competed in the Midwest Color Guard Circuit during the winter and year-round in the Badgerland Association. Open to girls from 12 to 21 years old, the Liberty Belles were very successful in competition. Highlights include winning the Wisconsin VFW State Color Guard Championship in 1970 and 1971. (Courtesy of RHM.)